IRELAND, BRITAIN AND GERMANY
1871–1914

FELICIAN PRILL

Ireland
Britain and Germany
1871-1914

Problems of nationalism
and religion in nineteenth-century Europe

A NATION NEVER DIES
W. E. Gladstone
The Irish Question

GILL AND MACMILLAN, DUBLIN
BARNES & NOBLE BOOKS, NEW YORK
a division of Harper & Row Publishers, Inc.

First published in 1975

Gill and Macmillan Limited
2 Belvedere Place
Dublin 1
and in London through association with the
Macmillan International Group of Publishing Companies
Published in the U.S.A. 1975 by
Harper and Row Publishers, Inc.
Barnes & Noble Import Division

Gill and Macmillan SBN: 7171 0707 8

ISBN 0-06-495729-2

Printed in Great Britain by
Bristol Typesetting Company Limited
Barton Manor, St Philips, Bristol

Contents

List of Abbreviations

Germ.	*Germania*
Köln.Ztg	*Kölnische Zeitung*
N.A.Z.	*Norddeutsche Allgemeine Zeitung*
V.Z.	*Vossische Zeitung*
Pr.Jb.	*Preussische Jahrbücher*
Dt.Rev.	*Deutsche Revue*
H.Z.	*Historische Zeitschrift*
Mar.Rdsch	*Marine Rundschau*
I.H.S.	*Irish Historical Studies*
P.A.	Political Archives of the German Auswärtige Amt
Rep.	Diplomatic Report
Instr.	Instruction
England 69 vol. 3 (or other numbers)	Series of the records and volume numbers

Preface

GREAT BRITAIN and Ireland are drawing closer to the continent under the influence of a common European heritage and actual common interests in the political, economic and social fields. A better knowledge of the views of one of the continental partners about an important period in the history of both islands may further mutual understanding which seems to be indispensable, at the present time, for common political and economic work.

This book aims at contributing fairly and honestly to this purpose. It should not be understood as a new systematic description of English-Irish relations in the time between the two wars of 1870/71 and 1914/18. While presupposing the acquaintance of most readers in English-speaking countries with the main historical facts and persons concerned, the book intends to embody the reactions, comments, impressions and feelings of German statesmen, politicians, diplomats, historians, journalists and others, including my own. It should be of interest to everybody who is working in the field of historical research, in practical politics and diplomacy, as well as to all those who, in a spirit of reconciliation, are striving for a common feeling of peace and justice in a century which has taught mankind so many lessons.

It was Professor T. W. Moody, Fellow of Trinity College, Dublin, who gave the first impulse to this work and who encouraged its completion with great interest, help with research and valuable advice. I wish to thank him for his most generous help.

I feel extremely indebted, furthermore, to the Embassy of Ireland in Bonn as well as to the Directors of the Libraries of the German Foreign Office and of the Friedrich-Wilhelm University in Bonn, Dr Grundmann and Professor Lohse, for having provided me with literature, in English and in German, including the contemporary press and periodicals. I also wish to express my gratitude to Dr Sasse, Dr Weinandy and Dr Gehling of the Foreign Office in Bonn, for their unreserved support in collecting material and their kind assistance and advice. Finally I wish to thank most heartily everybody who so generously helped me in completing the manuscript, in particular my son Norbert who reviewed and typed the handwritten text.

Bonn, December 1972.   F.P.

Introduction

IT IS beyond doubt that the Irish question became one of the most important issues in European political history. Its international significance and worldwide impact were obvious when in the last decades of the nineteenth century it developed into a handicap for British foreign policy and in the twentieth century it turned out to be a threat to Britain herself.

Reacting to the Irish question, the two most outstanding British statesmen of the relevant period, Disraeli and Gladstone, had quite contrasting approaches. Disraeli's view was one of blunt realism:

> It is the Pope one day, potatoes the next . . . a starving population, an absentee aristocracy, and an alien Church and . . . the weakest executive in the world.[1]

Gladstone's diagnosis was, as Curtis expressed it, 'more apocalyptic and ominous'. In a letter from Germany, in 1845, he wrote to his wife:

> Ireland, Ireland! That cloud in the west, that coming storm, the minister of God's retribution upon cruel and inveterate and but half-atoned injustice! Ireland forces upon us these great social and great religious questions—God grant that we may have courage to look them in the face, and to work through them.[2]

The first interpretation seems to be merely a description of facts without any indication as to what conclusions are to be drawn from such a state of affairs, typical of a statesman whose interests and merits were to be found mostly in the field of foreign policy. Gladstone's view, on the other hand, reveals already, at an early stage of his career, the political insight into the real substance of the question.

The assessments of the Irish problems by Disraeli and Gladstone, as well as by other British politicians and scholars, appear to be indispensable to a description of the German approach. As regards the reactions of the people in Germany when they heard about Ireland and British-Irish relations, one must admit that only a limited number were conscious of the implications of these problems. Ireland's destiny was not of particular interest to the Germans, at least not before the 1880s. It only concerned some Catholic circles where parallels were drawn between them and their co-religionists in Ireland, especially at the beginning of the Kulturkampf. The literature on Ireland was meagre, and newspapers wrote mostly on current German affairs. The wars with Austria and France and the struggle for German unity and, after 1871, the internal problems of the German Empire, were the prevailing topics in the political literature and in the daily press.

Interest in English-Irish affairs intensified in Gladstone's time, and the space granted to these matters by the papers, including headlines on the front-pages, increased considerably until the Great War broke out, when ideological and strategic propaganda did their work. In the last decades before the war the most important German newspapers gave very valuable reports on the actual problems, sometimes in a passionate and colourful way. Through the reports, editorials and comments of the daily press, the German public became fully aware of the complexity and difficulty of the Irish question, influenced, however, by the general political line followed by the editors running the papers. It was only through the reports of the special correspondents sent to Ireland that the German people learned of the Ulster crisis in the months and weeks before August 1914.

The contemporary press was not only a worthwhile but an indispensable source of information as regards German thinking and feeling about Ireland. The demands of the educated, scholars and men of political influence, as well as experts on German-British affairs and on ecclesiastical and cultural life, were met by the excellent articles of politicians and historians, published by the political periodicals.

The leading personalities in Germany strictly avoided expressing their opinions on British-Irish affairs in public, except on a few exceptional occasions. They felt committed to the general political principle that in peace time, under normal circumstances, no political leader should criticise the home politics of a friendly power. There were so many differences between the

Germans and the English, particularly in the last decade before the war, and occasionally so much uneasiness on both sides, that responsible politicians in Germany would have provoked un-favourable reactions and repercussions abroad and would have undermined their own position and career at home if they had poured oil into the flames burning in England and Ireland. No intrusion into English-Irish affairs was, in principle, the guiding line of official German policy. This attitude did not change until the outbreak of the war.

But behind the scenes everything that happened on the other side of the Channel was meticulously observed by the German authorities. Reports on Ireland from London filled up many files in the Foreign Office in Berlin and came to the attention of German diplomatic missions in other places, as well as ministries directly concerned and others interested in particular aspects of the question. Many briefings and instructions, which were very often drafted by the heads of the Foreign Office themselves, reached the German diplomats in London. The reports and reactions from Berlin form the backbone of the official German political assessment.

At this point it should be remembered that at that time the mentality of the diplomats was somewhat different from today's. The German ambassadors to the Court of St James were members of the higher nobility, brought up and living in the spirit of the nineteenth century, with the self-assertion of their role as representatives of the Sovereign of a re-established Empire. The way of life in diplomatic circles differed from today's in so far as a great deal more time was spent on social activities—week-end visits, which usually lasted longer than a normal week-end, hunting and shooting parties and other commitments. The routine work was generally done by the Counsellor, the number two of the embassy. That kind of social life presented many opportunities for contacts and information, similar to the possibilities that exist in our time. But the diplomats lacked one very valuable opportunity of modern diplomacy, namely the direct contact with the people of the host country, an opportunity which is now open in principle to all accredited diplomats in the free world. Strong barriers were put up at that time by protocol. The reports of diplomats were therefore exact and reliable in substance, but sometimes they revealed a lack of open-mindedness and, with some exceptions, of courageous and critical personal comments.

On certain occasions the diplomats sent these reports directly to the Emperor, thus neglecting the instructions of their superiors, including Bismarck's who was rather upset by this kind of hot line.[3] The Chancellor in particular felt very strongly about the activities of the diplomats, having himself been Prussian Minister to Russia and to France. He once remarked 'My ambassadors must wheel like soldiers.'[4]

The German envoys abroad were in an awkward position. On the one hand they were committed to their general instructions—watching carefully the maintenance of unperturbed bilateral relations with the host country—and, on the other hand they had to work in accordance with the particular instructions given by the Chancellor or the Head of the Foreign Service and had to act also in conformity with the wishes of the Sovereign whom they officially represented.[5] The endeavour to reconcile the sometimes divergent instructions and wishes led to collisions, because the superiors jealously guarded their prerogatives, especially personalities of such a singular character as Bismarck and William II.

The reports were received and carefully studied by experts on English-Irish affairs, who were able to endorse or reject the proposals, before eventually they could form the basis for political conclusions and measures.

The unwillingness of official circles to pass their information and views on to the public was balanced by the unofficial makers of public opinion. Bismarck himself filled the gap in so far as he gave orders to publish diplomatic reports in German newspapers which he found to be along the lines of his own political thinking (e.g. *Norddeutsche Allgemeine Zeitung, Kölnische Zeitung, Die Post,* etc.). Usually the reports were published unaltered, occasionally abridged, and always with the normal make-up of newspaper articles. They were introduced by the stereotype formula 'It has been reported to us from London.'[6]

CHAPTER 1

Two Empires

A new epoch in European history—Alsace-Lorraine—British-German relations—A community of interests—Britain's home politics—Bismarck and Windthorst before the Reichstag on Ireland and Alsace-Lorraine

THE day of the proclamation of the re-established German Empire, 18 January 1871, was a milestone in European history as a long period of tension marked by a series of revolutions and wars had come to an end. A new epoch began, lasting until 1914, the year of the outbreak of World War I.

The victory of the allied German Forces over France was decisive, but this did not, contrary to Ensor's view, inaugurate a transfer of the real political ascendancy over Europe from France to Germany.[1] Due to Bismarck's masterly policy, Prussia and her allies had managed to finish the war without being harassed by other powers, but Bismarck continued to be very much concerned about the attitude of the European countries. He took into account that, even after the defeat of France, Germany might have to run the risk of four or five further wars. On 15 June 1877 he remarked, 'A French newspaper has recently stated that I am suffering from a *cauchemar des coalitions*. This justified nightmare will accompany a German Minister for a long time to come and perhaps for ever.'[2]

Because of the Franco-German conflict, however, maintenance of peace depended to a large extent on Anglo-German relations. At the beginning of the war Bismarck had renewed the guarantee of the neutrality of Belgium, stipulated in the Treaty of London in 1839, thus safeguarding an important British interest.[3] Britain remained neutral like the other European powers, even after the downfall of Napoleon III when Thiers pleaded for intervention.[4] Although British public opinion was inclined to a more favourable feeling towards France, particularly after the battle of

Sedan,[5] Napoleon III had never been a popular figure in England.[6] Upon him 'the majority of his contemporaries saddled the responsibility for the outbreak of the war'. This attitude, reported by Erich Eyck, was shared by Gladstone and *The Times*.[7]

The intention of the Germans to annex Alsace-Lorraine to the new Empire caused some bitter feeling in Britain, particularly the threat to transfer these provinces without the consent of the inhabitants. Gladstone, however, failed to obtain a decision of his cabinet aimed at a common démarche of all powers not involved. Russia was certainly not in favour of such a démarche, not only 'owing to her Black Sea intrigue with Bismarck', as Ensor puts it,[8] but obviously also because of her territories with Polish populations. Before the treaty of Frankfurt was concluded, the German ambassador in London, Count Bernstorff, reporting on the address-debate in February 1871, pointed out that the members of parliament had cheered all remarks warning Germany against making too severe peace-terms. Disraeli recalled the lenient peace-conditions conceded to Russia after the Crimean war. No cheer was heard when the unification of Germany and the formation of the Empire were mentioned.[9]

Bismarck, however, did not prove as steadfast as he had been in 1866 when he opposed the proposed annexation of Austrian territories. The Emperor and the army leaders pressed for the annexation of Alsace-Lorraine. Bismarck did not like the idea, but yielding to this pressure, and influenced by a kind of popular movement, he eventually gave in. He later justified the measure by pointing to its military advantages,[10] fully aware that the annexation would probably turn out to be a serious handicap to himself and his successors.

Apart from the question of Alsace-Lorraine, the relations between Britain and Germany were on the whole almost unperturbed in the first decades after 1871: Britain dominating a worldwide empire with a powerful navy and immense resources, Germany having a growing population, full of skill and acquisitiveness, and disposing of efficient land forces on the continent. In Britain it was the heyday of the Victorian era; in Germany it was the beginning of a time of prosperity under the reign of the Hohenzollern emperors. A widespread euphoria, particularly among the upper classes, characterised the general feeling in both countries. It included some temptation for the people in

Germany who began to show the first signs of a hubris which later had fateful consequences in the field of domestic and—after Bismarck had been deprived of his power—foreign policy too.

Competition was not yet a word of wider political implications between the two countries at that time. The English press was full of admiration for the founder of the German Empire, particularly when dealing with the role of the Chancellor in the conflict between the State and the Catholic Church in Germany. The royal families in both countries were closely linked by the marriage of the Princess Royal to the Crown Prince of Prussia and Germany, Frederick William.[11]

In the United Kingdom, British/Irish relations continued to give rise to concern on both sides of the Irish Sea. The various rebellions in the nineteenth century, especially the Fenian uprising in 1867, were not forgotten. Gladstone's Disestablishment Act and the Land Act—which Lyons describes as disappointing[12]—had come into force in 1870, but had not paved the way to pacification and conciliation. Gladstone himself had not yet become a convert to Irish autonomy, and the Conservatives regarded the Irish as a primitive people, uncivilised and deeply superstitious. Ireland was for them a kind of backyard.[13] The Queen never wasted any affections on the Irish, whom she had not forgiven for refusing to send a delegation to Prince Albert's funeral.[14] At a later date she wrote to Sir Stafford Northcote, 'These Irish are really shocking, abominable people—not like any other civilised nation.'[15] Curtis expressed the view that the argument in Victorian England about the unfitness of the Irish for self-government belonged to the pattern of thinking which he called Anglo-Saxonism.[16]

It was quite clear that Bismarck, in the framework of Anglo-German relations, had to take into account these views as a basis for his attitude towards the Irish question, which he regarded as an internal British problem. As the discussion amongst the British public on the annexation of Alsace-Lorraine was still going on, no German politician could have afforded to express himself favourably with regard to Irish interests. In that case he would have provoked official British reaction in favour of Alsace-Lorraine and, probably, in favour of Polish-speaking Prussian subjects as well. On the other hand, any German move in favour of Ireland would have given rise to reactions and claims in the south-west and east of the German Empire. This had to be avoided at all costs.

Thus an unexpected and perhaps not very welcome community of interests between the two countries resulted from the parallel aspects of these political issues; it was a handicap for both and not even popular with many people, particularly not with the Catholic Church leaders and their flocks who never understood why Irish moves towards autonomy and more liberty were met with concern and misgivings by the German authorities.

The German leaders' approach to Britain and to British-Irish affairs—particularly Bismarck's—formed the guiding rule for the instructions issued to German diplomats and especially to the ambassadors in London.[17] The ambassadors, in their turn, were anxious to word reports so as to meet the expectations of their superiors. A great many reports were written in an emotional way, sometimes with exasperation and irony, rarely in obvious contradiction to the guiding rules of Berlin. In private letters, however, Count Münster, 'Bismarck's insubordinate ambassador', as he was called in a biography by his great-grandson von Nostitz,[18] expressed unorthodox opinions. He wrote in a very clumsy style, frequently repeating the same words.[19]

In the first year of the German Empire, not many reports dealt with Irish affairs. One might have the impression that the instructions received were followed literally. There were just a few remarks on the visit of the Prince of Wales to Dublin, where 'the police came into conflict with the mob and a rally took place in Phoenix Park with a resolution passed in favour of the arrested Fenians'.[20] Furthermore there was a report about the tactlessness of the French Count Flavigny, who had come to Dublin with a delegation from his country to express gratitude for the help granted during the war and who was said to have praised the identity of Irish and French interests.[21]

More attention was paid to the internal policy of England and her political leaders. It is curious to note that the ambassadors, right-wing people themselves, were less critical of the Liberals than of the Conservatives. Count Bernstorff, in a direct letter to William I,[22] expounded the ideas of Gladstone; he remarked that the Conservative Party, in its composition and following the experiences of the last Tory administration, presented little hope of success in the general election, due to the reduced confidence in it of the bulk of the people. At an earlier date he had already reported sarcastically that Disraeli was the best ally of the Liberal cabinet, because his friends and foes were full of apprehension of an administration under his leadership. Moreover, Bernstorff did not refrain from critical remarks about the Royal Family, including the Queen and the Prince of Wales. In a letter to the Emperor he strongly criticised the Queen because 'of her innate shyness and timidity'[23] and in another direct report to the Emperor he referred to the moral conduct of the Prince of Wales.[24]

Count Münster's reports dealt mainly with internal policy, including those on Church-State relations to which a special chapter is devoted. The situation of British political parties and their leaders was his hobby at the time. He was an aristocrat from Hanover, born in London, and in his eyes England was the only country with a really vigorous people and an advanced civilisation. He was a man who liked the English way of life, who behaved like an Englishman,[25] and who deeply regretted that the aristocracy in England was no longer a reservoir for coming statesmen 'owing to the enormous wealth, the materialistic mentality and pleasure-seeking of the nobility'.[26]

In an instruction to the embassy Bismarck had paid tribute to the working of the British parties and their machinery, pointing out that it was indispensable for a minister to have a strong party supporting him. The party would follow the principle, 'men not measures', as long as the 'men' would not have forfeited the party's confidence.[27] In this context he blamed the German parties: 'We have no parties, but only parliamentary groups.' This instruction gave rise to a long report by Münster on the English party-system, strongly criticising some party leaders, especially Disraeli and Salisbury. Several times he mentioned Disraeli's Jewish descent,[28] and as a man who felt that democracy was a fateful illness[29] he furiously condemned the introduction of the secret ballot—'the most dangerous change'—and although he recognised him to be a good leader of the opposition, he expressed his doubts about Disraeli's abilities as a statesman.[30]

The Conservative leader, in his turn, is said to have told Lord Derby that Münster was not a friendly man, 'He is full of distrust and stupidity.'[31]

Salisbury was characterised as a clever and wilful man, with

B

agreeable manners, but ruthless as a statesman and violent in his speeches.[32] In this context it should be mentioned that neither Disraeli nor Salisbury had ever been to Ireland, whereas Gladstone had been there in 1877—for three weeks only, however. Salisbury was not at all anxious to visit Ireland, 'an uncivilised country, where the priests and the Fenians contended for the leadership of the people,'[33] as he said.

The cool reserve as to the Irish question which had been observed in public by statesmen and other political leaders, was abandoned by Bismarck at a debate in the Reichstag on the administration of Alsace-Lorraine.[34] The subject of this debate on 16 and 17 May 1873, which appeared as item 2 on the agenda, was a report of the Bundesrat on the legislation for, and the administration of, the provinces for the years 1872-3. After a strong attack by Windthorst, the leader of the Catholic party, who blamed the administration for the unjust treatment of members of religious orders, Bismarck took the floor. After mentioning the 'difficulties between the British government and their Irish subjects' he drew parallels between the situation in Alsace-Lorraine and in Ireland. 'Everybody can imagine what would perhaps be done by certain people guided by the same sort of known and unknown chiefs under comparable circumstances in Alsace' he said, hinting at the 'chiefs' in Ireland. Subsequently he quoted from a diplomatic report which read as follows:

'The demeanour of the ultramontane press, which does not go so far as to advocate open rebellion, like the radical papers, is nevertheless turning out fatally for the welfare of the country. The leaders of the ultramontanists are fully aware that an uprising at the present moment would end with a total defeat of the rebels, followed by a reaction and coercive treatment of the ultramontane party, if it had participated in the rebellion . . . The leaders of the ultramontanists, while keeping themselves formally within the limits of law and order, are stirring up the people against the Protestant section of the population. With the admonition to endure the injuries suffered, they are furthering the discontent and strife among the people in order to keep the wounds open and to preserve hatred and contempt against the government by distorting and exaggerating the real facts. While keeping the poor people in emotion, they see only one target: Rome's power, without any respect to the country's prosperity. The ultramontane leaders are actually seeking to rock the confidence of the people in the legal authority of the judges and are giving support to the new Home Rule movement.'

Bismarck commented on this quotation with a remark that in Alsace-Lorraine also, certain people agitated against Protestants, and he repeated that for political reasons he would have preferred to object to the annexation of the provinces, but that military reasons had proved stronger.[35]

The parliamentary duel between Bismarck and Windthorst continued the following day. The Catholic leader criticised the quoted dispatch, observing ironically that there had been no positive and concrete facts in it. 'It was no more than the idle talk and gossip which can always be heard from young diplomats at social functions,' he said. Windthorst went on: 'We in Prussia know from experience that blaming the ultramontanists is a good recommendation for anybody prepared to behave in that way.' He concluded by saying: 'The Irish are not responsible for the sins committed by anybody in Alsace-Lorraine.'

Bismarck then spoke about 'the regrettable impossibility of living in accordance with the constitution in Ireland, unless the ultramontane party were to cease its activities'. Windthorst retorted: 'Catholics are not ultramontanists in my opinion.'

The first act of this parliamentary drama had taken place in Belfast, where an ambitious Consul wrote a report to the Chargé d'Affaires in London who transmitted a copy of it to his superiors in Berlin.[36]

Bismarck availed of this opportunity to draw parallels between Ireland and Alsace-Lorraine by quoting from the Consul's report, which obviously was a 'terrible simplification,' the superficial product of a subaltern member of the consular service. British newspapers hailed Bismarck's arguments and applauded this last act of the drama.[37] One could have the impression that compassion for the annexed provinces had declined. A community of interests had become manifest, confirmed by the leading German statesman, at least for a certain period. In any case, this parliamentary debate did not bode well for the future of both countries.

CHAPTER 2

Religion and Politics

*Church and State in Germany—Bismarck's position—Liberalism
in Germany and in England—Gladstone and the Vatican Decrees—Peace with the Pope—Sympathies and Antipathies—The
English-Irish implications of the problem—Count Münster's
blunder*

BISMARCK'S outburst during the debate of the German Reichstag must be seen against the background of the Kulturkampf.[1]
It happened in the same month in which the severest legal measures against the Catholic Church in Prussia came into force, the
so-called Maigesetze.[2] The entire debate disclosed the parallels
between the purely political and ecclesiastical fields, each of
which influenced the other.

An assessment of the Church-State relations in the United
Kingdom from the German point of view of that time requires
a brief analysis of those relations in Germany as a whole in the
1870s and 1880s, and in particular, in Prussia.

One of the most gifted and cultivated German diplomats in
Bismarck's time, the Prussian Minister to the Holy See, Kurd von
Schlözer, a Protestant and a sincere follower of Bismarck himself,[3] depicted the ecclesiastical state of affairs in Prussia as
follows:

By the beginning of the eighties, there was a state of anarchy
in almost all Catholic dioceses. The two Archbishops of
Cologne and Posen-Gnesen, who had been deposed by the
state, lived abroad. The Prince bishop of Breslau as well as
the Bishops of Paderborn, Münster and Limburg were removed from their sees by decision of the Royal Court for
ecclesiastical affairs; the Bishops of Fulda, Trier and Osna-
brück had died. Only the Bishops of Kulm, Ermland and
Hildesheim still held their sees. Thirty-four posts were vacant
in the Cathedral Chapters, 981 in the parishes and about 300

in the curacies. The revenues of the Church from the State were stopped; religion had become a means for instigation.[4]

In May 1884 Schlözer wrote to his brother:

In Berlin, one takes only an historical interest in the world-wide power of Rome, and merely through literature without any live contact. We have to pay here for the ignorance of the arrogant and bureaucratic brains of the continental people in Berlin.[5]

On another occasion he expressed the view that the laws of the Kulturkampf, in particular the Maigesetze, were a typical product of the lawyers in Berlin, composed without any knowledge of the Catholic community and the Canon Law.[6]

Those were the comments of a man whose statesmanlike views were praised by the leading Catholic newspaper after peace between Church and State had been restored.[7]

Ever since the end of the Kulturkampf much pondering has taken place in historical research and discussion upon the motives and the immediate causes of the struggle, particularly on Bismarck's role in it. Bluntly, it would be a superficial and summary judgement to hold him responsible for everything that happened at the time. He was said to have had a certain amount of sympathy for the Catholics in Prussia before 1866; it was even assumed that he intended to make a deal with the Catholics in order to initiate a reform policy social-conservative in character, aimed at overthrowing the predominance of capitalism and Judaism.[8] After the occupation of Rome by the Italian troops in 1870 he considered inviting the Pope for a permanent stay in Germany—at Schloss Brühl near Cologne, an area with a strong Catholic population, Catholic nobility and with mainly Catholic soldiers in the neighbouring garrisons.[9] In February 1871 he said that he regarded the Pope in the first place as a political figure, and as a man who had always preserved an innate esteem for all real powers, a great monarch controlling the consciences of 200 million Catholics. 'I would not hesitate, at the right moment, to advocate his mediation and even his arbitration in political questions,' he concluded.[10]

It should be recorded here that these remarks were made after the Promulgation of the Syllabus (Encyclical *Quanta cura* on the errors of modern liberalism, of 8 December 1864) and the Decree on Infallibility, of 18 July 1870, which were regarded as provoking a reaction from the State that was aimed at counter-acting any interference of the Pope in State affairs.

Most German bishops as well as the outstanding leaders of the Catholic (Zentrum) party in Germany had expressed themselves in favour of a postponement of the Decree on Infallibility.[11] They probably felt that the time was not yet ripe for the definition of the dogma, or they possibly held that, on the whole, it was too late for it. But in any case, the promulgation of the Decree was in fact not more than a poor pretext for the reactions of the governing parties and the administrations of the powers concerned, particularly in Germany where the Liberal parties formed the parliamentary majority.

On 14 May 1872 Windthorst, before the Reichstag, characterised the mentality of the German Liberals, saying that they had quite a different understanding of liberty than people in North America and the Anglo-Saxon race in general. 'According to your understanding, gentlemen, the State should be endowed with the utmost power, and you intend to make full use of it in order to strike down everybody who holds an opinion different from yours,' he exclaimed, aiming at the various representatives of liberalism.[12] He claimed the Liberals were illiberals who had acted against the principles of equality before the law and of liberty of conscience. And on 29 November 1881, another Catholic leader, Reichensperger, reproached the Liberals from the same rostrum for having altered their principles on civil and religious freedom, reminding them of their conviction in former times that those who did not observe the principles of ecclesiastical freedom could never further political freedom. 'In the long run political freedom can never persist when the Church is in chains,' he said.[13]

It should be emphasised here that the theory and practice of German liberalism differed, in fact, substantially from the Liberal thinking in England, at least at the relevant time. There was all the difference in the world between the protagonists of English political liberalism as represented by Gladstone and their opposite numbers on the German side, in particular with regard to the approach to religious freedom. Gladstone himself, for example, was a very religious man. His liberal policy applied only to matters purely secular in character. This does not mean that certain liberal people did not share the feeling that was behind the slogan, No Popery. The anti-Catholic mentality of the era before the Emancipation still persisted in both conservative and liberal circles of Britain and revived after the Vatican Decrees which were criticised by Gladstone as well as by other politicians and churchmen.

But political liberalism in Britain at that time was guided by a spirit of tolerance, whereas many Liberals in Germany followed political principles and ideals emanating from Hegel's doctrine of an Almighty State.[14] It is against this background that the declarations of statesmen in power and in opposition in Britain and in Germany have to be assessed. One cannot say that the common opinion in Britain was expressed by *The Times*, when the newspaper, commenting on the conversion of the Marquis of Ripon, observed that the Catholic faith was not in accordance with the thinking and feeling of a 'thorough Englishman'.[15] In Germany, on the other hand the various shades of Liberals, supported by a large section of the community, strenuously attacked the basic principles of Christianity under slogans like Freedom of Thinking versus Revelation, Civilisation, Culture and Progress of the modern states, etc.[16]

Bussman[17] takes the view that Bismarck—not at all a Liberal —went deeper into the struggle than originally intended, challenged by the stubbornness of Pope Pius IX. The Chancellor, also Prime Minister of Prussia for some time, looked upon the Jesuits, the members of the Catholic party, the inhabitants of Alsace-Lorraine, of Hanover and subjects with Polish as their mother tongue, as enemies of the re-established Empire. The Polish question was of particular importance to him, and he apprehended the close links between the Church and the Polish population.

But Bismarck underestimated the steadfastness of the Catholic party and the power of resistance of the Church, particularly in those regions mentioned above, where this resistance was supported by the national minorities. The power of the State, which he overestimated, failed to succeed in this struggle.[18] Thus he very soon had to reconsider his position.

Here we should consider the position of Gladstone as to Church-State relations, particularly as regards the Vatican Decrees. After his resignation from the Premiership he published an essay in the *Contemporary Review* dealing with ritualism and ritual—aimed at the conversion of the Marquis of Ripon—and a pamphlet entitled 'The Vatican Decrees in their Bearing on Civil Allegiance' which appeared in November 1874. The essay in which Gladstone took the view that conversion to catholicism meant abandoning man's moral and spiritual freedom as well as his loyalty to the State, provoked a sharp reaction on the part of Ripon, one of the richest and most outstanding members of the English nobility. Münster remarked on this occasion that Gladstone availed of this opportunity to dissipate the suspicion of being in favour of catholicism.[19] Earlier in the year he had expressed the conviction that Gladstone had been in favour of catholicism.[20]

The pamphlet, in which Gladstone strongly attacked the Decrees, gave rise to many comments and reactions both in England and in Germany as well as in Ireland and in the Vatican. It goes without saying that the strongest reaction in England came from Manning, the Archbishop of Westminster. He and Gladstone had been friends in Oxford, both of Anglican denomination at that time. In 1851 Manning, then an Anglican clergyman, was converted and later he became a Catholic priest. Eyck describes the moving scene when Manning and Gladstone knelt together in an Anglican chapel and Manning left the service, saying that he could no longer take holy communion in the Church of England. When he asked Gladstone to go with him, the latter refused and remained in the chapel.[21] As early as 1854 Gladstone, while in Munich, became a friend of Döllinger who later defied the Decree on Infallibility and was eventually excommunicated. In 1874, after his resignation, he came to see Döllinger again, before he published the pamphlet.

Manning's vehement criticism is understandable in so far as they had always been on good terms with each other, even after Manning's conversion. It must have been a spontaneous and genuine reaction, when Manning emphasised that never before had he felt so disappointed in a friend as in Gladstone.[22] Bismarck's press-organ, the *Norddeutsche Allgemeine Zeitung*, dealing particularly with the views expressed by the English Catholics, quoted from a letter by Manning to *The Times*, in which he pointed at the safeguarding of internal peace through non-discrimination of denominations and stated that the German Empire could have lived in peace if its statesmen had not been induced to pour oil on the fire of religious dispute, particularly through one man. In the same edition the paper quoted from a *Daily News* article on the Pope's criticism of Gladstone's pamphlet: 'This man is now affected by the actions of a minister in another country who is attempting to start a feud with the Church.' The *Daily Telegraph* stressed the fact that Döllinger had not participated in writing the pamphlet. The German paper underlined that now Gladstone could no longer be suspected of being a Catholic in secret.[23]

In Morley's opinion Gladstone was one of the very few people capable of discerning that the fall of the temporal power of the Pope marked a more startling change and a profounder crisis in human history than the unification of Italy, the unification of Germany, the reconstructed Republic of France, perhaps even than the preservation of the United States.[24] Although the course of history has proved that this prognosis was wrong, Gladstone's pamphlet nevertheless seems to be a testimony of that opinion and of his personal views on Church-State relations at that time.

There were manifold reactions in Germany. The publication came as a surprise to Bismarck, who had always looked upon Gladstone as a *Jesuit à robe courte*.[25] Münster sent the Chancellor a copy of the pamphlet, which was translated and disseminated to all German envoys abroad, following Bismarck's expressed appreciation, which was conveyed to its author by the ambassador.[26] A few weeks later Bismarck received the following message from the Liberal statesman, conveyed to him again through Münster: 'Tell the Prince that having studied this question, I understand that the new German Empire was condemned to fight out this struggle with the Pope; the Prince had to take action against the ultramontanists unless he was prepared to jeopardise his work. I wish him well and tell him that he has no better follower and ally in this struggle than myself.'[27]

In February 1875 Gladstone published a second pamphlet under the title 'Vaticanism, an Answer to Replies and Reports', dealing again with the Syllabus and the dogma of Infallibility. He presented the first copy, with a dedication in his own hand, to the German ambassador, to be dispatched to Bismarck, telling him that 'His Highness might accept the copy as a token of my sincere admiration'.[28] In his report on the event Münster mentioned, by the way, that Döllinger had seen the proof-sheets of the pamphlet before its publication.

Bismarck's letter of thanks of 1 March 1875, drafted by Bucher[29] and signed by the Chancellor without any alterations, contained the phrase, 'It fills me with a deep and hopeful gratification to see the two nations, which in Europe are the champions of liberty and conscience, encountering the same foe, standing henceforth shoulder to shoulder in defending the highest interests of the human race.'[30] Eyck observes rightly that this was the only occasion the Prince applauded Gladstone unreservedly.[31]

In the course of the struggle in Germany, the political leaders, including Bismarck, became aware very soon that the adversaries had not got weaker but stronger. The Chancellor was now far ahead of the liberal spirit of the age which he did not represent like Cavour in Italy or Gladstone in England.[32] Bismarck very often declared himself in not very flattering terms against the formalism and perfectionism of the ministerial bureaucracy in handling the struggle.[33] These people were the main opponents of the Chancellor when he, without being supported by William I and the Protestant clergy, took the first steps aimed at restoring peace between Church and State.

When the endeavours of both parties had produced a peace which seemed to be acceptable to them, one of the most fateful periods of modern German history had come to an end.[34] 'It is very difficult to unravel the Church-State policy of our leading statesman. Bismarck must be compared to Hegel who said: "Only one of my students has understood me, and this man has misunderstood me." These words, written by Derneburg in the *Nationalzeitung* in December 1893,[35] demonstrate the enigma of Bismarck's position with regard to the Kulturkampf, an enigma which cannot be solved with complete certainty. Probably it was his intention to neutralise the worldwide power of the Pope, as he had maintained the neutrality of the European powers during the Franco-German war; it was his concern to avert dangers from an Empire so vehemently shaken by that fateful internal struggle with its impact on the international field.[36] Bachem, an old parliamentarian of the Catholic party himself, speaks with admiration about the peace-making policy of the Iron Chancellor: 'At no time in history has a similar reversal been inaugurated by a statesman who had been the leading figure in a mistaken policy' and 'he was a Titan indeed, but not one who in his blindness wanted to storm an Olympus which had proved to be impregnable'.[37]

Anti-clericalism, being a product of the age of enlightenment, had to be reckoned with in the policy of all western countries in modern times. But deepfelt antipathy against ecclesiastical life and freedom had always led to a political weakness of the countries concerned. It appears to be obvious that the period of internal struggle in Germany during the nineteenth century was met with a certain sympathy abroad, not only because of the anti-Church measures but also because of the political weakness this struggle brought on Germany. Although Eyck's opinion, that an overwhelming majority of Protestant Englishmen were the only people who followed the Kulturkampf with unreserved sympathy,[38] seems to be exaggerated, it should not be denied that certain English circles of various political affiliations had backed the protagonists of the Church-State confrontation and their followers. To put it bluntly, there were people in England who —like a good many people elsewhere—behaved in a more Bismarckian way than Bismarck himself. On the other hand, other voices could be heard, speaking cautiously about the German situation and pointing out the bad experiences of Britain in the past and at that time.

In December 1873 Münster reported on a letter from Manning to the editor of *The Times*, in which the archbishop strongly criticised the Kulturkampf laws, which ruled that the education of the clergy should be handed over to the State, stating that they were aimed at a separation of German Catholics from the Pope and interfered with the assignment of the parish priests; he also maintained that the establishment of a Royal tribunal for ecclesiastical affairs was in contradiction to Canon Law.

The ambassador, assuming that the letter was written by a member of the German Catholic party, commented that the letter was obviously 'aimed at the Red Hat'.[39] The reaction of *The Times*[40] was very realistic, if not apologetic, in its arguments. The paper defended the clergy, arguing that its members are bound by conscience which cannot be forced by law. Any unjustified act of force would turn out to be impossible. In contrast to this reasonable comment, Odo Russell, the British ambassador to Berlin, talking to the State Secretary von Bülow a few weeks later, remarked that it was high time to restrain the activities of

Manning and the Jesuits. 'Nothing makes Germany more popular in England than the great struggle with the Vatican,' he said.[41] Some other noteworthy reactions in both countries with regard to Church-State relations in Germany should be recorded here to illustrate the heat of the discussion in private and in public. An exchange of letters between Pius IX and William I late in the summer 1873 gave rise to manifestations of sympathy in England for the Emperor who in his letter had emphasised the German view in rejecting the Pope's arguments. At a meeting in London on 27 January 1874, organised by Earl Russell, a resolution was passed thanking the Emperor in the name of the English Protestants for his steadfastness in the Church versus State debate. Russell, who was prevented by illness from presiding over the meeting, wrote a letter to the chairman, Sir John Murray, which contained the following phrase: 'The cause of the German Emperor is the cause of liberty and the cause of the Pope is the cause of slavery.' In a letter of 29 January 1874 Münster, in his euphoria, wrote to William I 'that there is nobody more popular in England than Your Majesty' and 'I am convinced that the manifestations should be regarded as sincere and that they will influence permanently the relations of both countries with each other.'[42]

Sir George Bowyer, a Catholic member of Parliament, in a letter to Earl Russell, had on his part expressed his concern about the meeting 'in the interest of Ireland'. Gladstone was said to have been against such a demonstration on the same grounds, too.[43] Manning, in a pastoral letter, condemned the meeting in strong words. 'Every man who took part in that meeting is now an accomplice in these acts of tyranny' (namely in Germany) he wrote. Shortly after the meeting in London, German Protestants who had met in the Town Hall of Berlin, after addresses delivered by certain outstanding protagonists of their denominations, thanked their English brethren for their support against 'the ultramontane party in the Church'.

But on the other hand there were the voices of those in Germany who did not share the euphoria expressed by Count Münster and who had a far more cautious and cooler approach to this kind of Anglo-German collaboration. In a memorandum, which is to be found in the Political Archives,[44] the writer, whose name is not revealed, warned the German diplomats that English politicians were generally reluctant to react favourably to the cause of the State in Germany's Church-State problems: first, they feared that the resistance of Ireland would turn into a national question, and, furthermore, they did not wish to arouse too much sympathy for Germany, because of the possibility of German co-operation with Russia which could be unfavourable to Britain in the future. The Irish implication, however, appeared to the writer of such an importance that he suggested that the situation in Ireland and particularly the newspapers written in Irish, which were usually ignored in England, should be carefully observed.

This allusion to English-Irish relations should lead us to note some facts in the context of the German Church-State complex.

Gladstone's Irish University Bill[45] had given rise to reflections, in both public and private English circles, on the various implications of Church-State problems. It was the purpose of the bill to set out appropriations for the endowment of a non-denominational university in Dublin with the aim of establishing colleges guided by laymen and uninfluenced by the Catholic Church.[46] But neither the Protestants nor the Catholics were satisfied by the bill. The Archbishop of Dublin, Cardinal Cullen, condemned it 'as richly endowing non-Catholic and godless colleges'.[47] The bill was in part Gladstone's own concept, and when it failed to pass by three votes against an Irish-Conservative majority, the question of the resignation of the Prime Minister arose, which he decided against in the end.

On 9 and 16 March the embassy reported on the case, quoting from some newspaper comments (*Spectator* and *Observer*) which held that the bishops, by their gamble and their selfishness, had unleashed a great aversion against the Catholics in England and, moreover, 'that dealing with the question of Irish education constitutes the English form of the struggle between secular and ecclesiastical power which is actually going on in Germany'.[48]

The bill was one of Gladstone's ideas for conciliation of the Irish Catholics. Unfortunately it was initiated against the background of events in Germany, and met with mistrust in influential parts of the English and Irish populations. Gladstone, who was obviously somewhat discouraged by this futile attempt, admitted to Münster some months later that he would have to face conflicts with the Irish Catholic clergy, presuming that the Pope was anxious to seek such conflicts in Ireland as he had found in Germany. Münster pointed out the 'aggressive attitude' of the clergy in the education issue and the support given by the Home Rule movement, adding that no English government could make concessions of that kind. The Liberal administration had to confront formidable agitation fomented by the ultramontane clergy who had been treated in such a friendly way by the actual government.[49] Gladstone was reported to be upset by an article of the *Osservatore Romano* which had stated that an unjustified reproach had been levelled against the clergy in Germany because of its anti-national feelings. 'The clergy is always in support of the oppressed national minorities as in Ireland' the *Osservatore* had said.

The *Norddeutsche Allgemeine Zeitung*,[50] at the request of the Foreign Office,[51] turned this report into an article, writing with satisfaction that a Protestant movement was apparently rising up in England and that Bismarck's policy was applauded with enthusiasm. 'The change in favour of the German Church-State policy is terrific.' Concluding the article, the paper remarked that 'Old England in the spirit of Elizabeth and Cromwell, in full conscience of her true mission, is joining us as an ally against Rome.'

Münster repeated, time and again, his warnings against the 'aggressive Irish clergy' and the Home Rule movement. The Bishop of Cloyne was said to have expressed in public the claim that Home Rule was the 'assertion of an outraged right'. Münster reported that the bishop had received his instructions from the Archbishop of Dublin who, on his part, had got his orders from Rome. In the ambassador's eyes the Home Rulers were to be regarded as the offspring of the Fenians.[52]

This account of Münster's reports on Church-State problems should not be concluded without mentioning a reported comment of Disraeli's. In a talk with the ambassador he paid enormous tribute to the Chancellor's courage. Comparing the German Catholic party with the Irish Home Rule movement, he said that the position of the government in Ireland was clear: the Irish party would be regarded as an enemy of the State.[53]

Many people in Germany felt very satisfied when they heard of such opinions, drawing parallels with the situation in Germany's east and south-west. The following very emotional and angry comment made by Pauli in the *Preussische Jahrbücher* was typical of the feeling of many people in Germany in the relevant period: 'If it came about that Ireland and Poland—Rome's instruments for combating freedom of conscience in England and Germany—were able to stand on their own feet at any time to come, the treacherous Jesuits would do all they could in order to poison the national development of the country concerned.'[54]

The responsible leaders, however, began to regard this community of interests from a more sober and a cooler point of view, appreciating this community and collaboration under the auspices and in the framework of European politics. They felt that, in the long run, Church-State trouble could only become a disagreeable handicap.

Endeavours to improve the awkward position of the leading statesmen both in Whitehall and in the Wilhelmstrasse suffered an unpleasant setback following a speech delivered by the German ambassador before the Protestant National Club in London on 12 May 1875. In reply to a toast Count Münster mentioned that 'our Protestant Emperor is not prepared to go to Canossa',[55] and then said that the reason was the Thirty Years War. Continuing, he remarked that: 'It is the Protestant Empire which the dark people of Rome do not like . . . It is the fear that in countries where the national feeling grows—where morality and education grow with the national feeling—the consequences must be a National Church. I hope that struggle will be spared this country for some time but I think you had better look out in time. I think you see in Ireland what is going on; I think you have not to look too far to see what is preparing and what will be the case in this country.'[56]

These utterances of Münster caused prompt reactions in the newspapers, both on the continent and in the British Isles—and of course, in the centres of official policy. The *Germania* urged the ambassador to resign from his post 'for which he has never furnished proof of his abilities as he did when he wrote his cookery book,'[57] and in a leader with the headline 'Declaration of Religious War by the German Ambassador in London', a few days later, the paper maintained that Münster had spoken *expressis verbis* for the Emperor and Bismarck.[58] Not only the

Catholic press but other papers like the conservative *Kreuz-zeitung* came out very critically, too.[59]

The Times,[60] dealing with the incident in a rather long article, gave a very balanced, but fundamentally critical assessment of Münster's speech, alluding to Bismarck's Church politics in general. Mentioning Münster's idea of a National Church, the paper reminded the ambassador that perhaps it might have been possible to isolate the clergy from Rome 300 years ago, but that this was impossible at the present time. With regard to the remarks on British policy towards Ireland it said that, after the experiences in the past, coercive measures would lead to nothing. Criticising Bismarck's policy, the paper pointed out that, as Münster had underlined, the nationalism which was prevalent among the progressive and educated people of Germany, supported Münster instinctively, and finally it posed the question whether strong legal and administrative measures were necessary for nursing such a feeling.

The reactions from Berlin disclosed the embarrassing position of the German leaders. Bülow, in the quoted letter to the ambassador,[61] expressed his concern at the bad impression given to the Catholic electorate, especially in Bavaria, and he intimated to Münster that even the Emperor was not happy about the speech. 'The matter has caused a sensation here' he wrote. Bismarck, as Bülow said, had appreciated Münster's courage, but had advised him to take care lest the ambassador ran into difficulties. The State Secretary concluded by writing that he felt obliged to declare that Münster's manifestation of protestantism appeared to have irritated those Catholics who were true subjects of the Empire.[62] Münster, in his reply to Bülow,[63] expressed his satisfaction that the Prince and the State Secretary shared his opinions in principle (Bismarck's marginal note: 'Scarcely, but I support them when they are expressed'). He felt disappointed that the wording of the speech, which was only directed at the audience, had been published in full by the papers and had caused such a sensation. 'Thus, it has become clear to what extent the English press is guided by ultramontanists as well as by French people and German and Austrian separatists who, on their part, are exercising a great influence on the Jews, surprisingly even in religious matters' he wrote. He had declined to allow a mass meeting to be arranged for an address of thanks

to him (Bismarck's marginal: 'That is right, too great interference in internal affairs'). Concluding, he said: 'I don't mind
the attacks of the *Kreuzzeitung* and of English and Irish newspapers. The national Empire cannot tolerate the ultramontane
Catholics in the long run; therefore the German Catholics will
have to establish a German Catholic National Church'. (Marginal
note: a big interrogation mark.)

Bülow brought the matter to a close by instructing Münster
on 3 June 1875, on behalf of the Chancellor, that he should decline, without comments, any further requests to speak at a
public meeting.[64]

In the meantime the Irish member of the House of Commons,
Mr Sullivan, had put a question to the Prime Minister regarding
Münster's utterances.[65] Disraeli replied in a tortuous way, intima-
ting that although the speech delivered by the ambassador was
not in conformity with diplomatic practice he did not intend to
restrict his freedom of speech. When Münster intimated his
dissatisfaction with this kind of reply to the Prime Minister, the
latter answered courteously that he had had no intention of
blaming the ambassador or of putting him in an awkward position.[66]

The German press, of course, took note of the parliamentary
sequel in the host country of the ambassador. Whereas Disraeli's
reply was interpreted as a rebuff by the *Germania*,[67] the *Norddeutsche Allgemeine Zeitung*, as an organ of the government,
tried to minimise the event by arguing that the National Club
was a kind of religious society.[68]

Nearly everybody felt shocked at the ambassador's speech: the
Emperor himself, Bismarck, in whose eyes Münster had always
been an 'insubordinate ambassador', the German Conservatives,
the Catholics and even part of the Liberals. It also shocked the
British Prime Minister, who was not Münster's friend,[69] the Irish
people, and last but not least, *The Times* from which the ambassador got a plain lesson. All in all a sad résumé of Count
Münster's blunder.

CHAPTER 3

Land War and Home Rule

AFTER his defeat in the general election of 1886 subsequent to the failure of the first Home Rule Bill in the House of Commons, Gladstone wrote the following words which well sum up the background to the problems described in the preceding chapter:

> Had Mr Pitt in 1801 carried Roman Catholic Emancipation, as we suppose he wished, many an Englishman would have thought him precipitate. Precipitancy was avoided, but at what cost? For twenty-nine years the question was trifled with on one side of the Channel, and left festering on the other, and Emancipation was at last accepted as an alternative to civil war. Such is not the manner in which I desire to see the business of the Empire carried on.[1]

This long delay in carrying the Emancipation turned out harmful to the Union. The cost Gladstone alluded to was very high indeed. Immense damage to property and heavy loss of human life would have been avoided, if the only fair and suitable consequences of the amalgamation of the Kingdoms had been implemented, creating peaceful coexistence on equal terms for the various denominations and religious communities in Britain and Ireland. The heavy burden of a memory of long periods of discrimination would have been eased, the more so because the problem of religion and politics as a matter of decisive importance for mankind has always run like a red thread through English-Irish history. In his political career Gladstone at all times did his utmost to achieve a well-balanced relationship between Church and State in implementing the justified requirements of the State and the freedom of religious life and organisation. It seems clear that the lessons Bismarck and his followers had learnt—at high cost—served as an awful example to those statesmen of the civilised world who were anxious not to endanger the strength and security of their States by furthering hostility between Church and State.

The Germans, whose sensitivity was sharpened by the terrible experiences of the Middle Ages and of more recent times, could never neglect the relationship of Church and State when viewing each phase of English-Irish history; though there were many points of view on the subject, as became evident through the utterances of politicians, the press and other factors influencing public opinion. This applied to all the national, social and economic movements, particularly to those of an agrarian character, to the role of the Church in these movements, at the grass roots as well as at the Roman centre, and particularly to the assessment of the Irish leaders and their achievements.

The following analysis of the Irish situation in the eighties, made by the Counsellor of the London embassy, Herr Stumm (after 1888, Baron von Stumm) may serve as a kind of outline before dealing with the events of that decade in detail. This German diplomat, after a journey all over Ireland, during which he had formed contacts that went beyond those sanctioned by convention for a foreign envoy,[2] kept a record of his impressions, which forms an interesting and valuable, though summary, assessment of the situation as seen through German eyes.[3] An abridged version of the record reads as follows:

In spite of the measures taken under the Coercion Act 1881, the number of agrarian crimes and the spirit of uprising and discontent are spreading rapidly through all classes of the population. Ireland of today appears, as it did 300 years ago, as a conquered island whose land was divided up by the conquerors among themselves and whose possession they have to defend by force against the hostile attitude of the native population.

For centuries the Irish people have had no other contact with their landlords except through the agents who collect the rents or through the policemen who confiscate the cattle. Forty-four thousand agrarian crimes have been committed in the course of the last year. The Land League, banned and outlawed by the Government, is still persisting in unweakened vigour. Rallies are taking place by night or are camouflaged as dances.

Miss Parnell appears to be the evil spirit of her brother who is not unreasoning. As a prophet of the liberation of Ireland from the English yoke, she travels about all over the island, welcomed like a saint by the peasants.

Religious motives do not play an important role under the present circumstances, due to the atheistic and socialist doctrines imported from America. The influence of the Catholic Clergy has therefore diminished.

The rents do not appear excessively high in fertile districts in the east, Kilkenny or Cork, contrary to those in Galway or many parts of the midlands where, moreover, the land is owned by shopkeepers, speculators and societies who have forced up the rents ruthlessly and who have squeezed the tenants.

. . . 2,715,604 Irishmen have left their homes since 1851, and the whole population has decreased by more than three million people since 1846.

This record was sent to the Chancellor with an approving comment—an interesting fact considering how Münster used to express his opinions in other reports—and was then circulated, by order of Bismarck, to all German ministers of State and Empire as well as to all German diplomatic missions. This indicates the noteworthy fact that Bismarck did not object to the general line of the assessment made in the record. On 20 April 1882, the Emperor wrote the following marginal note to this paper: 'The author of this interesting and clear, though gloomy, description is to be commended.'

MOVEMENTS AND MEASURES

The New Departure and the Land League—The Land Act and the Coercion Act 1881—The Phoenix Park murders and coercion again—Count Herbert Bismarck in London—The Arrears Act and the National League—No optimism—The Home Rule Movement and the Irish Party—The Caretaker Government and Gladstone's return—Bismarck, the Poles and the Parnellites—The first Home Rule Bill—Salisbury's 'twenty years'—The Plan of Campaign—Gladstone's second Home Rule Bill.

The end of a long period of economic prosperity in Europe caused a disaster in Irish agriculture. Subsequent to the boom which had lasted for a quarter of a century, the Irish tenants were badly hit by the recession, particularly that on the agrarian sector. The poor results of three consecutive harvests had been made more acute by the increased importation of agricultural products which were not met by any import levies as in the continental countries. The total value of Irish agricultural production had fallen from £36 million in 1876 to £32 million in 1878 and to £22 million in 1879. The potato harvest had gone down in the same period from 4 million to 1 million tons.[4] The tenants, however, had to pay the same rents as they did before the recession. Arrears at an incredible total amount had been accumulated and evictions of tenants were quite common. The refusal of protective measures for Irish agriculture by the British politicians in power indicated their lack of insight into the particular economic situation of Ireland. A migration from the country to the towns, so characteristic in Britain as well as in large parts of the continent, did not occur in Ireland because there was no employment in the towns, except in some parts of Ulster where industrialisation was in progress. A recurrence of the Great Famine of the early forties had to be reckoned with in the late seventies.[5]

It is against this background that the economic and political development has to been seen. Unfortunately people on the continent and their responsible leaders, owing to quite different situations in their countries, to their different outlook and to the important geographical distance between Ireland and central Europe, became aware of the situation in Ireland comparatively late, and their envoys did not take note of it until the Land War was raging. Thus, it should not be taken as a surprising fact that in the first period of the disturbances the German representatives reacted with reluctance and on few occasions.

The New Departure, as Moody describes it, involved the open participation in public movements by extremists, the intention being to bring an advanced national spirit and revolutionary purpose into friendly rivalry with moderate nationalists.[6] It meant a change in Fenian methods but not in the essential aim of Fenianism; a plan for open instead of secret action in which a radical settlement of the land question figured as one of a series of subsidiary objectives[7] which involved no action not strictly within the laws and no alliance between constitutionalists and revolutionists.[8] The main principles of the new policy are outlined in detail in a telegram of 25 October 1878 from Devoy to Parnell, in which Devoy offered the support of the Irish-American nationalists under the following conditions: self-government; vigorous agitation in the land question on the basis of peasant proprietorship; exclusion of all sectarian issues from the platform; Irish members of Parliament to vote united on all imperial and home questions; adoption of an aggressive policy and energetic resistance to coercive legislation; support for all nationalists struggling in the British Empire or elsewhere.[9]

The Land League founded by Michael Davitt in April 1879 was something different. It was, 'in the first place, an emergency organisation with exclusively agrarian purposes, the immediate defence of the tenant farmers threatened with eviction'.[10] The New Departure was 'an outline of aims and methods as to handling future politics in general, whereas the Land League was to serve as a means for remedying injustice in the land questions'.

It goes without saying that these differences and subtleties were far too complicated to be fully grasped by uninvolved contemporary observers—in particular, diplomats and journalists from the continent who were not fully conversant with English/Irish history and relationships and who saw the situation, partly at least, through glasses coloured by their informants. One cannot avoid the impression, for example, that Parnell as a political leader and as president of the Land League since October 1879 was regarded, at least in the first years of his activities, as a kind of civilised Fenian.

Most foreign observers, as mentioned above, were hardly aware of what was happening until violence and outrage shook the political stage, providing the correspondents with headlines for their newspapers and the diplomats with sensational material for their information and reports. At least, the attention of the respective authorities in the countries abroad was eventually drawn to that stage where a drama with worldwide impact was developing, seriously affecting the position and reputation of Britain as a European power.

The limited interest on the European continent should be regarded under a double aspect. On the one hand, people in Britain whose main concern was the maintaining of the political and economic status quo in Ireland propagated this aim systematically through the channels of the press, of diplomacy and of social relationship; on the other hand, the Irish organisations laid the emphasis of their propaganda upon the United States where they found their moral and financial support through Irish emigrants who had come to influential positions in political and economic life.

No wonder that under these circumstances the reports of the German embassy were insignificant and meagre, at least in the first year after the foundation of the Land League. Early in 1880, the ambassador, after a conversation with Disraeli and with reference to the Irish parliamentary obstruction, pointed to the necessity of taking energetic measures against the Irish members of Parliament who were 'striving for an undermining of Parliament's authority'. He added that the distress in Ireland was being exploited by the current agitation and that coercive measures would be unavoidable.[11]

It is not surprising that Bismarck was dissatisfied by the style of Münster's information. Shortly before the general election took place in which Disraeli was defeated—contrary to the ambassador's prediction—an instruction was sent out to the embassy requesting urgently a report 'on the economic and political situation in Ireland, on the measures taken in order to avoid famine, on the procuring of means and how they are spent, and on the extent to which plans and preparations for legislation to settle the Land question had developed'.[12]

Münster's reply[13] was a typical product of his mentality, a mixture of triviality and exasperation, though not entirely without realism and truth. He went so far as to blame 'the credulous Irish' because 'they think they are the true proprietors of the land', obviously in complete ignorance of Cromwell, in particular, and of Irish history in general. Then he spoke about the revolutionists, the over-population of some districts and the parcelling out of the crofts while taking the view that the Irish tenants were a lazy lot who were drinking as much as they could get to drink, comparable to the muzhiks. 'Not the landlords but the money-lenders are responsible for the evictions of the tenants' he wrote.

The measures of relief taken by the British government were palliatives. 'It cannot be denied', he wrote, 'that the English administration in Ireland is weak and badly organised and that the handling of purely domestic affairs could be left to the Irish themselves, to the advantage of both sides; so far the wishes of the moderate Home Rulers might appear justified'—one remarkable admission, at least.

It was clear to those who knew the Chancellor and the purpose of his instruction that he was not satisfied by Münster's reply. It did not deal, as a matter of fact, with the questions put to the ambassador. As Bismarck was very anxious to know about the internal situation of the United Kingdom as a world power, he was very keen indeed to be informed on a question which gave rise to genuine concern. Bismarck did not insist this time, but Münster obviously felt committed to inform more frequently on events in the future, the more so as newspaper correspondents became more interested in Irish affairs. The *Norddeutsche All-gemeine,* a government paper, for example, informed its readers about the evictions of tenants in Connemara where 'the police mutilated four people with the bayonet', and it described the situation in Ireland as 'partly anarchical', because the government was not able or not willing to provide for law and order. 'While destitution is increasing, hungry-looking people of the working classes are marching through the streets with black banners and a loaf of bread at the staff's point' the paper wrote.[14]

The *Germania* in an article on 'Ireland's past and future' reminded its readers of Henry VIII, Elizabeth, Cromwell and William of Orange, mentioning the discrimination against the Catholics, Grattan's Parliament, the Act of Union, Emancipation, the Famine, Emigration and the Fenians, all in all a brief summary of Irish history. The paper discussed the ordeal of the Irish people, their oppression and age-old enslavement, while hailing Gladstone because of the Land Act and the Disestablishment of the Church of Ireland. 'He has done more for Ireland than the Tories, who did almost nothing' the paper declared.[15]

In his next report Münster described the activity of the Land League which 'propagates the expulsion and extermination of the landlords'.[16] He predicted the failure of the investigation against the Irish leaders. 'The whole procedure is ridiculed in Ireland, the defence well organised—£20,000 have been subscribed to it on the first day.' Gladstone, Bright and Forster, the Chief Secretary, were called up as witnesses for the defence 'because they had propagated rebellion in the same way as the Land League'. 'Intensive gun-running is going on, an American pistol can be bought for seven to eight shillings.'[17]

In a speech at the Lord Mayor's banquet on 9 November 1880 Gladstone stressed the necessity for reforms in Ireland on the one hand and for coercive measures against infringements on the other. 'Not only landlords are threatened by the League but also the tenants who are paying their rents' he said. Reporting on the speech, Münster added that in Gladstone's view the landlords were obviously fair game.[18]

In the following report he told the story of Captain Boycott 'whose harvest has been gathered by 50 people from Ulster under the protection of 900 men of infantry and cavalry with two guns'. He also wrote about the situation in the south-west of Ireland 'where the Land League has full power, and where the rents payable on St Michael's Day have been paid nowhere. The unfortunate landlords are in frightful distress because credit has been almost entirely cut off,' he said.[19]

In a letter to the Emperor,[20] Münster blamed Gladstone and his cabinet for having admitted to organising the revolution in Ireland where the Land League was in full power, aiming at the separation of Ireland from England, the establishment of an Irish Republic and union with America, as well as the allocation of the land to the lower classes of the population. In this context he mentioned voices in favour of the Irish, for example, that of the Archbishop of Toronto who had called England 'a cruel stepmother to Ireland'.

Apart from his reply to Bismarck's instruction of 23 March 1880, Münster's reports and opinions were, partly at least, unbalanced and of a summary character, not always based on uncontested facts, and they tended to ignore the lessons of the century in which he lived. Obviously he was not fully aware of 'the fear of famine, or rather of having to choose between starvation and eviction, was the great underlying political reality of the late seventies and early eighties of the nineteenth century in Ireland'.[21] The land legislation from 1801–70 was in general in the interest of the landlords and against the interest of the Irish tenant; the Irish landlords enjoyed great influence in the leadership of both the Whig and the Tory parties and in both Houses of Parliament, out of all proportion to the number of members from their ranks.[22] Winston Churchill, on his part, described the situation in Ireland in the most impressive way as follows:

'The Queen's speech (1880) contained no suggestion of Irish land legislation; and the supporters of the ministry had assembled at Westminster eager to discuss every subject—from the

Treaty of Berlin to the shooting of hares and rabbits—except the subject of Ireland.'[23]

He added the wise words 'that a political movement to be dangerous must find its substance in social evil'. He then quoted from a record of General Gordon who had visited the west of Ireland in 1880 and who had described the situation 'as worse than of any people in the world, let alone Europeans' and who had declared 'that the people are patient beyond belief, lying on the verge of starvation in places where we would not keep cattle'. Obviously the content of such records had scarcely come to the notice of foreign diplomats at that time.

In 1893 Gladstone remarked that 'without the Land League the Land Act 1881 would not now be upon the Statute Book'.[24] Beckett believes that the League's influence on British opinion had made it politically possible for Gladstone to carry his conception into effect.[25] Although it meant an important progress compared with the Act of 1870 which only seemed to be satisfactory as long as agriculture prospered, the Land Act of 1881 did not prove to be a final solution. It satisfied the wishes of the tenants in so far as it met their demands regarding the 'three F's' (fixity of tenure, fair rents, freedom of the tenant to sell his share of the holding)[26] and the establishing of the Land Court. Gladstone had to fight very hard before he reached his goal; in the third reading only fourteen members voted against while the conservatives and Parnell with his followers abstained.[27] Eyck, however, takes the view that the bill was diluted in the House of Lords,[28] and the Queen was said to have blamed Gladstone by remarking that justice should be done to the tenant but not at the expense of the 'non-responsible landlords'.[29]

Parnell's attitude was understandable, the more so because the Irish members had not been consulted by the government and were in no way responsible for the measure. The weakness of the bill could have been avoided if such a consultation had taken place.

The German embassy followed the legislative proceedings with interest, reporting continuously on the various phases. Gladstone was said to have declined to call the majority of the Irish landlords 'tyrants', but—according to a report—there were people who behaved as such.[30] Some months later Münster informed Berlin on the 'good progress of the Land Bill'. Even the

Conservatives were now convinced that legislative measures were necessary in order to avert further calamities in Ireland.[31] Frederick William, the Crown Prince, mentioning the proceedings of the bill in a letter of 17 August 1881 to Bismarck from Morris Castle, made the following remarks:

'Parliament here is in great anxiety because of the Land Bill which is felt as a necessary evil for Ireland in order to avoid greater nuisance in the coming winter. Several Lords have abstained from voting by yachting or shooting grouse instead; other Lords are speaking against while voting in favour.'[32]

After the passing of the bill Münster expressed his doubts as to whether the Land Act would appease the discontent in Ireland, because the Land League was regarding it merely as the first rung of a ladder. He recorded that Parnell had declared before the League 'The land is yours'[33] and that *The Times* had reported on a procession of 30,000 people in Dublin, where Sexton declared 'The City of Dublin has broken loose from the Lion and the Unicorn and has arrayed itself under the sacred banner of the Shamrock and the Harp.'[34]

Beckett,[35] pointing to the unstable political situation outside Ulster, holds that the success of the Land Act depended on its being supported by Parnell and the Land League, and that 'their attitude was decidedly hostile'. Parnell's position is described as awkward. Sitting between two fires he was on the one hand threatened by extremists who were defying the government and waging direct war on the landlords, and on the other hand he had to face the possibility 'that the act, if generally accepted, might so far conciliate the tenants as to undermine their support for the Home Rule party. He did not, therefore, denounce the act completely but complained that it did little or nothing for tenants who were already in arrears.'

When dealing with the activities of the Land League, Münster several times took the opportunity to attack Parnell. In his report on the adoption of the Coercion Bill[36] he commented on the leader's attitude by declaring that 'he had unmasked himself by his contacts with the French red revolutionists' and that 'he and his followers are in reality democratic revolutionists in the worst sense of the word'.[37] Later on,[38] when the Land Bill had been enacted, he maintained that Parnell as head of the Land League had declared that 'everything will have to be done to prevent the execution of the act which is entirely unsatisfactory'. Curiously enough, this information was not accepted by the Foreign Office in Berlin. Münster was corrected by the marginal note: 'Not correct; he had asked the tenants to assume an observant attitude with regard to the experiences made with the act in each county.' Owing to this inaccuracy the report was not presented to the Crown Prince Frederick William who was interested in the act.[39]

Following the arrest of Parnell and other League leaders, the reports dealt first of all with the emotional discussions which took place in the cabinet, with Bright's and Chamberlain's warning of an open rebellion and bloody fights in the case of Parnell's arrest and with Gladstone's and Forster's advocating of energetic measures.[40] A few days later the embassy informed Berlin on Gladstone's disappointment at the events, following his expectation that the unrest would cease and that the agitation would be halted through the act (Bismarck's marginal note: 'Stupid!').[41] Another report described the many arrests in Ireland, taking the view that a body of 40,000 soldiers and 12,000 policemen could suppress the rebellion but not restore law and order, in particular because doubts had arisen about the legitimacy of the proclamation of the Lord Lieutenant who had declared the League an unlawful association on 19 October 1881.[42]

The last reports of that year were pessimistic in outlook. They gave a depressing description of the situation, emphasising that the League despite its suppression continued to act with unweakened vigour, that boycotting was going on all over the country and that Parnell's manifestos even found their way through the iron bars of Kilmainham. Far-sighted Englishmen could find no way out of the situation and were growing more and more indifferent to Ireland. 'Landlords who are abandoning deliberately one quarter of the rents are not in a worse position than their equals in England and Scotland . . . The Irish question on the whole presents nothing but difficulties.'[43]

According to Lyons, Parnell had already grasped the central fact that the Land Act had beaten the League and that there was no longer a future for a predominantly agrarian agitation. But the practical end of the Land League, he continues, did not mean the end of unrest, as the arrest of the leaders opened a new phase of violence.[44] Thus one can state that contemporary assessment and the results of historical research coincide in this case.

Looking back upon the period described, a period marked by the implementation of coercion, one should recall how coercion in theory and practice was viewed by English people who had a calm approach to the situation. Speaking on the Coercion Bill in the House of Commons, Randolph Churchill declared that 'Coercion is a double-edged weapon and has before now fatally wounded those administrations which have been compelled by their own folly to have recourse to it.'[45] Winston Churchill said that Forster's policy was unfortunate, that his position, although supported by overwhelming majorities of both big parties, was certainly unenviable and that there was an impression that he was a man particularly repugnant to Irish feeling.[46] Eversley's attitude towards Forster as that of a contemporary and of a member of Gladstone's cabinet was not as severe as Churchill's. He was against coercion and regarded the act as a great error. 'It had greatly aggravated the position and prevented the Land Act from having effect in quieting the country.' But in his opinion, Forster went to Ireland with high ideals, with great determination to do justice and to ameliorate the condition of the lower class of tenants. He administered an odious Coercion Act with great leniency to those who were imprisoned under it. But Eversley nevertheless criticises Forster's dogmatic self-confidence and his brusque manners.[47]

Forster's term of office ended when he resigned after the Kilmainham Treaty by which Parnell and the other leaders were freed. The Phoenix Park murders, whose victims were Lord Cavendish, Forster's successor, and his Undersecretary Burke, demonstrated in a frightening way the complexity of the Irish question. Nobody knew from which part or class of the country a new dragon would arise when other dangers had been neutralised.

In Münster's opinion the discharge from custody of Parnell was a gain for radicalism, Gladstone in his ingenuity being its unconscious tool. In his view, the moving spirits were Chamberlain and Bright whose plans were based on common action of the Radicals and the Irish. Münster took the view that Gladstone had underestimated the danger and had failed to demand powers for suppressing the 'rebels, trouble-makers, murderers and

arsonists'.[48] The murders were described as 'part of the programme of the Fenians written in blood, which was meant to
convey the message: No Englishman on Irish soil'. The murders
were said to be directed against Parnell, too, who had received
threatening letters because of his attitude in the agrarian conflict.[49] After the funeral of the murdered Chief Secretary,
Münster informed the Foreign Office about the extraordinary
measures taken, adding the comment 'that Gladstone's position
has been strengthened through this action'.[50]

In this context it must be noted how the German press reacted to Gladstone's policy during those years. While the papers
close to Bismarck wrote in a rather cautious way, the *Germania*
dealt with Irish affairs frankly and critically. The paper had
obviously not forgotten what Gladstone's position had been with
regard to the Vatican Decrees,[51] and the first articles of the paper
after his return to power convey the impression that certain misgivings had persisted. But the English Liberals were viewed
differently from the Liberals on the continent 'who regard the
struggle against Christianity in general and the Catholic Church
in particular as their principal mission'. Liberalism in England
was praised on the ground that it had achieved the Emancipation
of English and Irish Catholics. 'Lord Ripon, a convert, as Viceroy
of India: this is an indication that Gladstone has abandoned his
illusions about the Old Catholics after the Vatican Council and
has got rid of the velleities of the Kulturkampf as outdated and
unpractical.'[52]

According to a correspondent's report it was originally envisaged that Lord Ripon should be appointed Lord Lieutenant of
Ireland but this was finally not accepted. Eventually, Lord
Cowper was appointed. 'As a politician he is a mere cipher, a
fact which seems to be characteristic of viceroys in Ireland.'[53]

The comments of the paper on the events in 1881 had been
poor and absolutely inadequate, whereas the situation after the
Phoenix Park murders was carefully observed. On 11 May 1882,
the correspondent informed readers about Trevelyan's appointment as successor to the assassinated Lord Cavendish and about
the condemnation of the murders by the bishops.[54] In a leader
with the headline 'The new Irish Coercion Bill' the newspaper
pointed out that the murderers had achieved their goal: the truce
between the Government and the Land League was broken, the

Land War continued. 'We are not in favour of emergency laws, but we understand that Gladstone yielded to the pressure exercised upon him by the English people when introducing that Bill.' The article criticised Parnell: He should be more helpful in oppressing the moonlighters whose activities had caused the coercion measures.[55] This comment is an indication for the paper's approach to Parnell who was for the most part regarded with a certain reserve.

In a report from London the paper defended the Irish party against the accusations of other press organs in Berlin which held the party responsible for the assassination of the two politicians. 'This is quite untrue; on the whole, the Irish people are furious about this foul deed.' The paper concluded the report by quoting Michael Davitt: 'I had rather stayed in jail for a lifetime instead of taking note of this shame my country has to endure.'[56]

In another report the correspondent dealt with the secret societies, remarking that the Church had always condemned them. 'England has used the secret society of the Free Masons for creating unrest in all countries of the world.' It appeared to be doubtful whether it would be advisable to employ the same means in Ireland as in India for the extermination of secret societies, the correspondent declared, 'for Ireland is not India'.[57]

In the following articles the *Germania* described the reactions and repercussions in England following the developments in the Irish situation, in particular the positions of the parties and England's role as a world power. It regretted the aggravation of the difficulties caused by the murders and the setback Gladstone had suffered by it on the one hand, but blamed the statesman for his wait-and-see policy on the other. 'It cannot be denied that Gladstone was not himself, free of the fault of British politicians, which is not to deal with very urgent matters unless compelled by force.' The indignation of the Tories was hypocritical, the paper declared; they were fully aware that in England reforms could only be achieved under the heavy pressure of a threatening rebellion. Each country had its hereditary troubles, but England's were too numerous and too great. According to the paper, the Irish question had become a dangerous illness for England as a world power. The country's destiny was closely linked with Ireland; England's position in the world and her internal development were at stake. Further coercion would provoke reactions of the Irish in the United States. 'What is going to happen if England runs into difficulties in Egypt, Turkey or on the continent?' the article concluded.[58]

In this context the paper quoted from remarks of *Die Post*, a conservative press organ, which were not less critical of the British as to their handling of the Irish question. 'When, eventually, the English saw that their way of administration was of no practical use and when they resolved to change the situation, they did it unwillingly and to such a limited extent that this fact paralysed the envisaged effects completely. The Irish could not be satisfied by measures taken half-heartedly, feeling that they were treated like hungry dogs fed with a few bones.'[59]

With regard to German views on the relevant phase of Irish history, another important source is Count Herbert Bismarck, the son of the Chancellor and later his State Secretary in the Foreign Office, who spent almost two years of office in London (from 1 January 1882) as First Secretary to the German embassy. His reports and personal letters to his father no doubt considerably influenced the Chancellor's assessment of Gladstone's dealing with the Irish question and of Ireland generally. In his introductory observations to the published letters of Count Herbert,[60] Bussmann, who has edited the collection, describes the political and parliamentary situation of England during Gladstone's second ministry as a situation which proved enormously instructive for the young diplomat. His opinions as expressed in his letters frequently reflected the chancellor's approach to England's political landscape in the 1880s, confirming it, however, through personal experiences and observations.

It is small wonder that Irish affairs attracted the attention of the Count considerably, because the handling of this matter was regarded in Germany as one of the touchstones of parliamentary democracy in England. In one of the first letters to his father from London he dealt with the qualities of the parties. He accused the Conservative opposition of aimlessness, and quoting Lord Bedford—'they have no first-class capacities, the Liberals have the abler people, Gladstone is the most popular man and if he, the shrewdest popular orator, were sitting on the opposition benches, any Conservative cabinet would be in distress'—he gave a gloomy picture of the future of conservatism.[61] In a letter of 21 February 1882 to his brother, he described the bearings and the implications of the Land Act with regard to the Irish Peers, deploring deeply that according to estimates 'Gladstone will take twenty-three per cent from the Irish Lords in order to put this amount into the pockets of the Irish farmers whom he intends to secure for himself'. These remarks were preceded by passing shots at the liberal Whigs who regarded the Irish Lords as ship-wrecked persons who could not expect to save their entire property and should be content to save seventy-five per cent. It is robbery, organised by the government', he wrote.[62]

In a letter of 9 May 1882, Count Herbert recorded his impressions after the murders very bluntly. In his view Gladstone should be compelled to resign, parliament ought to be dissolved and Ireland should be put under martial law. After describing Gladstone's behaviour in parliament in unmistakable terms he mentioned Parnell 'who is in difficulties with the American Fenians and whose reputation is shattered'.[63] Bussmann describes Count Herbert's approach to the Irish question in these words: 'It is typical that Count Bismarck regarded the social misery of the Irish tenants and its consequences from the point of view of the State attacked, and that he integrated the particular events in Ireland into a greater political-social context.'[64] There is nothing to add to this judgement. After the setback in his Irish policy caused by the Phoenix Park murders, Gladstone showed no signs of discouragement. By virtue of 'his trust in the healing power of justice'[65] his faith in the measures he had inspired remained unshaken. After the failure of the Compensation for Disturbance Bill in 1880 which was defeated in the Upper Chamber after its adoption in the House of Commons—a fateful decision of the Lords which aggravated the Land War—[66] Gladstone took another initiative aimed at sweetening coercion[67] and at guaranteeing the effects of the Land Act. He introduced the Arrears Bill. This bill, when enacted, had a more appeasing effect upon the country than the severity of the coercive measures.[68]

In October 1882 the dissolved Land League was replaced by the National League, which was closely linked with the Irish party. The League formed the backbone of the party in organising the electorate at home and it convened the mass meetings. 'The effects of meetings like this will be to enable those parliamentary representatives to tell the Government that when they are making demands in the House of Commons for proper and

D

remedial legislation for this country the entire population may be said to be behind them.'[69]

Internal difficulties in the Irish administration hampered the efficiency even of the security forces.[70] And the Lord Lieutenant's opinion, reported by Münster, 'that the state of affairs had improved, that the League had lost power and that the Clergy exercised restraint',[71] was too optimistic.

Contrary to this, the *Germania,* in an article entitled 'Famine in Ireland' reported that in Donegal 8,000 people faced death by hunger. Some priests had directed an open letter to Trevelyan, the Chief Secretary, who in his turn, when travelling around the country, had not visited the parishes of the authors of the letter, the *Germania* declared. The paper asserted that the main diet of the population of coastal regions consisted of submarine plants, and that no help had been granted to the people for weeks after the visit of the representatives of the administration.[72]

No wonder that the subsequent diplomatic reports no longer viewed the situation with optimism. They dealt mostly with the effects of coercion and the increasing tension between Dublin Castle and the Irish population as well as with the feeling of British politicians. Count Bismarck, in his capacity of Chargé d'Affaires, informed the Foreign Office on his conversations with these politicians. Lord Hartington—later Duke of Devonshire—took the view that the Irish behaved peacefully as long as coercion prevailed, whereas Chamberlain expressed himself in favour of Home Rule—an opinion he was to abandon very soon. 'Most of the British population is not interested in foreign policy as they are carefully following the situation in Ireland; the popularity of the cabinet depends on it,' Count Herbert wrote.[73]

In a private letter to his father he had written that fear was the actual political stimulus in England. According to Count Bismarck, Gladstone was also in fear of his constituents in Midlothian. He had been informed that the Scottish Presbyterians were irritated because of the rumours that he was in negotiation with the Pope. 'He is afraid that his reception would be lukewarm and that he would be greeted with crys of No Popery. Thus he preferred to stay at home instead of going to Midlothian.'[74]

Further letters and reports in 1883 described the personality of Lord Spencer, the Lord Lieutenant, his outlook and reputation. Herbert Bismarck, in a letter after a conversation with Sir

W. Harcourt, wrote to the Chancellor that more trouble with the Home Rulers was lying ahead, but that the censure of the government by the Conservative opposition was handicapped because of Lord Spencer's firm implementation of the Coercion Act; no Tory administration could do it better.[75]

In another private letter to his father he informed him of a talk with Spencer. Spencer was said to have remarked 'that they would cope with Ireland very soon; the Irish, like all people of Celtic race, prefer to have a strong administration, they expect orders and obey with enthusiasm'. In addition to these absolutely foolish views Spencer expressed his opinion about the Irish and German immigrants in the United States. 'The Germans do not get along well with the Irish in America. If the German immigration were to continue at the same rate in the forthcoming years, the Irish would be thrust into the background and would lose their influence in the elections.'[76] It is inconceivable that the Chancellor could have taken these reports as a basis for making up his mind about the future of American politics and the mentality of the Celtic race.

Optimism is ill-timed, could be the motto of the subsequent reports. Bitterness towards England despite the concessions on the agrarian sector, as well as terrorism, lawlessness and agitation had increased due to the influx of money from America, and the intervention of a Home Ruler in parliament, who said that 'ninety per cent of the Irish people hate you, the rest despise you'. These were the catchwords of Münster's reports. Spencer was hailed as an energetic man 'who has weakened the power of the rebels considerably,' whereas Gladstone was said to have admitted that the Irish behaved ungratefully despite his reform legislation.[77]

The clearest indication as to the real situation in the period before Gladstone's resignation in 1885 was to be found in the behaviour of the Irish during the visit of the Prince and the Princess of Wales in April 1885. Münster gave the following portrait of it: everything was well staged, although the assistance of the police and the necessity of protective measures could not remain unnoticed. No flag on the Town Hall; flags on other buildings had to be watched-over by night. In the country many signs of dislike such as black banners, coffins, whistling and jeering. At Mallow and Cork demonstrations of a very unpleasant character with much whistling and grumbling, the royal coaches stoned in a very disgusting way. In Ulster and Derry whistling and grumbling too, at the instance of the National League. 'The deep discordance prevailing in Ireland was not concealed, and there are apprehensions that the visit has not produced the effect the Viceroy and the authorities had reckoned with. There is no conciliation of the hostile elements and the antagonism has deepened,' Count Münster declared.[78] In this context one should take note of Bismarck's attitude towards Gladstone and his policy in those years, which he expressed in a letter to William I: 'The decay of England's power as a possible result of Gladstone's policy cannot be assessed as a useful development for Germany's political situation'.[79] At this crucial point of Irish history one should recall the role the Home Rule movement and the Irish party had played up to the time when Gladstone's second term of office approached its end. Dibelius pays great tribute to the role of this party during the Victorian era in taking the view that 'the internal history of Victorian England is dominated by the impulses Ireland has given to English politics' and 'no description of English political parties can therefore ignore the most powerful lever arm of England's internal policy, the Irish party'.[80] Alter[81] gives a concise description of the origins of the constitutional Home Rule[82] movement in Ireland which started in 1869 at the suggestion of Isaac Butt, the son of a Protestant clergyman in Donegal, thus initiating the revival of constitutional nationalism in Ireland for a period of almost five decades. He emphasises the merits of the Home Rule party in the agrarian issues, in presenting a model of organisation and discipline for the parties in England, and, eventually, its considerable contribution to the enacting of the Parliament's bill. In Alter's view Butt's concept was a synthesis of national, conservative and liberal ideas, with the aim of neutralising the radicalism which was threatening as a consequence of the growing power of the masses. Butt's feeling was 'There is no people on earth less disposed to democracy than the Irish. The real danger of democratic or revolutionary violence is far more with the English people'.[83] Butt's originally very vague suggestion proved attractive to both Protestant conservatism and Irish catholicism and led to the constitution of the Home Government Association for Ireland in May 1870,[84] an association at first composed of Protestants and Conservatives but later on of

Liberals, as well, which aimed at the creation of a decentralised United Kingdom, federal in character. But the successor organisation, the Irish Home Rule League founded late in 1873, was dominated uncontestedly by the Liberals. After the remarkable success of the Home Rule candidates in the general election of 1874, a party programme was adopted declaring the Home Rulers an independent party 'united on the principle of obtaining self-government for Ireland, as defined in the resolutions of the conference held in Dublin last November' (1873).[85] The Home Rule party was not revolutionist, owing to the social standing of its members and the change in social structure under the influence of the emancipated middle classes which, however, were rather weak in Ireland.

Butt has been characterised as a 'man of great ability, courage and public spirit, but the victim of drink and debt[86] who 'died of a broken heart . . . with a bitter sense of failure, of ruined fortune, and of political defeat by insurgent members of his own party, unredeemed by any generous appreciation of his great services to the Irish people'.[87] He remained a Conservative until the end of his life.[88] He felt that he was taking the best course to maintain upper-class leadership and to preserve Ireland from revolution. Had any considerable body of Irish Conservatives followed his lead, the history of the following thirty years might have been very different. Looking back upon the last decades before the war, there seems to be a lot of truth in this opinion expressed by Beckett.[89]

When Butt died in 1879, Parnell had, as MacDonagh points out, practically seized control of 'the flaccid, directionless and disintegrating Home Rule Party in the House of Commons and began to fashion it into an instrument of his own'. Very impressively he compares Parnell with Bismarck, 'Like Bismarck, Parnell created a situation or series of situations, in which he appeared to the relevant power groups to be indispensable.'[90] Like Butt, Parnell was not a revolutionist. During the coercion period he was under heavy pressure to secede from parliament, but he stayed at his post 'apparently opting for a constitutional rather than a revolutionary role'.[91] But he had resolved to stand up to the English. 'That is the only way to treat an Englishman.'[92]

The German comments on the first stages of the Home Rule movement were poor and superficial, mostly summaries which were limited to a minimum. Home Rule was felt to be a dangerous word with regard to similar problems in Germany as mentioned above.

Münster reported briefly on Butt's activities in the House of Commons, mentioning his motions for amendments in the address-debate and his argument that 'the situation in Ireland is not in conformity with the constitution'.[93] In his reports on the Irish obstruction he confirmed that Butt had been against obstruction, contrary to other eminent members of the party. 'This extreme ultramontanist party' [whose leader was a Protestant!] is anxious to lead Ireland into bloodshed' he wrote.[94] Alluding again to the Irish obstruction in parliament and reporting on the sharpening of the standing orders, the ambassador characterised the Irish question as England's most dangerous problem in the near future, asserting that 'the party which agitates for the separation from England in the open is growing steadily and behaving in a very impertinent way, dreaming already of an amalgamation with the United States'.[95]

Münster mentioned Parnell's activity for the first time on 12 February 1880, declaring that 'this activity is regarded as treacherous'.[96] Early in 1881 he reported Parnell's trial in Dublin 'which is regarded as a bad joke as everybody knows that the jury will never dare to return a verdict of guilty', adding that the government was beginning to regard the Irish rebellion as something dangerous (marginal note of William I: 'high time').[97]

A few days later he spoke about 'the impertinent behaviour' of a minority in the House of Commons and expressed his regret that the governmental power had descended 'from the Crown and the aristocracy into the hands of the masses'.[98] In this respect a remark of an Italian paper (*Aurora* of 7 February 1881) criticising the behaviour of the Whigs and Tories towards the Irish party is noteworthy. With regard to the Coercion Bill, which was called 'despotism' by the paper, it blamed Gladstone and expressed the opinion that the Irish would go ahead with agitation but would never go as far as civil war, because they were too clever:

> 'Il bravo Patrizio
> Ha troppo giudizio'

the article concluded.[99]

Gladstone resigned in June 1885 and Lord Salisbury took over, forming a cabinet without a majority in parliament, the Caretaker Government. Shortly before, Münster had reported that the followers of Home Rule were increasing, particularly among the young Conservatives. 'Up to now this was regarded as a revolutionary claim which was beyond any discussion, but at present it is taken as a necessity by many people.'[100] These were ominous words with regard to the tactics of the Conservatives aiming at a conciliatory position towards the Home Rulers in the coming general election. It is very interesting in this context to take note of a letter of 4 July 1885 from a Briton (his surname is unknown, his first name was Malcolm) to Count Bismarck in which he predicted that Gladstone would return to power 'at the end of the year with a large majority'. In the view of this Mr X who was obviously very close to Count Herbert, the Conservatives had played their cards very badly. 'For the sake of six months' office they have thrown away their chance of six years' office. Now Mr Gladstone will lead the Liberal host to battle with a united front and I have no doubt that he will achieve a greater victory than he won in 1880. His popularity in the country is at this moment greater than it has been at any stage of his career; and he owes no small part of his popularity to the persistent and savage attacks made upon him in the German press. It is commonly believed in England that His Highness your father has used all his influence and skill to thwart and discredit Mr Gladstone's foreign policy with a view to drive him out of office.' The author of the letter continued by pointing out that Gladstone was the victim of foreign malevolence and that this belief had raised in the constituencies a determination to send him back into government at any cost. 'Nothing contributed more to Lord Beaconsfield's fall than the support he received from the press in Germany and Austria. Lord Salisbury is believed to be in office by the favour of Germany and Austria who are supposed to have influenced the Queen in pressing him to take office.' (Bismarck's marginal note: 'There was no need for my assistance. The papers rather did it against my will. It was the English policy which incensed them!')[101] At any rate this letter seems to be a noteworthy contribution to the history of the Salisbury interlude and its international background.

Notwithstanding this prospect of the life-expectancy of the Conservative cabinet, the German ambassador was optimistic.

After a visit to Windsor he expressed the opinion that Gladstone's regime was regarded as 'entirely pushed out'. Gladstone was said to have been pushed out by the radicals, first in Ireland and later in other matters of reform. 'One cannot assume that the Queen will call upon Gladstone again.'[102] But he remarked that the government had at least made a truce with the Irish party. His next report followed the same line. Parnell was said to have offered his support to the Conservatives while the Liberals had strongly expressed themselves against the Parnellites. Thus it might be possible that the Conservatives could go hand in hand with Parnell in the next parliament, but this collaboration would break down very soon. On this occasion he predicted that the situation in Ireland would grow worse than it had hitherto been. 'Parnell is not able to prevent the outrages, no matter what he has to say in this case.'[103] In one of his last reports from London Münster repeated his warnings. 'Boycotting is directed against everybody who refuses to join the National League or who does not obey its orders rashly.' Boycotting measures had gone so far that a whole congregation had left a church apart from the boycotted members who remained alone with the priest, he wrote.[104]

An interesting report regarding American interference in Irish affairs dealt with a speech of the U.S. Vice President Hendricks who had depicted the misery in Ireland as truly appalling and had hailed Parnell's political triumph. 'Ireland will find devoted and steadfast friends in the United States. Every Irishman here tonight, every Irishman in America is a protest against the bad government of England in Ireland', an adopted resolution said. The *New York Herald* was reported to have pointed out the tactless misuse of the Vice President's position, and the government was advised to put a curb on him.[105]

The developments between Gladstone's resignation and the general election incited the German press to raise its voice also. While all papers close to Bismarck, which were expecting Salisbury's victory, observed a certain reserve,[106] liberal papers dealt intensively with the election issues, particularly with the Irish question. The *Vossische Zeitung*, one of the oldest German newspapers, took the forefront in reporting on Irish events. In a leader of 2 August 1885 with the headline 'The English Cabinet allied with the Parnellites'[107] the paper dealt with the controversies within the Conservative party and pointed out that Lord Randolph Churchill, who was characterised as a 'young cuckoo in a hedge-sparrow's nest', had succeeded in insulting the Tory squires to such an extent that they were prepared to fight their leaders who had just recently come into office. Conservative M.P.s were said to differ with the government on important issues. According to the paper the Conservatives were upset mainly because they were suddenly requested to approve a policy which they had hitherto rejected unanimously. The question had arisen, what advantage the party could derive from the new tactics. The paper took the view that the 'cold and intriguing leader of the Home Rulers in no way conceals his aim to exploit the weakness of the Government for his party's purpose'. When asked how long he would behave in such an agreeable manner, Parnell was said to have replied 'As long as you are not a Government in reality'. In another article the paper foresaw the return of Gladstone because of 'the incomparable attraction of his name to the English people' and reminded its readers that during the Franco-German war Salisbury had declared himself in the House of Lords as an adversary of Germany.[108] A leader of 30 September 1885 gives a portrait of Michael Davitt 'who bears the aureola of a martyr in the people's fantasy—he is the most successful agitator among the most eloquent people in Europe'. Yet this man, the writer concludes, was thrust aside by the cool-headed Parnell whom the farmers preferred while at the same time disliking the nationalisation of the land.[109]

Important events had happened in the meantime. It goes without saying that both English parties did everything in order to attract the Irish party for their own purposes and aims. Salisbury's cabinet was in a precarious situation. But he was very lucky to have sent Lord Carnarvon to Ireland as Lord Lieutenant. He became very popular in the country. He walked freely about Dublin, unattended, while Spencer had always been escorted by a cavalry detachment.[110] Carnarvon's secret conversation with Parnell on 1 August 1885 led to a rapprochement between the two parties. Winston Churchill, most impressively, speaks of 'the two rulers of Ireland—coroneted impotence and uncrowned power'.[111] No doubt Salisbury was informed about the meeting, but in Winston Churchill's view there was no certainty as to whether it took place by personal initiative or by authorisation of

Salisbury. 'A sufficient explanation is that Lord Salisbury allowed the interview to take place in order to pacify the Viceroy and soothe Mr Parnell and that he did not communicate the fact to his colleagues because he thought the matter would make more trouble in the Cabinet that it was worth.'[112]

The tug-of-war of the parties continued. Chamberlain's intention to go over to Ireland in order to explain his Local Self-Government plan failed because Archbishop Manning and Archbishop Walsh of Dublin thought that such an action would be interpreted as hostile to the excellent tenor and promise of Lord Carnarvon's regime.[113]

There is some discussion in historical literature about the question of exactly when Gladstone became a convert to Home Rule. In Hammond's view Gladstone understood Home Rule as the realisation of the liberal idea of self-determination, very conscious of the parallels on the continent.[114] But nobody who thinks in terms of practical politics would deny that every statesman in England at that time looked out for allies who supported his own party in case a majority for his party was not assured. From this point of view it appears to be irrelevant whether the attitude and the tactics of the party-leaders were dominated by a certain ideology or by pragmatic thinking.

Gladstone remained silent until his son Herbert on 16 December 1885 communicated his father's position with regard to Home Rule. Mansergh[115] speaks of Gladstone's 'dislike of "bidding" for the Irish vote, the danger of arousing uncompromising and unrelenting Tory opposition to all proposals for Irish self-government, the risk of Liberal division' as reasons for his silence. But Gladstone's silence obviously lasted too long. He had requested the Irish to express their demands while Parnell claimed that the Irish votes would go to the highest bidder and asked the Irish in England to vote against the Liberals,[116] a request which caused a loss of twenty to forty seats to the Liberals.[117] Parnell's tactics turned out to be a grievous error because these seats lost by the Liberals were of crucial importance in the vote on the Home Rule Bill in 1886. It was too late when he had to admit this. Eyck's opinion[118] that his attitude expressed retaliation for his arrest does not seem very credible.

The general election took place against the background of too much tactics, too little strategy. It returned 331 Liberals, 251

Conservatives and 86 members of the Irish party. Parnell held the balance of power.

The German embassy's comments following the election were rather poor, probably because Münster had left his post after a term of office of twelve years. A colourful period in the history of the German embassy had come to an end. Münster had been one of the most wilful personalities in German diplomacy. All his reports must be seen as the products of a man who felt that concepts like democracy, self-determination, secret ballot etc. should be classified as mortal sins or at least as sins against the spirit of the age.[119]

His successor, Count von Hatzfeldt-Wildenburg, was a career-diplomat; he was State Secretary in the Foreign Office before he came to London. He was not in command of the English language and had to speak in French. He was very fortunate in bringing with him to the embassy something very valuable; the unreserved confidence and esteem of Bismarck.

In the meantime German newspapers and periodicals commented on the issue of the election and prophesied on the future development of English-Irish policy. One of the most interesting comments on the Irish question after the election of 1885 appeared in the 'Politische Korrespondenz' of the *Preussische Jahrbücher*. The author stated bluntly that there was some doubt as to whether it would not be England's wisest policy to repeal the Union as it stood, limiting the links to a dynastic personal union with a common foreign policy. This could be based on the following points:

1. Oppression of the Irish race as hitherto practised would cause increasing and unbearable danger to England
2. A reconciled Ireland would be able to recruit soldiers for defending England's worldwide power
3. There was no longer any concern that France or Spain could use Ireland as a stronghold for an attack on England
4. The incalculable element of people belonging to the Irish race would no longer remain in Westminster Parliament.

Randolph Churchill, 'the only man of genius among English statesmen', was said to nurse such thoughts, but the 'English pride would resist an apparent dictatorship of the Irish part of a majority'.[120]

The only daily paper that reported continuously on the Irish situation after the election, the *Vossische Zeitung*[121] applauded Parnell because he had expressed himself in favour of the weaker party in order to take his advantage from a balanced state of the parties. Parnell—following the principles of a party tactician working in accordance with diplomatic use—was said to have declared with cynical frankness that he would prefer to sell his support to the Liberals at a fair price. In a further article the paper published a letter from Hartington to *The Times* in which he gave his first warning of a possible split in the Liberal party if there was an alliance between Gladstone and Parnell.[122] The paper then quoted from a report of the *Germania* which took the view that Parnell was aiming at national independence for Ireland, Home Rule being almost 'a discarded idea and a payment on account'. 'Could England run the risk of a civil war? Only an absolutely foolish statesman could do that and that is not what practically thinking Englishmen usually do.'[123]

Hatzfeldt's first prognosis on Salisbury's future had been favourable, and Bismarck was delighted,[124] but a few days later the ambassador had to admit that Parnell—taking into account the Fenians—could not conclude any compromise according less than an independent parliament to the Irish. 'Gladstone will have to demonstrate he is prepared to make concessions which are not even approved of by Chamberlain.'[125]

In a telegram of 27 January 1886[126] the embassy informed Berlin on the defeat of Salisbury's government in the vote on the amendment concerning the Irish farmer's situation. The Caretaker Government's term had expired and Gladstone took over again,[127] although the Queen had worked very hard to create an anti-Gladstone party.[128]

In the outgoing cabinet Lord Carnarvon had been the most tragic figure. A highly cultivated man, he was, like Derby and Gladstone, passionately devoted to the classics. The Government did not behave generously in the field of Irish education as Carnarvon had suggested. They were constantly influenced by the reactions of the Protestants in England and Ireland. Only a few concessions were made, due to the intervention of Randolph Churchill who was always interested in good relations with the Irish hierarchy.

The Irish population was very kind to the sympathetic Viceroy, but the success of his work depended on his abilities to convince the Parnellites, the hierarchy and the tenants that their interests were best guarded by collaboration with the Conservatives. In private, Lord Carnarvon made his view quite clear that an audacious step in the direction of Home Rule was unavoidable.[129] 'He had ventured into the quicksand that awaits all politicians who stray from the straight and narrow path of party interests, and, although acting out of the loftiest motives, his behaviour earned him nothing but reproaches from his colleagues.'[130]

In the 'Caretaker' term the Conservatives missed a great chance for conciliation with the Irish. Winston Churchill wrote that 'they had office but not power',[131] and Balfour spoke of 'seven months eating dirt'[132]—a very sad balance.

Immediately before and shortly after Salisbury's defeat another flash of lightning from Berlin struck Ireland and the Irish party when once again parallels were drawn with Prussian subjects of Polish descent. Bismarck's intervention in the Prussian Abgeordnetenhaus (Lower House) on 29 January 1886 in the debate on the motion of a group of deputies 'on the protection of German national interests in the eastern provinces' was preceded by an article in the *Norddeutsche Allgemeine Zeitung*[133] which reported first on a speech of the Duke of Westminster in Chester where he, according to *The Times*, had asserted that the Parnellites had secured their position by the means of cruelty, blackmail, assassination and murder, shamefully supported by some Roman Catholic priests.

Commenting on this report of *The Times*, the German paper wrote: 'if one exchanges the words Poles and Parnellites, the situation in our country is very similar to that beyond the Channel. Polish propaganda against Prussia is exactly the same as that of the Parnellites against England. Both in this country and Ireland the subversives are finding zealous support for their aspirations in certain radical circles and from a number of ultramontanist priests. Our situation is still more dangerous in so far as in Germany the Social Democrats, the Guelf, French and Danish elements are supporting the Poles with the common aim of destroying the re-established Empire'—undoubtedly a relapse into the phrases of the Kulturkampf.

This sheet-lightning in the press announced a thunderstorm which broke out in the Prussian Parliament in the debate mentioned above.[134] Bismarck, obviously instigated by the press article of 25 January, began his intervention along the lines expressed by the paper. 'Regarding the situation of the parties, we are in a similar position as the English nation. There, too, there exists a basis of an intransigent opposition, represented by the national opposition party of the Parnellites. It is their principal desire to be separated from the British Empire and therefore they are not very interested in its destiny', he said.

'By analogy with the Parnellites, we have got a number of intransigents who, partly due to their affinity for France'—pointing at Alsace—'could be characterised as our Fenians because they do not recognise our political aims and do not follow them. They are not powerful enough, neither the Parnellites in England nor the Poles and other admirers of foreign countries here; but they are joined by certain elements who, though not sharing the aims of nihilism, prefer to go hand in hand with them for a certain period instead of making the task of government easier for the others. Thus, the English "Progressive Party", as I like to call it, joins the Parnellites in creating a majority which leads again to a change of power, as we have seen happen in these days. We have a similar situation here. There exists a certain number of intransigents, and a "piedestal" which is jumped on by everybody who wants to cause trouble to the present Government or intends to attack it', he continued. 'Politics is not a science to be taught, it is an art, and people who are not able to handle it should stay away from it . . . Gladstone will have to demonstrate for the second or third time that he avails of the abilities to assume the responsibility of the State', he concluded.[135]

It is noteworthy that Bismarck on the occasion of this second outburst with reference to Ireland, which may also be regarded as the strongest attack on Gladstone he ever made in public, never mentioned the ultramontanists nor the Church nor any other adversary of a former period. The Kulturkampf had almost come to an end, and at this stage of the relations with Pope Leo XIII he could no longer lump together Catholics and members of the national minorities. He felt free in his attitude with regard to these minorities, for the Vatican was no longer his powerful and dangerous foe in the Church-State conflict. Like in 1873,[136] the British press, reporting on the debate, supported the Chancellor. 'It is time to recognise the truth, written large in history,

in contemporary events and in human nature, that there are antipathies which have to be accepted as ultimate facts and which
neither justice nor generosity can soften.'[137]

It was on this shrill note from Bismarck that Gladstone began
his third term of office. But the Chancellor was not the only
politician who behaved that way. The attitude and actions of
members of Gladstone's party, his new cabinet, and Conservatives who, at least to a certain extent, had been in accordance
with him as to Irish affairs, proved more damaging than the out-
bursts of Bismarck. Resignations of prominent cabinet members,
for example, Trevelyan and Chamberlain, and the trip to Ulster
of Randolph Churchill were a bad omen for his term.[138] Hatzfeldt informed the Foreign Office that the Conservative party did
not agree to Lord Randolph's Ulster Campaign ('Ulster will
fight, and Ulster will be right') because he had worsened the
situation by using sectarian arguments. The Liberal press had
characterised him as a rebel instigating civil war.[139]

Gladstone's Irish effort—his first Home Rule Bill—was an
uphill battle against two of the deepest instincts of British politics,
as Hammond puts it; the belief that the English social system was
suitable to Ireland and that Ireland could remain what she was
when the Union had been enacted, a country governed through
the agency of the Protestant ascendancy.[140] But he did not give
in when old friends deserted him, and the struggle for Home
Rule began.

On 19 March 1886,[141] Hatzfeldt reported that Count Karolyi,
his Austrian colleague, admired Gladstone in his dealing with the
Irish question and held that England, according to her traditions
and political mentality, was not in a position to rule Ireland by
dictatorial principles. Coercion laws had not proved adequate
(Bismarck's marginal: 'Because they were of exceptional and
temporary character'). The only alternative left by which to end
the discontent in Ireland was to grant more independence and
concessions (Bismarck's marginal: 'Will not be successful'). Resistance in England against concessions could be overcome.
Aversion against concessions was decreasing more and more and
Gladstone would have an obedient majority in a new parliament
(Bismarck: 'May be, Parliament will ruin England'). Pacification
of Ireland would be of great importance for the other powers,
too. England, actually paralysed by strife, would again occupy

her proper position in European politics (Bismarck: 'Ireland will then show a tendency to France or the United States').

Hatzfeldt criticised Karolyi's utterances, 'The feeling of hatred among the Irish, based on a memory of long periods of violence and deprivation, will not disappear and one must assume that an Irish parliament with a limited authority—as it is envisaged—will have in mind the abolition of that limitation as soon as possible' (Bismarck: 'Of course').

With regard to the first phrase of Karolyi's remarks (about English traditions and mentality) Bismarck gave instructions to the embassies in London, Vienna and St Petersburg, criticising Karolyi in the following way: 'Even those who are studying the history of the Tudors and of the Lord Protector Cromwell only in a superficial way, know that the various governments of England have, even before the Battle of the Boyne, exercised an unparalleled despotic rule in Ireland. Count Karolyi should know that in Ireland, the government of England has acted ruthlessly in modern times also.'[142]

This record substantially clarifies, on the one hand, Bismarck's feelings with regard to the historical background of English-Irish affairs in the past, and on the other hand his approach to actual problems which was dominated by his political philosophy as that of a statesman who had won an empire for his king and who regarded the British Empire as a power whose political substance, at home and abroad, had to be watched over carefully.

The following weeks of that year, full of surprising and dramatic events, were observed in Germany with close attention. Hatzfeldt reported continuously on the developments in parliament and on the national implications of party-life. 'Gladstone is prepared for a small majority against the Bill. It must be presumed that he will never take drastic measures against Ireland.'[143] In further reports he pointed out that the Irish policy was not accepted with enthusiasm as Gladstone had expected and that the outlook was gloomy. 'The Army will take part on both sides of a Civil War.' General Lord Wolseley was said to have expressed his intention of resigning rather than fight against the 'loyal North of Ireland'.[144]

In a letter to Bismarck, enclosed in the report of 19 April 1886,[145] a German-born manager of the Ulster bank asked the Chancellor for protection for the families of German descent living in Ireland 'and to tell England that Germany does not sympathise with the efforts of a well-meaning but infatuated enthusiast to force the loyalists out of the Imperial Parliament and to hand over German flesh and blood into the power of the friends of midnight assassins, burners of living cattle and destroyers of public buildings'.

In this context it is well worth noting a report of the German embassy in St Petersburg[146] in which Russian reactions to the bill were described as follows: 'The Home Rule Bill produces sensation and gloating, the autonomy of Ireland can no longer be blocked. The problem will rise time and again, even if Gladstone should fail.'

Prince Kantakutsen was said to have declared that he hoped Gladstone would succeed. 'The Home Rule Bill has caused more damage to the British prestige than the indulgence of England in the Afghan question' the embassy added.

The reaction in the United States was, of course, quite different. The German Legation informed on the country's interest in the bill: 'If Gladstone succeeds in realising his project, he will have done just as much for the vindication of our policy as for the advantage of his country,'[147] an American periodical was quoted.

But already in May 1886 Bismarck received personal messages from Lord Rosebery telling him that he (Rosebery) expected a defeat of the government on the Irish question and Gladstone's resignation after a majority of twenty against the bill.[148]

After sending reports on the parliamentary proceedings in which Hatzfeldt described Salisbury's intentions with regard to Ireland as 'ruthless' and Gladstone's closing address as an 'oratorical work of art', the embassy wired the result of the vote and Gladstone's defeat (Bismarck's marginal 'What is going to happen now?').[149]

The German papers followed the proceedings attentively and informed their readers continuously. The *Norddeutsche Allgemeine* dealt with the reaction of British public opinion which was described as partly alarmed, partly surprised. However, the paper had to admit that the Irish problem could not be solved by negation. 'England is still looking forward to listening to a debater who might speak with serious arguments in favour of

E

Gladstone' the paper wrote. Further reports described the ups and downs in parliament, the Liberals wavering between yes and no and eventually of the refusal of Chamberlain and the letter of Bright, which decided the position of the Liberal Unionists.[150]

The *Germania* also reported daily on Gladstone's position and the different opinions expressed in parliament and by the public. A London correspondent, quoting from a report of the conservative *Post*, passed on the information that armed Orangemen had invaded Catholic churches during services. However, 'Gladstone is a deeply religious man with true Christian humility'.[151]

The liberal *Vossische Zeitung* was one of the most ardent observers of the British parliamentary scene. In the same way as the other Berlin papers, its correspondents in London—people of high standing at that time—gave their impressions of the progress of the Liberal party through the secession of the Whig Unionists under Hartington and some Radicals, led by Chamberlain and Bright.[152]

Already early in April 1886, the paper predicted that perhaps seventy to eighty members of the Liberal parliamentary party would secede from the party because of Gladstone's Irish policy.[153] In a leader a few days later, it took the view that the Irish question did not touch the people in Britain. It was a remainder from the old time of aristocratic rule that modern England had to deal with, a foreign rule over an unwilling neighbouring people, a foreign rule which present-day England would never have imposed on Ireland by force. Gladstone was playing the diplomatic role of a fair broker.[154] 'Ardour against the Irish reform has not only clouded the judgement of *The Times* and of other press-organs in England but has also incited these papers to falsify facts' the paper wrote.[155] In a rather long article dealing with Ulster, the paper pointed out that 'to emphasise denominational differences is an anachronism. The problems between England and Ireland, which are regarded by both sides to be due to a difference of race, are in reality the result of historical influences of the preceding years, that is of the absurd policy of England during the last centuries which implanted the arrogance of the oppressor into the English and the bitterness and hatred of the oppressed into the Irish.'[156]

The paper launched heavy attacks against Chamberlain and his followers whom it took—rightly—to be responsible for Gladstone's defeat. 'The bill was in his hands and he could not resist the temptation to exercise his power.'[157]

Also the *Preussische Jahrbücher*, in some critical remarks dealt with the enigma of Chamberlain. In the periodical's opinion there seemed to be great confusion among English radicals on the Irish question. According to the paper, it was their intention to convert English catholics and Irish nationalists to enlightened radicalism, and they felt that they could reach this aim by measures against the landlords, while the Irish were in the first line struggling for Home Rule in order to expropriate, by their own authority, the Irish soil held by English landlords. It was Chamberlain's belief that he could amalgamate English and Irish radicalism and that, by maintaining the Union, he could establish the rule of the middle classes in the whole United Kingdom after having considerably limited aristocratic privileges.[158] In another article, some time later, after Chamberlain's resignation, the periodical compared Chamberlain with the farmers of Baden who in 1848 'aspired to a republic'. Chamberlain wanted neither Home Rule nor land purchase, he wanted to compel the landlords to sell their land to private persons at low prices. 'He is less well-meaning than the peasants in Baden in 1848. Gladstone is to be congratulated that he has got rid of this man—please God, for ever'[159] the article concluded.

It is interesting to note the author's opinion that all presumptions of Irish wishes to join the United States or the French Republic were nothing but 'foolish twaddle'.[160]

Historians' assessments coincide in a striking manner with the observations of correspondents and politicians of that time. In an interview with Barry O'Brien in 1898, Chamberlain admitted, with regard to his motions for amendments 'I wanted to kill the bill.'[161] And as Mansergh puts it, Chamberlain's opposition to Home Rule was bitter and unrelenting for the remainder of his life: 'not only were his speeches in Parliament decisive, but the loss of the Radical vote in industrial England was a blow from which the Liberal Party never recovered . . . Parnell was right when he said Chamberlain had killed Home Rule—and today it may be asked whether he had not signed the death warrant of the Liberal Party as well.'[162]

Winston Churchill recollects the violent scenes in the House of Commons and the declarations of hatred against England reiterated by Irish nationalists, 'however historically excusable', which together with the long nightmare of outrages and unrest had 'bitten deep into the British mind and memories', but with regard to Chamberlain his judgement is rather severe. In pointing out that Chamberlain was not likely to be turned away from his purpose by the difficulties and dangers of his position, he writes the meaningful words: 'The determination of such men is only aggravated by these elements. Their doubts are hardened into convictions at the whisper of compulsion.'[163]

It seems to be very doubtful whether Churchill is right when he says that Gladstone might have carried the second reading, if he had made a lame and ineffective speech so as to give the impression that he was hesitating and uncertain. 'Seldom has rhetorical success been more dearly purchased' he says.[164] The rift between Gladstone and Chamberlain had become too deep, both had arrived at the point of no return.

The Queen had written to Gladstone shortly after the bill had been introduced and had spoken of a danger to the Empire.[165] After Gladstone's parliamentary defeat she wrote into her diary: 'Cannot help feeling relieved.'[166]

After the dissolution of parliament, the *Preussische Jahrbücher* wrote: 'Every sensible Englishman must wish Gladstone victory. Until the Irish question has been settled there is no chance of having a viable government except under his leadership. The mismanagement of this problem, either by the use of force or by half-conciliation, makes it more dangerous.'[167]

Hatzfeldt had expressed his uncertainty with regard to the issue. He mentioned Lord Rosebery's feeling that he would not support the Irish policy unless he were convinced that this policy was the only way to restore order in Ireland and to prevent a partition of the Empire. He believed that another victory for Gladstone would lead to a full engagement by England in Irish affairs, thus preventing her participation in European matters. 'A democratic England would not be a reliable friend of the German Empire.' He reported that some people were convinced that only an inner crisis or a great war would rouse the nation, which had become indifferent through wealth and luxury, and restore it to a normal political situation. 'One can count the number of friends of Germany within the ranks of the Liberal party.'[168]

Apart from this report, the embassy refrained from comments of any substance after the dissolution of parliament. However, the German papers continued to report on the Irish situation and both the *Norddeutsche Allgemeine*[169] and the *Germania*[170] commented that despite Gladstone's defeat Home Rule would remain on the table. 'No big reform has been passed at the first go, due to the tough character of the Anglo-Saxon race. For the Emancipation of the Catholics a stubborn struggle of a generation was needed.'[171]

The *Germania*[172] and the *Vossische Zeitung*[173] reported on the outrages in Ulster after the defeat of the bill and described the bloody conflicts between Catholics and Orangemen in Belfast. The Liberal paper informed its readers on the demolition of pubs owned by Catholics. In one incident it described how a Protestant mob had broken the doors and windows and had thrown out the furniture, which was set on fire, strong liquor barrels were smashed and everybody got drunk, shouting 'to hell with the Pope', and soldiers had to be called to restore order and clear the streets with bayonets fixed. 'Gladstone and the Paper-Unionists' was the headline of an article of the same paper in which it commented on Gladstone's manifesto for the electoral contest. 'Time after time the modest demands of the Irish were rejected; now the Irish people claimed a higher price—self-government with increasingly wider powers—for its conciliation with England.' The existing Union was compared to that of Russia and Poland. Gladstone was considered to be right when he described it as a Paper Union.[174] The paper described Randolph Churchill as 'a man with a tongue similar to that of Thersites' who 'swears like a fish-wife'.[175] The *Preussische Jahrbücher*, alluding to the fact that Churchill was now fighting against a plan he was formerly willing to accept, at least in secret, felt that he was acting in a way 'which caricatured his extravagance and affectation'.[176]

After the election, which had turned out unfavourably for Gladstone, Hatzfeldt took the view that the defeat was not a final negative test for him, because the outcome had been relatively successful.[177]

The *Vossische Zeitung* hailed Gladstone's achievements in a similar way. 'One can expect that the defeat may be an early sign of the victory of the policy advocated by him, taking into account the particular circumstances which have made the Irish question one of the most burning issues of today' the paper declared, adding that within one year's time one man had exercised such an influence on his countrymen that he had persuaded the Scots and the Welsh, as well as, one-third of the English to vote in favour of sweeping reforms.[178]

The outcome of the election gave rise to some noteworthy observations by the *Preussische Jahrbücher*. The periodical declared that Ireland should be left to her own fate, but that such a decision was very difficult for John Bull. All his various qualities, including his national pride, barred him from this insight. This national pride, however, was still the least obstacle. It was fear, the worst of all advisers, which worked as a deterrent. People in England believed that all the enemies of their country would settle down in Ireland (armed of course) in order to conquer England and Scotland. 'One could burst out laughing at this nightmare' the article concluded. In this context the author of the article quoted from Frederick the Great of Prussia: 'L'espèce humaine est moutonnière, elle suit aveuglement son guide.'[179]

Coming back to its former arguments regarding Chamberlain's policy, the periodical repeated its opinion that he needed the Irish as allies in parliament. 'All in all, one must say that the prospects for the Bill are favourable. Very soon Gladstone will muster a majority' the periodical dared to prophesy. Actually the English were still full of misgivings as to his policy. 'They prefer to keep the Irish in the House of Commons and the Fenians in Ireland in order to save everything that can be saved. They behave like a blind man who passes flints and clods through his hands believing that they are pearls.'[180]

Salisbury's renewed regime was burdened with his ill-advised and fatal utterances on Ireland during the election campaign and in previous years. Worst of all was his speech on 15 May 1886 in St James's Hall where he compared the Irish with the Hottentots, disputing the contention that one ought to show confidence in the Irish People by granting them independent representative government. And then followed the ominous words which were taken as a programme: 'My alternative policy is that parliament should enable the government of England to govern Ireland. Apply that recipe honestly, consistently, and resolutely for twenty years and at the end of that time you will find that Ireland will be fit to accept any gifts in the way of local government or repeal of coercion laws that you may wish to give her.'[181]

Already in 1872 he had declared with regard to Ireland that 'there is no precedent either in our history or in any other to teach us that political measures can conjure away hereditary antipathies which are fed by constant agitation'.[182] And on another occasion he said that 'Ireland must be kept, like India, at all hazards, by persuasion, if possible, if not by force'.[183] It is not clear how these declarations can be reconciled with another opinion once expressed by him, that 'Coercion is, [not] in and by itself, a faith to live and die for'.[184]

With regard to Salisbury's denial about his speech in St James's Hall the *Vossische Zeitung* made the comment: 'Although he did not use the word "coercion", the policy advocated by Lord Salisbury for twenty years is the coercive policy which has been applied for decades in all possible shapes and which has frequently proved a failure. His declaration seems to be proof that he has not yet learned the art of denial.'[185] The *Germania* also came back, time and again, to the 'twenty years' policy. Salisbury's utterances are the best propaganda for Home Rule, the paper stated. One should wish, in the interest of Ireland, that no coercion government would accede to power, for this would call up all the anarchist elements of the Irish people, a fact which would be followed by immense trouble both in England and in Ireland.[186]

The first days of Salisbury's second term were overshadowed by unrest and violence in Ulster. Both the embassy and the daily papers reported on it. The embassy and the *Vossische Zeitung* underlined that Randolph Churchill must be held responsible for the fact that the Protestants had attacked first. The police, however, had acted in favour of the Catholics.[187] In further reports the paper spoke of 'an Irish religious war' and gave a detailed description of the troubles and the casualties.[188]

Dealing with the formation of the cabinet, the paper alluded to the difficulties of Salisbury, who had to take into account the wishes of 'political invalids', and regarded the new ministers—apart from Salisbury and Lord Randolph Churchill—as men 'of fair average qualities without any outstanding characteristics'.[189] The Prime Minister could reckon with the support of the Whigs so long as he was pursuing 'a moderate conservative or a moderate liberal policy'. In case of a new election Salisbury would try either to get rid of the Whigs or to fraternise with the Parnellites. Churchill in particular, as an ambitious man, would prefer not to depend on the support of the Whigs in the long run; the alternative would be an adoption of the Home Rule policy.[190]

In a concluding article on the new government the paper maintained that 'time is fighting for the Irish ideas', which were gaining more and more ground in Unionist circles. The Gladstonians could therefore wait.[191]

Official circles in Germany, of course, welcomed Salisbury's return to power, not only because it was Gladstone who had been ousted from office, but also due to the expected reactivation of England's foreign policy as a world power. But the Prime Minister himself was fully aware what the Irish handicap meant for his liberty of action in foreign affairs. Once 'a wise and careful Foreign Minister, the best who served England in his lifetime',[192] he had to admit in a letter to the Queen of 24 January 1887, 'that the prospect is very gloomy abroad, but England cannot brighten it. Torn in two by a controversy which almost threatens her existence, she cannot, in the present state of public opinion, interfere with any decisive action abroad.'[193] Unfortunately he had not done much for a remodelling of his image in Ireland, which he described as an "ultra clerical state" and declared that the Catholic majority contained "all that is unprogressive, all that is contrary to civilisation and enlightenment",[194] 'only steady and unyielding government would reduce the threat of this tyranny [of the Catholic majority] to manageable proportions'.[195] He could not expect a better reputation in the country, at least not as long as he held the opinion 'that the Irish must take a licking before conciliation will do them any good'.[196]

'Killing Home Rule by kindness' was, nevertheless, the slogan of the Salisbury-Balfour regime for Ireland. They hoped to achieve this in the same way as Peel, who had little sympathy with Irish landlords, had outlined it in the early forties during his second term of office.[197] Although the Land Act of 1887 gave a minimal degree of relief to the farmers—the Land Commission not being empowered to reduce the rents—the agrarian crisis continued and served as a stumbling block on the road to conciliation and to an effective improvement of the social position of the tenants. No wonder that in this case the Crimes Act of 1887 failed[198] like all its predecessors.

In April 1887 Hatzfeldt reported on 'evictions of tenants by force, which seriously hit and embitter the population', and he spoke of the harshness and cruelty of the landlords.[199] In November 1887 he had to admit that the Home Rule movement was making great progress, supported by Gladstone whose party was obviously increasing. According to the report, Parnell's party was looking forward to the further evolution with confidence. 'Even if Gladstone were to die Home Rule would triumph after all,' the ambassador concluded his report.[200]

Lord Rosebery had strongly criticised the Irish policy which in his view had provoked civil war in Ireland. England had frequently felt entitled to criticise other countries, including Germany, on matters concerning these countries. How would England react if other states would now feel entitled to criticise the English government for the treatment of the Irish and to characterise the situation in Ireland as a stain of the nineteenth century? (Bismarck's marginal: 'This has happened very often, years ago'.)[201]

In summer 1887 the ambassador criticised several members of the government, principally Balfour, the Chief Secretary, and the Home Secretary, Mr Mathews.[202] So far as Balfour is concerned, this brief reference might be typical of diplomatic reporting at that time. One can have the impression that the embassy spoke of Balfour, the nephew, but that it really meant Salisbury, the uncle, who was then persona grata in Berlin. Historians looking back on Balfour's term of office describe his activities and manners in unflattering words.[203] A long time after he had left the Irish office he contested the existence of a genuine Irish national feeling,[204] declaring the Scotsmen had a better claim to be a nation. Eyck takes the view that the coercion which was enacted for an unlimited period was met with growing dislike in Britain; people were embittered about the fact that Balfour treated political prisoners as criminals.[205]

It was not surprising that under these circumstances agitation fell on fertile soil, particularly on the agrarian sector. The 'Plan of Campaign', which was launched in 1886, was not a new organisation but a method to secure the farmer's interest in the continuing agrarian crisis, based on the principle that it should be left to the farmers themselves to decide what a 'fair rent' was.[206] The Plan, of course, produced many reactions from the State and the Church too. Dillon and O'Brien headed the new campaign together with the two Redmonds. Obviously Parnell himself had no strong feeling about the movement, he laid more stress on the success of the Home Rule movement than on the agrarian policy. In a conversation with O'Brien at Greenwich, Parnell did not conceal his objections to the Plan.[207] In Lyons's view the Plan of Campaign was a straw to be grasped at by the farmers in the south and the west, perhaps 'more than a straw but less than a life belt'.[208] Balfour had to admit that the Plan was better organised in winter 1889/90 than before.[209] [210]

By-elections, which produced several defeats for the Conservatives and Liberal Unionists, indicated that Salisbury's term was about to run out. The prospects for Gladstone's comeback appeared to be promising and bright. The Grand Old Man started his campaign at the age of eighty-two against the background of a considerably altered political scene, both in the United Kingdom and in Europe. Parnell had died in his forties and Ireland had inherited a divided party; on the continent two German emperors had died within ninety-nine days, leaving the throne to a successor of twenty-nine years of age who believed that the founder of the Empire should retire at the age of seventy-five.

Regarding the pre-election time and the contest, the embassy was not very talkative; Hatzfeldt was apparently more cautious in his predictions than his predecessor had been. In a report of May 1892 the Chargé d'Affaires however, informed of Salisbury's views on the importance of the Irish question for the general election. The Prime Minister had particularly underlined the consequences which Home Rule implicated for Ulster. 'Although Parliament is entitled to make laws binding the population of Ulster, it cannot sell them into slavery.'[211] The same demagogic references were made by Balfour, when he spoke in Belfast one year later on an 'unscrupulous majority desiring to destroy a loyal minority' and went on to say 'that the tyranny of a majority could be as fatal as that of a tyrannical King, to whom resistance could be justified'[212] (William II's marginal: 'Typical for a free Briton'). In any case, these utterances of Conservative politicians in the early nineties, which were borne out by events thirty years later, became significant for many forthcoming decades.

Among the German newspapers the liberal *Vossische Zeitung* informed its readers in Germany on all details of the developments in almost daily reports, comments and articles. The commentaries of the paper became noteworthy in so far as they viewed both the external and internal implications of the outcome of the election, from a different angle. The politicians most mentioned were Gladstone, Salisbury and Chamberlain. The paper had obviously found the range of Chamberlain whom it had never forgiven for his alliance with the Conservatives in 1886.

There was one concern which a good many German circles had in common: what would be the British foreign policy if Salisbury had to resign? On 18 June 1892 the paper wrote: 'The well-balanced concert of power in Europe, in which Salisbury supported the policy of the Triple Alliance with ability and reliability and which proved so adequate for the maintenance of peace in Europe, would be upset if Gladstone came back. The unpredictability of Gladstone is a danger which makes us hope for a victory for Salisbury. In spite of Home Rule, the English voters would be well advised to take into account the position of their Empire in Europe.'[213] In other reports the paper laid stress on the necessity of Gladstone saying something about his foreign policy. 'The Conservatives and the Liberal Unionists are rightly playing their trump card—Salisbury's foreign policy.'[214] After Gladstone's victory the same paper expressed the wish that he might strengthen internal peace in the Empire with the aim of maintaining England's foreign relations along the old lines. 'Misgivings should very soon be thoroughly dissipated.'[215] A fortnight later the paper said that foreign policy was Gladstone's vulnerable spot,[216] and it was relieved to tell its readers that 'Rosebery's appointment to the Foreign Office is a guarantee that Salisbury's foreign policy, which has proved absolutely successful, will be upheld'.[217]

With regard to Ireland the paper reported that the situation in that country and the solution of the Irish question was felt to be 'an Imperial matter of the highest importance by the English voters, but the people expected that the fulfilment of all other wishes in the political, economic and social field should not depend on Home Rule'.[218] Alluding to the difficulties in Ulster, the *Vossische Zeitung* said that Gladstone had mentioned the possibility of a partition.[219]

In spite of the misgivings expressed as to his foreign policy, the paper hailed Gladstone in many articles and comments after his victory, although the difficulties he would have to face in the Home Rule question and other issues were not concealed.[220]

As regards Chamberlain, the paper's comments were in no way flattering. He was said to be an 'unattainable master in parliamentary guerrilla warfare', 'his weapons are not clear; his checked ambition and the awareness of not being in a rank adequate to his ability have poisoned his tongue'.[221]

The *Preussische Jahrbücher* characterised Chamberlain as a 'bewildered, wilful and shoppy wholesaler'. The periodical criticised his opinion that the Irish members should be kept in the House of Commons and gave the following comment on this issue: 'So long as there are a hundred Irish members in the House of Commons, who could be put out only through Home Rule, the functioning of the British Parliament is blocked. The situation is similar to that in the Reichstag which, as long as a hundred ultramontanists are members, can hardly do its work'[222]—an allusion to the influence of the Catholic party in the German Reichstag which had been considerably enhanced through the Kulturkampf.

'Popular modern politics has led to an irreconcilable contradiction, because its aim is to appease national feeling, with the intention of ruling the population of a great power composed of several races through the system of universal suffrage, a system which requires a thoroughly homogeneous population. This contradiction is obvious, almost trivial. However, a policy which cannot unravel this contradiction is unsatisfactory. It would be more pleasant for us to witness these events in England if her weakness did not prove harmful to world politics'—these remarks reflected the assessment of the problems of the national minorities in Germany[223] and elsewhere.[224]

When Gladstone introduced his second Home Rule Bill in February 1893, the embassy was optimistic about the position taken by the Protestants. 'They will be convinced very soon of Gladstone's sense,' the embassy reported to Berlin, submitting in the same report the guiding lines of the bill.[225] 'Reaction in Parliament is no longer unfriendly, Unionists are not opposed in principle but only against certain provisions'—that was the impression of the ambassador. The bill, which was described as impossible in Great Britain six years ago, had now numerous supporters: it became a burning political question and nobody was able to predict whether it would be settled in the sense of its author or in that of the Unionists, the report said. Hatzfeldt took the view that 'the bill will eventually be adopted in the House of Commons, the position of the Government has not worsened'. 'Gladstone must have a strong majority in Great Britain if he will amend the United Kingdom's constitution in the outlined way, and also with regard to the position of the House of Lords which will probably reject the bill' he wrote.[226]

The ambassador confirmed his optimism about the bill in a further report, mentioning the flight of capital from Ireland, the drop in the assets and the import of weapons for the use of the loyalists in the north. Hatzfeldt also made an allusion to a possible fight against the House of Lords in case of a rejection of the bill, predicting that 'Gladstone could in such a case dispose of the sympathies of the masses' (William II: 'Jolly nice prospects!').[227]

Despite heavy attacks against the House of Lords following the rejection of the bill early in September 1893, Gladstone, taking into account his age of eighty-three, was said to have renounced launching a fight aimed at parliamentary reform.[228] In Hatzfeldt's view Gladstone intended launching a new election campaign in order to return a greater majority.[229]

The German daily press observed the parliamentary proceedings of the bill with interest. The *Germania* had no doubt that the new bill could lead to a solution of the Irish question. 'Great Britain and Ireland are to be congratulated on the prospects of the adoption of the bill.'[230] The *Norddeutsche Allgemeine*, formerly Bismarck's press organ, remarked after the first reading that no further argument had been produced: 'The pros and cons are a matter of opinion after all.' According to the paper, Anglo-Saxon race-politicians, sceptics and people with special historical knowledge were, in general, inclined to regard the attempt of Home Rule as a hopeless and dangerous experiment.[231] With reference to an utterance of Justin McCarthy that in the view of the Irish members the bill could present a final solution, 'so far as a prognosis is possible,' the paper compared this wording with the reactions of the Czechs in Bohemia who used to change their opinion 'when radicalism believes that the time has come to make new claims'.[232]

The *Vossische Zeitung*, commenting on the introduction of the bill, came back to the question of the position of the British Empire in relation to Home Rule. It held that the appeasement of the Irish desires would not impair the weight of England's foreign policy.[233]

In the following months the paper reported continuously on the progress of the bill, frequently condemning the efforts of Conservative and Liberal Unionist politicians to play the Orange card by instigating Ulster against the parliamentary majority. The weakest point of the bill was said to be the admission of Irish members to Westminster. According to the paper, this provision was meant as a shield against the reproach that the bill could destroy the unity of the Empire. 'Preservation of this unity should be fairly sympathetic to the Conservatives and Unionists, but the thinking and acting of the parliamentary opposition is not guided by generally accepted principles. The reason of the party commands that they fight this provision bitterly' the paper commented.[234]

In the *Preussische Jahrbücher*, Emil Daniels tackled the Ulster problem, especially the apprehension of the Protestants that they would be ill-treated in Irish courts, and wrote as follows: 'These apprehensions of the Unionist opposition are unjustified. The Irish have always proved to be a tolerant people. Neither a heretic nor a witch has been burnt at any time on the Emerald Island. . . . Their modern literature, including the Catholic one, hails the idea of tolerance and treats the Protestant Irish in Ulster in such a unanimous and unreserved spirit of conciliation that the parallels drawn between Catholic Ireland and Spain seem to be futile'.[235] In another part of his essay the author pointed at the unjust treatment of Ireland with regard to the contribution to the imperial budget. 'Castlereagh assumed the Irish national debt after the Treaty of Paris but introduced the English tax rules in Ireland. From that time until this day Ireland, the poorest country in the civilised world, has borne the same tax burden as England, the richest country on earth . . . Such a robbery from helpless poor people organised by the state is without a parallel in the civilised world' the author said.[236]

The bill, adopted by the House of Commons with a fair

majority, was killed in the House of Lords, after a desperate fight by Spencer and Rosebery against an overwhelming majority of the Conservative and Liberal Unionist aristocracy.[237] The Liberal Lords were like voices crying in the wilderness. The *Vossische Zeitung,* however, dared to prophesy that 'the time will come when Rosebery's words, now ignored by the Lords, will get their historical confirmation'.[238]

A few days earlier the same paper had hailed Gladstone, who now had failed for the second time, for his devotion to the issue. 'Never before in England has a great work like this been so completely linked with one person.'[239] But he, too, had to learn the lesson that even in England the word 'liberalism' did not cover the idea unequivocally. In Hammond's view he was isolated because his fundamental outlook differed from that of the intellectual liberals.[240]

The settlement of the Irish question had been postponed for another thirty years and more, to the disadvantage of both islands and detriment of England's position in Europe and the world. 'With Home Rule for Ireland, England would be ten times stronger than before.'[241]

It is generally known that Bismarck appeared to be an adversary of the Parnellites and the Irish aspirations, mainly with regard to his concern about repercussions in Germany herself. If he behaved that way on domestic grounds, there is, nevertheless, reasons to believe that this farsighted statesman had once expressed the opinion—as reported but, however, unconfirmed—that 'England counts for nothing in European politics unless the Irish question has been settled'.[242]

HIERARCHY, VATICAN AND GOVERNMENT

The role of Clergy and Hierarchy—The Vatican between Government and Hierarchy—Errington's mission—Parallels again—Further British efforts and Bismarck's interest—The Congregation of the Holy Inquisition and the Irish tenants.

The movements and measures described above were the first stage of a conflict on temporal affairs, but in no way can they be regarded only as such because this conflict, as frequently happened in Irish history, was based on different approaches depending on individual attitudes to religion and politics. This problem became relevant again in the period of Land War and Home Rule. In a country whose Catholic population had been dispossessed of most of their lands centuries ago by a conqueror of another denomination, the question arose as to where the moral limits had to be drawn regarding the methods and means applied by the masters of the various movements to reach their political, economic and social aims.

It is against this background—late in March 1882, at a time of great tension in the Land War—that a conversation between Münster and Cardinal Manning, the leading Catholic churchman in England should be regarded. It is very interesting to notice that Manning's assessment of the Irish situation was rather similar to the findings recorded by Stumm[243] on his return to London from a mission in Ireland which took place in the same month as Münster's conversation with Manning. The Cardinal, having described the situation in Ireland as he saw it, pointed at the agrarian criminals 'who are recruited from a part of the population demoralised by poverty and idleness'. 'Gladstone's measures' Münster reported about Manning's views, 'are undertaken with the best intentions but have proved unpractical and unhelpful. The hierarchy in Ireland is quite aware of the dangers to be faced; protecting the country from Republicanism and anarchy is the problem that matters. This opinion is shared by the Vatican.'[244]

This seems to be a summary of the feelings of the Church leaders in general—with many exceptions among the local clergy and certain members of the hierarchy. The local clergy, no longer educated on the continent but at home, for the most part came from rural areas. They were sons of tenants and labourers, thus well acquainted with the life and problems of the country people due to the common social background. Therefore they felt called upon to assume leading roles, especially in cases of the absence of suitable laymen.[245] National movements exceeding the local basis could not be started without assistance or tolerance from the clergy. The Church was always prepared to support all efforts to improve the situation of the Catholic population in the framework of the existing political and social conditions, resisting, however, any movement aimed at abolishing these conditions by force.[246] The Land League and National League as well as the Home Rule movement were supported by the local clergy, the parish priests and the curates. At a later date they were followed by members of the hierarchy who took the opinion that Parnell's moderate policy was able to drive the pace-makers of the revolutionists in the national movement into the background. The local clergy, moreover, believed in a diminution of Protestant influence in Ireland and in an eventual end of the landlords' rule.[247]

The Vatican had come into an awkward position. The highest authority of the Church had to take into account the justified claims, the pastoral needs, as well as the moral position, of the faithful on the one hand and the diplomatic pressure of the British government and the tactics to be followed with regard to the interests of the world Church on the other hand. Thus, the impression could be that the Vatican was wavering in order to satisfy everybody. But, obviously, in the long run nobody was satisfied, illusions fluttered away and a sense of disappointment and uneasiness was felt by everyone who had thought to use the Papal Curia as a chief-witness for his own view, if not as an arbitrator.

Already in 1880 Gladstone had tried to persuade Cardinal Newman that the Pope should intervene with the aim of separating the clergy from the Land League. 'You will hardly be surprised that I regard the Supreme Pontiff, if apprised of the facts, as responsible for the action of these priests for I perfectly well know that he has the means of silencing them.'[248] Newman corrected him saying that he was overrating the Pope's powers in political and social matters.[249] But this mistake, committed by Gladstone, initiated a series of mistakes and led to the uneasiness mentioned above.

On 3 January 1881 Leo XIII wrote a letter to Archbishop McCabe of Dublin and the other members of the Irish hierarchy admonishing them to make a difference between lawful and unlawful movements aimed at redressing complaints. Ireland would achieve her aims in an easier and more secure way if she stayed in the framework of law and order, said the Pope. The German translation of the text was published in the *Germania*, and the German ambassador to the Quirinal reported at length on the reply of the Irish bishops of 25 January 1881, in which they

F

blamed the unjust and ruinous English laws. 'The people have woken up from their lethargy and have firmly demanded the abolition of these laws. Although we do not approve of all means of agitation, we approve, however, of all its aims. One should not believe in the calumnies of English newspapers' the bishops wrote. The ambassador informed Berlin in this context that, according to a *Mot d'ordre* of the Vatican, the press was requested to write less on Irish affairs and to abstain from comments in favour of the English government. Cardinal Manning was said to have suggested establishing an Apostolic Nunciature in London in exchange for the Pope's personal efforts for the appeasement of Ireland.[250] A few months later the same embassy reported that the Pope would be unable to exercise his authority over the bishops in this case if they were to defy his instructions. 'The Pope would not do the government's work because Gladstone is a bitter foe of the Vatican.'[251]

The *Germania* criticised Gladstone because he had declined to accept the suggestions for amendments of the Land Bill made by the bishops. 'By this the English government had lost a weapon which proved most efficient in the struggle with the Land League: the Catholic hierarchy never ceased to curb the exuberant emotions of the League.'[252]

Late in 1881 the attention of everybody concerned was drawn to the presence and activities of Errington in Rome. The German embassy informed Berlin in several reports on the personality of Errington: 'Irish M.P.; a convert and to be regarded as a devoted Roman Catholic, a gentleman open to intrigues, seems to be an able agent of the Archbishop of Dublin.'[253] Gladstone was said to have denied that Errington went to Rome on an official mission, as Protestant circles suspected. Münster, however, asserted that Errington was provided with letters of recommendation from Gladstone and Granville and that he reported to the Foreign Secretary in private letters.[254] A few months later it was confirmed by the Government in both Houses of Parliament that Errington had gone to Rome on his own initiative, but it was admitted that he had offered his services to Lord Granville, who then received his confidential reports.[255] Certainly it cannot be regarded as a mere accident that Mgr Capel, a Canon of the Chapter of Westminster Cathedral, published just at that time a pamphlet with the headline 'Shall the Queen establish diplomatic relations with the Pope?' Pointing at the ten million Catholics as subjects of the Queen (without Colonies), the author gave an affirmative answer to the question, in particular with regard to Ireland. Mgr Capel sent a copy of the pamphlet to the Chancellor in Berlin, together with a personal letter.[256]

Obviously, the question of diplomatic relations had also been on Errington's agenda in Rome, but the government in London was quite aware that this was a delicate matter due to the attitude of the British Protestants on the one hand and of the Irish clergy on the other, for they both disliked the idea. Anyway, there is no doubt that the actual motive of Errington's activity, either with the active assistance or passive tolerance of the government, was to counteract the Irish political and agrarian movements in general and the collection for the Parnell testimonial fund in particular.[257]

On 15 May 1883 *The Times* published a Circular of the Holy See to the Irish bishops, which condemned collections 'raised in order to enflame popular passions and to be used as the means for leading men into rebellion against the laws. Above all things, then, the clergy must hold themselves aloof from such subscriptions when it is plain that hatred and discussions are aroused by them'. The Circular was commented upon by the embassy and German newspapers. Following news from London the embassy took the view that the Irish would only yield to the influence of the clergy if it were in conformity with them. According to the embassy the national feeling in Ireland was stronger than the religious.[258]

Following Bismarck's custom, this report was published in the *Norddeutsche Allgemeine Zeitung*.[259] The paper confirmed the news that the subscriptions for the Parnell Fund mounted quickly and that there was no longer any doubt about the success of the collection which might possibly have failed without the Pope's interference.[260]

Thus, Errington's activities proved a failure. Although Gladstone had again denied the official character of Errington's mission and although Fitzmaurice, the Under-Secretary of the Foreign Office, had declared that the Pope's letter had not been written on the initiative of the government, this rumour was maintained and circulated in the press.[261]

Taking sides with the Vatican, the *Germania* regretted the

fact that the letter had been rejected in Ireland and criticised the attitude of Archbishop Croke who had propagated the collection and who had published his decision after his return from Rome that he would not give up his role in the actual agitation because, as the paper wrote, 'he regarded the letter as a diplomatic step aimed at a rapprochement between the Vatican and the cabinet of St James'.[262]

Official German circles may have received the news that the Irish clergy defied the Roman reactions with mixed feelings. On the one hand this fitted into the efforts of the government to stir up the Catholic clergy against Rome, but on the other hand they had to regard it as a bad example for priests and laymen of national or linguistic minorities who could take the Irish attitude —'national interests first'—as a model. The endeavours of the British government to exercise some pressure on the Vatican with the aim of influencing the Pope in dealing with the Irish question found parallels in Germany at that time. Very often the Irish party has been compared—though unjustly—with the Catholic party in Germany, even by Bismarck himself. The Catholic party in the German Empire and in the various German states was a stumbling block for Bismarck and his followers, in particular during the Kulturkampf and earlier: an obstruction which the Chancellor wished eliminated by the mediation of the Vatican. Already in 1862, in the pre-imperial period, Bismarck had begun his efforts in this direction and he pursued this course up to a time shortly before his resignation from office. During the Franco-German war the Archbishop of Posen-Gnesen, Count Ledochowski, was the man Bismarck relied upon; he regarded him as a supporter of Prussian sovereignty, in the provinces where there was a Polish population or people of Polish mother-tongue.[263] All these endeavours to influence the Roman Curia failed, however, despite Bismarck's comparatively strong bargaining power at that time. There was no promising prospect for him so long as Pius IX was alive.[264]

In later years the Chancellor intensified his efforts, with a better prospect of success due to Schlözer's[265] excellent relations with the Vatican, in particular with Mgr Galimberti, Secretary to the Congregation for extraordinary affairs, with the Cardinal State Secretary and even with Leo XIII himself.[266] In the early eighties the political support of the Catholic party was needed for a parliamentary majority in favour of Bismarck's new tariff policy which was rejected by liberal deputies. The Kulturkampf was about to expire and a good deal of the laws discriminating against the Catholic Church and its priests and bishops had been repealed. The way for an active German policy towards the Holy See with the aim of making the best of a bad bargain was open, and Bismarck succeeded in convincing the Pope that influencing the Catholic party in favour of his policy would turn out in favour of Catholic interests. Thus the Pope instructed the Apostolic Nuncio to Bavaria in Munich, Mgr Angelo di Pietro—a nunciature to the German Reich was not established before the end of the 1914–18 war—to advise the Catholic parliamentary group to agree to a bill irrevocably fixing the peace-time strength of the armed forces for a term of seven years; the so-called 'Septennat'. The Catholic leader, Baron von Frankenstein, did not communicate this papal advice to the members of the group, and at a party rally in Cologne on 7 February 1887, where Windthorst addressed his political friends in a most remarkable way, it was declared that even the Pope must recognise the possibility of a free choice for each Catholic in temporal matters.

Leo XIII, obviously indignant at the reaction of the party to his advice, requested the Cardinal State Secretary Jacobini to express his disapproval about the party's attitude. This took place through a second letter to the Nuncio which was published in German newspapers just like the first one. As Eyck puts it, 'it was a thunderclap for Windthorst', but the Pope's word proved ineffective.[267]

After the dissolution of the Reichstag and the new election following a short but vehement contest, directed in particular against the Catholic party, the new Catholic parliamentary group, except for a few members, abstained in the crucial vote on the Septennat, whereas the group in the Prussian Lower House, by urgent request of the Holy See eventually gave its approval to the last Peace Law which practically put an end to the Kulturkampf and to most of the discriminating measures, except the expulsion of the Jesuits[268] and some other provisions of minor importance.

It is a fact that comparisons drawn between political matters in different states are usually rather poor because each country and its policy has a particular aspect due to race and tradition.

But in this special case the analogy is striking: the same period of history, the same denomination concerned with an almost equal political influence, the same methods aimed at neutralising this influence and a diplomatically homogeneous Pope who—though maintaining his claim for a restoration of the Papal temporal power—was regarded as a peace-loving and open-minded person.[269] The one important difference was the fact that the members of the German Catholic party were Germans—the national minorities having their own deputies at that time—while the members of the Irish party and the Irish churchmen were not of the people of the dominating power.[270] This, however, did not prevent Bismarck from taking the opportunity to exploit to his advantage the prima facie parallels and from giving advice grounded on his own experiences.

Information from Rome that Gladstone intended to take up new contacts with the Vatican[271] gave rise to diplomatic activity in Berlin. Following an instruction from the Foreign Office Hatz-feldt reported that Rosebery did not know anything and that it was not envisaged to do anything about the matter.[272] Immediately afterwards Schlözer was instructed by Bismarck to make a report and he informed him that: 'All rumours about a resumption of negotiations between England and the Vatican are unfounded. There is no doubt that a desire for a renewed rapprochement with Gladstone exists in the Vatican. The difficulties with Ireland cannot be eliminated without the Pope's help, but Gladstone would never again entrust a mission to Errington, who is no longer persona grata in the Vatican' (probably due to a letter which was published indiscreetly and in which the author had joked about the Papal Court).[273]

So the Errington affair was filed in the German diplomatic records, but a new contact with the Vatican attracted the interest of the German authorities—the mission of the Duke of Norfolk. Hatzfeldt reported to Berlin that Salisbury had not denied, in a confidential conversation, that the Duke was instructed to press for an influencing of the obstinate Irish clergy by the Vatican with the aim of persuading them to abandon their revolutionary activities. Officially, however, he would be compelled to deny this because otherwise public opinion would strongly blame the government for having caused interference by the Pope with internal affairs.[274] Following this report Schlözer was instructed by Bismarck to lend his support to the Duke 'It is in our interest that the Pope might give help to the Conservative government in England.'[275]

Also the press informed its readers about the mission. Quoting from the *Observateur Français*, the *Germania* declared that the Duke of Norfolk had asked for a political intervention by the Pope in exchange for official relations with the Vatican. The paper excluded such an interference because the principle of non-interference should be maintained and the Holy See did not appear to be inclined to abandon Irish claims in exchange for diplomatic relations, the more so because there was no unanimous feeling among the English bishops in this delicate matter. Cardinal Manning was said to have written to the Curia that the Holy See might limit the exercise of their influence to religious matters only.[276] A few days later the *Moniteur de Rome*[277] recalled the admonitions of the Pope that the Irish should keep themselves 'dans les limites légales et constitutionelles' and reported on utterances of Leo XIII, in which he referred to the attitude of the Catholics in Germany during the Kulturkampf. 'Pourquoi', s'est écrié le Saint Père, "n'en serait-il pas de même en Irlande?' It seems to be doubtful whether the Pope had made a remark like this, if one takes into account the different historical and ethnological background; in any case, the press report is an interesting contribution to the assessment of the Irish situation by certain Roman circles.

It is noteworthy that German diplomatic activity in the context of England's relations with the Vatican went on until Bismarck's resignation from office in 1890.[278] Hatzfeldt reported on 4 May 1888 on a question by Labouchère in the House of Commons as to whether the Duke of Norfolk had been acting on the instructions of Salisbury or not in Rome, and that Fergusson answered this question in the negative.[279] Schlözer wrote at the same time that Leo XIII was still to be regarded as being in favour of the British government with regard to the Irish question.[280]

In 1889 General Sir John Simmons was sent over to Rome on a special mission, in the capacity of Envoy Extraordinary and Minister Plenipotentiary to the Vatican, with the instruction to contact the Pope on the issue of the denominational situation in Malta. Bismarck reacted to Hatzfeldt's report with the marginal note: 'Is this the old drunkard who attended the Berlin Congress?' When Hatzfeldt confirmed the identity, Bismarck remarked: 'Effete ignorant person.'[281] On 11 December 1889 Schlözer informed Bismarck that the General 'will do his best to increase British influence over the appointment of bishops in Ireland,' commenting that the Curia would hardly accept this.[282] One month later Schlözer reported again on England's efforts to come to terms with the Vatican with the hope that the prerogatives of the Cathedral Chapters in the appointment of bishops would be restricted and the government enabled to use its influence in this matter. Bismarck commented in a marginal note: 'His Holiness will be on his guard.' To Schlözer's opinion that Leo XIII would have difficulties meeting England's wishes he remarked: 'He wouldn't dream of it, *numquam retrorsum*.'[283] These reports gave rise to a conversation between Bismarck and his collaborators at Friedrichsruh; as a consequence of which Hatzfeldt was instructed as follows: He could express himself confidentially that the English government's belief in the possibility of the Curia's renouncing their influence on the Irish Church, even by a hair's breadth, would disclose their ignorance in matters of history and particularly that of the Papacy.[284] Reporting after a conversation with Salisbury, Hatzfeldt took the view that the Vatican's influence over Ireland was rather poor, even if the Curia would be inclined to act in favour of the government.[285] Schlözer, however, reported[286] that, in the view of certain prelates in the case of a diplomatic rapprochement between England and the Vatican, the possibility could not be excluded that England might exercise more influence over the appointment of the bishops. In 1893, after the introduction of Gladstone's second Home Rule Bill, Hatzfeldt reported that according to the view expressed by a Papal prelate the Curia was inclined to wait for the enacting of the bill before taking up renewed contacts with regard to the re-establishment of diplomatic relations. Gladstone was said to have in mind sending a Chargé d'Affaires to the Vatican.[287] Some time later Bülow, the new Minister to the Vatican after Schlözer's resignation, informed the Foreign Office that the negotiations had come to a deadlock.[288]

With this, a very interesting period of German diplomatic activity came to a standstill. Bismarck's successors were not so much interested in this important matter as he had been. In his view normal relations between England and the Vatican were, obviously, a considerable contribution to the strengthening of her power in Europe, just at a time when he had proposed an alliance pact to Salisbury in 1889, which, however, was never accepted.[289]

The Plan of Campaign, like the Parnell Testimonial Fund, a few years earlier, proved to be another test of the relations between Vatican, hierarchy and government in their mutual efficiency and their influence on the people of Ireland. The measures of the plan (refusal to pay higher rents than deemed acceptable by the tenant, and, in the case of non-agreement with the landlord, depositing the proposed rent sum in a particular fund, indirect boycotting, concerning land-grabbers and other persons)[290] gave rise to renewed efforts by the government to engage the Church in the struggle. In 1887 the Pope sent Mgr Persico on a fact finding mission to Ireland. As a result of this mission the Curia put the following question before the Inquisitions' Congregation:

'Utram liceat in controversiis inter locatores et conductores fundorum seu praediorum in Hibernia uti mediis vulgo appellatis the Plan of Campaign et the Boycotting.'

And the Congregation replied: 'Negative.'[291] A Papal Rescript of 20 April 1888, therefore, condemned the Plan and the boycotting. With reference to the establishment of the Land Court it pointed out that contracts should not be violated, and the boycotting was declared to be in contradiction to natural right and Christian charity.

The reaction of the British government was disclosed to the German ambassador by Salisbury himself. After a conversation of 30 April 1888 Hatzfeldt reported that, in the Prime Minister's view, Mgr Persico was the man who had advised the Curia on the Rescript, but that the government had no illusions about its success. In Hatzfeldt's opinion the success depended on the attitude of the bishops.[292]

Parnell is said to have declared that the document was not binding on the conscience of the Irish, expressing the view that it could be regarded only as an advice in temporal matters issued by an authority whose advice had not always been wise.[293]

In a similar way Hatzfeldt reported that in Parnell's opinion the Catholics would not be influenced to neglect their duties towards the country. The ambassador added that the Papal decision had come unexpectedly to the Irish leaders and to the Liberals and that they were not so unconcerned as they appeared to be. Chamberlain had told Hatzfeldt that the decision would contribute to an appeasement in Ireland and that the government had been entitled to secure the consent of the Pope in a confidential way.[294] Some time later he informed Berlin that the Catholic members of the National League had expressed themselves against the Rescript and had declared that the Pope had been ill advised on the Irish situation. 'Hotspurs are preaching resistance to the Curia in case they would dare to sell the liberty of Ireland in exchange for concessions to England', Hatzfeldt said. 'The Corporation of Dublin had declared that they defied to be ruled either by Saxons or by Italians.'[295]

German newspapers reported the events after the Rescript with great interest, although, at that time, everybody's attention in Germany was drawn to internal matters, mainly to the hopeless illness of the Emperor Frederick III. The Liberal *Vossische Zeitung* expressed its doubts that the Rescript had hit the mainspring of the National League, and took the view that each attempt of Rome to influence a popular Irish movement had failed to succeed.[296] In a leader with the headline 'The Pope and the Irish Question' the paper reminded its readers that Leo XIII had been very courteous with Prince Bismarck in his attempt to secure Catholic support in the Septennat issue.[297] According to the paper, he now knew how to oblige the English government by supporting them in their struggle with the Parnellites; if the government were to accept this interference in favour of the cabinet, Rome would obtain a position in which the government could not object to an eventual action of the Pope against the interests of the landlords and those of the government. The English people will hold that Lord Salisbury has asked for the Pope's assistance against British subjects, the paper said; this suspicion must violate the English national pride to such an extent that the position of the cabinet could be endangered. The paper drew the conclusion that the State had been subdued by the Church.[298] In a later article the author remarked 'The cards are shuffled for an Irish Kulturkampf against the excessive temporal claims of Papal power.'[299] A correspondent of the paper drew the attention of the readers to the fact that 'it is a curious thing that the strongest supporters of the Papal interference in

Irish politics are Unionists who are using the protection of the Protestant minority as an argument against Home Rule'.[300]

The *Germania*, too, dealt in some articles with the situation after the Papal Rescript. Interpreting the decision taken by the Congregation, the paper pointed out that boycotting was not referred to in a general sense, but that this term had to be understood only in the context of the Plan of Campaign. Having described the hopeless situation of many tenants, the paper wrote: 'With regard to the circumstances as a product of the appalling sins England has committed for centuries, the assessment of Irish affairs has become immensely difficult, and even in cases in which the Irish have to be condemned, one must do it with a bleeding heart.' The paper quoted the warning declaration of the Irish hierarchy about the Coercion Bill of 1887 and stated that the outrages in Ireland were limited to some districts of the country. 'Despite unjust treatment and bad social circumstances, the crime statistics of Ireland are better than those of England and Scotland.' Coercion and absence of reforms—these facts have embittered the Irish people and will impede the acceptance of the Roman Rescript, the paper declared. Quoting from the *United Ireland*, which had blamed Mgr Persico who was said to have kept the representatives of the people at a distance while being flattered by the land profiteers, the *Germania* criticised the Irish paper because it had failed to express any approval whatsoever for the Roman decision. 'It seems to hide itself behind the well-known Jansenistic differences of "facts" and "matters of faith and morals".[301] In some additional remarks the paper appealed to the people of Ireland to listen to the voice of justice and morality and to get rid of atheistic and revolutionary elements.[302] Concluding the articles on the situation after the Rescript, the *Germania* published in full the declaration of the hierarchy of 27 June with its strong appeal to the British parliament.[303]

The *Vossische Zeitung* informed the German public that in a letter to the Vatican the Irish bishops had defended the condemned measures.[304]

Bauer[305] takes the view that in their dealings with the Irish question the Vatican had kept in mind the future of the Catholic Church in England and Ireland as a whole, neglecting the Church in Ireland, as well as disregarding the idea of an Irish parliament in Dublin. Rome had in mind to conduct the worldwide

Anglican community back into the Roman Church; national aspirations did not matter in this context.

Although it is true that the Catholics in England were afraid that they would be isolated if the Irish Catholics were separated from them, it may not be assumed that the Vatican's policy at that time was based on reflections which can only be assessed as illusions. No power in the modern world has proved more realistic than the Vatican. The peaceful end of the German Kulturkampf seems to be a striking proof of it. Both partners found their limits drawn by the principle propagated by the great master of German politics: 'Politics is the art of the possible.'

PARNELL

The Leader and his team—Parnell versus The Times*—His fall and the party's split—Last appreciations*

John Morley wrote about Parnell: 'The pen of Tacitus or Sallust or de Retz would be needed to do full justice to a character so remarkable. The horrid weakness of envy and jealousy was unknown to him. From that his pride saved him. For laurels he did not care.[306] No better characterisation has been made by a contemporary politician, friend or foe, or by his biographers than that of this most cultivated and gifted personality in modern English history. And in a very impressive way Cruise O'Brien emphasises Parnell's imposing stature and great attraction: 'Few leaders in modern times have looked so very like a leader.'[307] Eversley describes him as reserved, aloof and even frigid. 'His speeches were cold hard and unimpressionable. But he was endowed with a dogged and unperturbable will. Above all, he had the very rare gift of instinctive command over men, and the power of compelling them to follow him.'[308] The liberal *Vossische Zeitung* spoke of him as being cut out for a dictator whose fervour grows if one opposes him. 'One has the impression that everybody coming in contact with him is hypnotised. The power of this man is immense.' The paper compared him with Samson who was prepared to die under the ruins of the temple together with his foes.[309] Bonn holds him to be the greatest son of Ireland —'a mixture of childlike simplicity and a never failing intuitive grasp of what is politically possible and politically necessary; a hermit with a shy faint-heartedness, but gifted with an iron energy to make people serve his purpose'.[310]

It must be admitted that the bulk of the German people—as well as people in other continental countries—had no real idea about Parnell in his prime. Newspapers wrote on the Parnellites mostly in a despising sense, because they were only provided with news and opinions from anti-Irish sources.[311] What they knew about Parnell was almost nothing. No German schoolboy and no student, except one of contemporary history, would have given a reasonable reply when tested about his knowledge of English-Irish politics. In the twentieth century even less was known of Parnell on the continent, and gradually his image faded in the dusk of history.

In his time, however, attention was paid, in certain circles, to certain crucial periods of his life, for example to that of the first Home Rule Bill, to his fall from power and his death. When studying German newspapers and periodicals of the eighties one gets the impression that justice was done to Parnell only in the dramatic last year of his life and after his unexpectedly premature death.

What interested people was the question whether Parnell was a revolutionist or not. It is very difficult to define what a revolutionist really is. No doubt, through the eyes of the then ruling classes, both in Germany and in England, and in the view of certain British Conservatives, Parnell was regarded as a revolutionist in the sense of the Victorian epoch, although nuances are to be noted everywhere. Bismarck has mentioned the Parnellites but not Parnell himself. It must be assumed that he was aware of Parnell's real character, as that of a conservative nationalist, although men like Parnell appeared to him and his ruling contemporaries as unearthly. But Bismarck was in no way misled by the partly stereotyped reports of his diplomats and other information. As mentioned above, the Chancellor had a perfect knowledge of English-Irish history, including the Irish question, and as a man with a direct grasp of everything that was really going on in Germany and in Europe, he had an approach to persons and events which was quite independent from prefabricated opinions or from what is called public opinion. Of course, his approach to personalities like Parnell was along the lines of his approach to British-Irish problems in general; strong personalities and their emanations were regarded under the criterion of whether they made Britain, as a European power, stronger or weaker. He would never have despised or rejected revolutionists if they had served Britain in his sense. Up to this time few people in Germany had realised what the Irish question had meant to Britain in the nineteenth century. Bismarck belonged to this small number of people,[312] and there is no indication whatever that he underrated any important person who acted as one of the *dramatis personae* in that formidable play on the European stage.

So far as religion is concerned Parnell was said to be 'closely reserved and never disrespectful'. His contemporaries mentioned his superstition and his belief in the plurality of the worlds and their habitable condition. The Catholic Church was in his highest esteem.[313] Nevertheless, certain circles of the clergy and hierarchy were hostile to his followers. In Cruise O'Brien's view this 'sprang not so much from any doubts as to the religious bona fides of the candidates as from the church's general suspicion of all movements of a revolutionary or semi-revolutionary character'.[314] This position, taken by several churchmen in Ireland and in the Roman Curia had, no doubt, also influenced the approach of German Catholics and of their press. Their approach to Ireland and her destiny was full of warm-hearted enthusiasm while looking upon Parnell and his party—at least for some time of that period—with a certain reserve.[315] One cannot help feeling that Parnell's personality appeared to them in a somewhat unreal light. No doubt, there was another reason for this reserve. They disliked the analogies which were drawn rather frequently between Irish and German Catholics, in particular during the Kulturkampf, because they rightly felt that the Church-State trouble in Germany was based on a divergent approach to the historical role of Church and State, whereas they attributed the English-Irish conflict in the first place to national antagonism.

At the time when Parnell's influence was at its height, his team and its several members were entirely over-shadowed by their leader's personality. None of them reached such popularity as to become known to a broader public on the continental side of the Channel, apart from some men in the ministries and particular experts in British home politics. The names of Dillon,

W. O'Brien, Healy, Biggar, Sexton and others were to be found, however, in diplomatic reports and press articles, but not with such force that the name and the person left a lasting impression. Though gifted and able these men—Dillon, the medical doctor, with excellent qualities for leadership; W. O'Brien, an accepted writer, journalist and eloquent speaker, kind and humorous; Healy, the best debater and best legal mind, who 'felt himself to be the stuff of which leaders are made,' with an infinite capacity for hard work; Biggar, leading in obstructionist methods and tactics; and Sexton, an eloquent speaker in Parliament, particularly on financial questions—could not contend with the Uncrowned King for his invisible crown.[316] It seems not to be a mere accident that the Irish party was known in Germany under the name Home Rulers, before Parnell took over and as Parnellites afterwards. It is an indication of the feeling that the party was dominated by Parnell's spirit and that it was kept alive, during the coercion periods and other times of oppression, through his creative breath and power.[317]

Yet in the mental vigour of all Parnell's men and in their individual minds there existed a force restrained but highly explosive, comparable with a time-bomb. This became manifest after Parnell's fall.

But before this day *The Times*, his inveterate adversary, helped him to his greatest triumph as a political leader. The whole story appears incredible to an impartial observer and to anybody assessing the events of that period. One must put the question how such a blunder could occur in a paper of the highest standing and world-wide reputation. The outcome of the case confirmed once again that aversion and hatred founded on political hostility are the worst advisers for settling differences in the political or religious field. *The Times* had been taken in by an unscrupulous and criminal slanderer and impostor by the name of Pigott, 'a Fenian and degenerate nationalist'.[318]

The publication of the letters alleging Parnell's connection with the Invincibles, caused a sensation on the continent and in Germany and drew public attention to everyone connected with the case. The installation of the Parnell Commission and its proceedings from September 1888 until Pigott's confession on 27 February 1889 and then until the report of 18 February 1890 were profitable material for journalism and political speculation.

The German embassy followed the proceedings with unemotional and rather impartial reports. In October 1888 it reported on 'the difficult situation of *The Times*' and on the possibility that the paper could lose in the judgement.[319] On 27 February 1889 Berlin was informed of Pigott's confession, the report speaking of the carelessness of the newspaper and predicting that Parnell would 'carry the day'. A few days later another report spoke of actions for slander to be faced by *The Times* which could 'lead to the entire ruin of this paper with such a firm financial basis'.[320] With regard to the proportionally modest sum of £5,000 of compensation which was accepted by Parnell the embassy held that this moderation had to be explained by O'Shea's divorce suit which was already filed at that time.[321] The *Germania*, although reserved as usual in all affairs regarding Parnell, nevertheless, took the view that *The Times* had admitted being wrong by accepting the forfeit of £5,000.[322] A few weeks later the paper quoted from *The Tablet* which had pointed out that Parnell had been attacked in a way which made it difficult to say 'whether wickedness or foolishness had played the greater part'. The German paper criticised the article in footnotes, particularly the argument of the Commission that the agitation of the Land League had been due to the evictions, not to the misery of the tenants.[323]

Winston Churchill says that his father had expressed himself against the setting up of a Commission of three judges (Lord Hannen, Mr Justice Day and Mr Justice A. L. Smith), pointing out that political difficulties could not be met by unconstitutional methods. ' "Parnellism and Crime" is not criminal, it is entirely political.'[324] Under the headline 'Pigott's forgeries' the *Preussische Jahrbücher* told its readers that *The Times* had been duped by one of the dirtiest scoundrels and that Parnell stood justified after this shameless attack. The periodical took the view that the outcome of the case would not necessarily endanger the position of the government, because 'the English public is not the same as the French.[325] In France a party will be condemned on the whole, if there is a scoundrel in their ranks, whereas the Englishmen are cool people. There is no evidence that the government have supported or instigated *The Times*'—thus correcting Lord Randolph. Be that as it may, 'Never in this country', Gwynn says 'did Ireland stand higher than at that moment [of the acquittal] and never in the whole history of the British parlia-ment did there appear a prouder figure, a stronger or more com-manding personality.'[326] Later on, *The Times* ranked Gladstone, Gordon and Parnell as the three outstanding figures of the Vic-torian era,[327] a rather belated avowal.

The climax of Parnell's career was followed very soon by a nadir. Parnell had to experience how quickly all low human instincts can be set loose if there is a man who appears to be a suitable target. The whole story of Parnell's romance and fall is not unparalleled in political history, but in the nineteenth century there is hardly to be found another case with similar lasting consequences for the development of a political question like this, or a case which implicated more crucial decisions about the destiny of persons and properties, as well as about material and spiritual values. When the present-day generation looks back upon the year 1890, after having survived two world wars, the Russian revolution, the atom bomb, decolonisation, the explora-tion of outer space and other events either fruitful or not, they cannot but shake their heads with incredulous amazement at the pettiness, hypocrisy, envy, thirst for revenge, unleashing of pent-up minority feelings and other destructive qualities which became manifest in those days.

German comments on these events were naturally varied. While diplomats and most daily papers refrained from detailed descriptions, the remarks made by the *Preussische Jahrbücher*, one of the most outstanding political and historical periodicals, appear to be typical of the uneasy feeling in German circles which had a say in the chorus of contemporary political observers. 'In order to land a blow on the Home Rule movement, the advers-aries have thought out a typically English manoeuvre. Parnell has had relations with the wife of another man; perhaps it was adultery, perhaps not. Everywhere there are liaisons such as this, the particular circumstances, however, not being clear. If the husband is content the public is usually silent also. In this case the husband did not say anything for years; now he was induced to file a petition because of adultery. An English gentleman, indeed! What a public which allows a party leader to be ruined by such a gentleman!'[328]'

And some time later the same author reiterated his arguments in equally blunt terms: 'O'Shea had a beautiful wife whose lover

G

was said to have been Parnell. O'Shea connived at the liaison for years, because this eased, probably, the costs of his household.[329] Parnell's adversaries offered him a worthwhile deal if he would take action against Parnell, and honourable O'Shea seized the opportunity. That is the fact on which the question is based as to whether Parnell can remain the Irish party's leader, for in virtuous England a party leader can only be a man of impeccable virtue. That is the English difficulty which appears to be ridiculous to a cultivated continental. A mature and educated people would say that Parnell, as a human being, did not become worse after the trial since the stain of the deed had lain upon him for a long time and was notorious. To produce material for use in the courts with the aim to neutralise a political adversary is distasteful and dirty. The cad who accepted to be bought for noising up a long endured humiliation in order to ruin another man's political career is by nature such a scoundrel that his wife could not do better than despise him, as she had not been compelled to deceive him. The whole affair is not very pleasant, but one should forget about it; and it should not influence politics.'[330]

This assessment, though not very clear as to what was meant by 'deal' and 'bought' is in substance not very far from that of scholars. Various allegations had been made against O'Shea, the chief of which was that, apart from conniving at his wife's relations with Parnell, he had committed adultery with her sister.[331] According to the story told by Parnell's wife after his death, O'Shea in fact connived at the relationship between Parnell and his wife, and he did so partly in the hope of political advancement and partly in the hope of financial gain. It is the opinion of Lyons, however, that historians have argued too long on what version is the correct one.[332] The 'hope of political advance' seems to be proven by O'Shea's Galway candidature, which was supported by Parnell and Chamberlain.[333] Cruise O'Brien characterises O'Shea as 'ambitious with a small but sufficiently disastrous talent for political intrigue'. Both O'Shea and Mrs O'Shea played the role of mutual informants between Parnell and English politicians, chiefly Gladstone and Chamberlain, with whom O'Shea, apparently, had good political relations.[334] In the same author's view the suspicion that Chamberlain instigated O'Shea's action is not 'inherently improbable'.[335] In any case, many traces lead back to this chief-antagonist of Parnell who had become his irreconcilable foe since he was instrumental in defeating the bill in 1886. It is appalling that, very probably, some politicians of those days, had used a man like O'Shea as a tool for their tactics. Two major attacks on an irksome politician in the course of two years by using means of dubious character seem to be a bad indication of the moral standing of certain people in the Victorian era, perhaps an indication of the very rude methods which were to be used in the twentieth century when character assassination became popular in political disputes.[336]

As regards the German feelings on the repercussions of that decree in the Liberal and the Irish parties, the embassy remained reserved as to the moral side of the case. Hatzfeldt made no allusion to it, while dealing at length with the political consequences of the affair, in particular with Gladstone's position in the context of the Home Rule question. Two major topics seem to have been important in his view: Parnell's manifesto, which was described as a hard blow to Gladstone, and the indiscretion Parnell committed in publishing details of the conversation with Gladstone in Hawarden. 'Gladstone's Home Rule policy was founded on the argument that his plan would lead to a conciliation with Ireland without doing harm to the English who are sick of the Irish question. Parnell, having unveiled this fiction very rudely, has demonstrated that neither can the Irish aspirations be satisfied by Gladstone's vague promises, nor had he a perfect plan in mind.' According to the embassy, Parnell seemed to be prepared to resign, if Gladstone would guarantee a parliament for Ireland with full power in the land question and in matters concerning the police.[337] After Gladstone's refusal of any further collaboration with Parnell as party leader, and subsequent to the manifesto, the *Preussische Jahrbücher* criticised Gladstone and expressed itself in favour of Parnell. 'It is ridiculous to describe Parnell's behaviour as indiscretion. If two party leaders cannot come to terms, each of them must be free some day to tell his party the plain truth. In the long run Parnell underestimated the support he could expect from a collaboration with English radicalism. If he had believed in Gladstone's satisfactory intentions with regard to Ireland, Parnell, whom we take as a patriot, would not have caused the breach for the sake of his leadership. Instead of this he saw in his resignation—probably rightly—the danger of the Irish movement becoming futile. An important factor in the destiny of the English Empire thus depends on the negotiations of the leaders of an oppressed nationality.'[338]

The reactions of the leading German daily papers were different from each other in their emphasis. The *Germania* made hardly any remarks on the moral aspects of the case; it dealt mainly with the political side. After having reported on the events in Committee Room 15 in a businesslike fashion, it gave a résumé of the crisis in a special article of 2 December 1890. 'Parnell has provoked a crisis in England which threatens not only to do heavy damage to the Irish cause but to change the parliamentary situation of Great Britain, too.' In the view of the paper 'the manifesto is a document drafted with vicious cleverness'. It was said to be aimed at rendering the breach with the Liberals irreparable and to appeal to the Irish people, in case of an unfavourable decision of the parliamentary party, to regard Parnell as the true representative of Ireland's independence and nationality.[339]

The *Norddeutsche Allgemeine*, though no longer Bismarck's organ after the Chancellor's resignation, launched its attacks chiefly against Gladstone and described the Prime Minister's position as awkward: 'The maintenance of his puritan decorum can never be separated from his character-role as a statesman: Nobody should forget that the tradition of English radicalism has a tinge of puritanism since the seventeenth century. Even men like Labouchère are compelled to be morally exasperated by the adulterer Parnell.'[340] With regard to the Home Rule question the paper took the view that 'no love affair could do heavy damage to Home Rule, if it were to be recommended to the British people as an honest, patriotic and reasonable policy'. 'Since the moment the divorce case hit the Liberal internal policy, it became evident to the world that this policy had not been patriotic and statesmanlike but one of those party manoeuvres such as are, and will be, produced by parliamentarians' the paper declared.[341]

The national-liberal *Kölnische Zeitung*, in former times sporadically one of Bismarck's press organs, chose Parnell as its target by dealing chiefly with the divorce case, blaming him as a secret-monger who could not live without conspiracy. The paper called Parnell a 'taciturn, grim and melancholic conspirator' who exploited the secretiveness of his political role as a mask for his love-affair.[342] In a rather long report on the 'decision of the Parnellites'[343] the paper asks how it happened that this Anglo-Saxon joined the Celts. 'If the Irish spoke German, they would say "du" to each other while they would address Parnell as "Sie".' Having noted the low level of the arguments in Committee Room 15, the paper went on to declare that those present, had literally dripped with sweat, except Parnell—'the cold, white stone'.[344]

The liberal *Vossische Zeitung*, well informed as always and reporting in a balanced way, also mentioned the reactions of the middle class puritan circles who were the backbone of Gladstone's party. 'Neither *The Times* nor O'Shea can be amazed that there have been rumours on a deal between them and that these rumours are still persisting', the paper wrote.[345] Already early in 1890, when O'Shea had filed his divorce suit, the paper had apprehended the possibility that the reputation of the Irish leader, 'whose authoritative voice has done more for maintenance of law and order in Ireland than Balfour's tougher coercion laws,' could be affected.[346] During the crisis the paper expressed the opinion that Parnell's attitude was getting more and more incomprehensible, and after the manifesto it wrote that the Uncrowned King was about to destroy the entire cause he had hitherto served.[347] Committee Room 15, was the focus of the daily reports of the *Vossische Zeitung*, which could not help being stupefied by Parnell's stubbornness. In one of its last reports in those crucial days it informed its readers about Parnell's adversaries within the party and about the censorious attitude of the hierarchy.[348]

The secession of the forty-four members from Committee Room 15 was the end of a united Irish party. 'A united party—even poorly led—was preferable to a party torn asunder.'[349] MacDonagh, pointing at the consequences of Parnell's fall and the vulnerability of a movement which owed its coherence, meaning and life to a single man, takes the view that even after the restoration of substantial unity in 1900 the old wounds never healed completely.[350]

In his first report after the split, Hatzfeldt expressed the opinion that 'according to certain indications public opinion will turn out in favour of Parnell, although the hierarchy is against him'.[351] Maybe Hatzfeldt was thinking of Parnell's strong position in Dublin, which was 'fiercely Parnellite', and therefore over-estimated the number of Parnell's followers.[352] In any case, he was terribly mistaken in his prediction.

The German newspapers' comments after the split do not appear very remarkable. They were, in fact, anticipated necrologies. They dealt more with Gladstone than with Parnell. The *Kölnische Zeitung*, in a cynical manner,[353] compared Parnell's fall with Gambetta's funeral which was described as 'the greatest success of his life'. The paper had to admit, however, that Parnell had proved irreplaceable for the party. In their reports on the by-election contest in Kilkenny the papers underlined again the Church's opposition to Parnell, the temper of the Irish women and the violent conflicts of the members and followers of the split party.[354] Of all the comments of the papers, the leading article in the *Germania* of 13 December 1890—'The party crisis in Great Britain'—is the most noteworthy. Having mentioned Salisbury's efforts for peace in Europe, it continued: 'Gladstone's cabinet has been frequently an uncertain factor of foreign policy and not always in favour of the Central Powers'. The paper, however, expressed the wish that the Grand Old Man should win the next electoral contest, chiefly, in the interest of Ireland. While emphasising Parnell's outstanding political qualities on the one hand, it blamed his dictatorial manners on the other. 'Beside the Capitol is the Tarpejan rock; what had rendered him great, caused his fall, as well.' The paper concluded the article by warning Ireland of Parnellism.[355]

When the talks in Boulogne had failed to mend the split in the party and Parnell had refused to resign from the leadership of his own free will, at least for the time being, he continued his campaign to restore the lost confidence of the country. Despite his setback in the by-elections, 'He is going in triumph from one place to another, and in his instigating addresses he never forgets —apart from personal attacks and the ups and downs of politics —the real objective which he pursues: the legislative and factual independence of Ireland from England. By this means he has succeeded in sailing round the cliffs of the divorce scandal', the Chargé d'Affaires, Count Metternich, reported.[356] In criticising Gladstone's weak and vague Home Rule plan, Parnell maintained he was reluctantly presenting to Ireland only a sham Home Rule.

Parnell asserted that the Liberal party was not unanimous and that Ireland was being compelled to exchange the right of national independence for something which was, as yet, not clear. 'There is incontestedly a lot of logic in these arguments' the embassy commented. 'Home Rule has made much progress in England, partly because people are sick of it all, partly due to sympathy for it. When the land question is no longer under English jurisdiction, there is little interest shown by England, a fact which could lead to the decision to leave the Irish alone.'[357]

Parnell had never been in the best of health, but it had worsened in the last months. In an address in Creggs on 27 September 1891, directed to friends and enemies, he declared his last political intentions: 'We shall continue to fight. We fight not for faction but for freedom. I honour them [my friends] for their courage and I will not leave them until they get a better leader.'[358]

His death, a few days later, again aroused sensation on the continent. One has the impression that it was only at this very moment that people realised what Parnell's personality had really meant in British-Irish history. The *Kölnische Zeitung*, which during Parnell's lifetime was not very friendly towards him, stated that, looking back upon the career of the dead Irish leader in the course of the last fifteen years, one had to admit the extent to which Ireland and Parnell had influenced English history. 'One could say that during the greater part of that period Ireland and Parnell have played the leading role in English politics.'[359] The *Germania*, in an appreciation, told its readers that 'Parnell has had a position in the Empire and in parliament which can be regarded as similar to that of O'Connell. In parliament he fought with incomparable stubborness, steadfastness and inexorability'.[360] The *Vossische Zeitung* called him the 'idol of the Catholic Irish despite his Protestant faith', who, like Boulanger, had eventually lost his reputation with friends and foes.[361] The most remarkable obituary, in philosophical terms, came from the historians of the *Preussische Jahrbücher*. 'His death cannot leave unmoved any contemplative politically-minded man in our country. Human affairs advance chiefly by the pressure and thrust of divided masses which do not know their objective, having in view by instinct only the next point. At times it appears as if the objective cannot be attained but as the mechanical result of powers running into each other. But the great moments of history are those in which powerful and farsighted personalities determine the objectives and draw the masses behind them. In the actual perplexity of English state life, this personality appeared to be the late Parnell. It is a mystery how a people's genius propagates itself. It is futile to derive it from the blood. The greatest sons of many nations are descended from a foreign race—like Parnell.'[362]

There has been much written in favour of Parnell's great significance in history, and the contrary, too. Lyons has given a well-balanced description of his merits and his faults and errors, of his nobility and weaknesses.[363] In any case, 'the Parnellite decade profoundly changed the Anglo-Irish balance of power'.[364]

Morley[365] compared Parnell with Mirabeau, in whom 'private fault destroyed a saviour of his country', and with Robespierre, who was 'brought to the scaffold at the reaction of Thermidor'. Be that as it may, his portrait will assume many different colours in history, like Schiller's Wallenstein.

Parnell's destiny was like that of a Greek tragedy. It was the result of an enchainment of everything and of anyone concerned. Everybody was a captive, either of his principles or passion or of the spirit of the age, but there was no *deus ex machina* to enter the stage with the power to disentangle the knot.

Three eminent men in Europe left the front benches of their countries' parliaments in the early nineties, Bismarck, Gladstone and Parnell. Bismarck had to resign when he had mastered the great crisis of the Kulturkampf, but he had to pass over to inadequate successors his enormous mission in the field of foreign policy with its looming dangers. Gladstone left the Premiership without having completed his life work, the solution of the Irish question, and Parnell had to die in the awareness that his place remained deserted and his party split. Rarely was Europe struck so fatefully as in those crucial years.

CHAPTER 4

Greatness and Insufficiency

Gladstone through German Eyes—Lord Rosebery—The Cecil Decade and Parnell's successors—Wyndham and the Devolution Scheme—The Liberals again—The Irish Council Bill and new unrest.

LOOKING back from the late 1900s, even now one can feel how quickly and dramatically the political landscape of Europe had altered after the retirement of Bismarck and Gladstone, as well as after the decease of Parnell. As regards Gladstone, whose personality dominated the Irish question, one should remember Asquith's remark in his memoirs: 'The retirement of the greatest figure in politics was the signal for the letting loose of the waters.'[1] This was the parallel to the great event in German history when 'the pilot had left the ship'. Greatness dwindled away, and the heyday of two empires had begun to fade.

It is known that both figures did not have friendly feelings towards each other. While Gladstone regarded Bismarck as a 'nation-builder, only to be paralleled with Cavour, but unscrupulous and full of the devil',[2] Bismarck said of Gladstone: 'With such an incompetent politician, who is nothing but a great orator, one cannot account for England in our political strategy.'[3] 'Professor Gladstone' as he called the Liberal leader disparagingly, was a source of unease for him which was nursed from time to time by the remarks of his son, Count Herbert.[4] In an instruction early in 1874 to the embassy in London—when Gladstone was still in power, however, and before his pamphlets on the Vatican Decrees—Bismarck spoke of him as 'a statesman with crypto-Catholic feelings'.[5] Münster, who had once been full of admiration for Gladstone, 'not as a statesman and leader of a party' but as 'one of the most cultivated and most benevolent persons, who will always exercise a great influence through his excellent eloquence and his diligence, as well as, through his learning and his charming character,'[6] took him for 'an utterly radical man, unpredictable in foreign policy, more Russian than the Russians, a Slavophile, a bitter foe of Austria and a sympathiser with the wildest Italian revolutionists'. To the opinion expressed by Münster that the Queen would never again call him, even after a Liberal victory, and that the Whig leaders would do everything to keep out of power 'this ingenious but dangerous statesman,' Bismarck wrote the marginal note: 'You are mistaken, Count Münster.'[7] Schnabel[8] takes the opinion that there was 'no other statesman so despised by the Chancellor as the Grand Old Man, whose policy was dominated by humanitarian and pacifist ideas, who opposed the rising imperialism and complied with the national movement of the Irish and who extended the franchise'. Bismarck believed that his German adversaries (chiefly within the ranks of the liberals) regarded Gladstone as their ideal.[9] In April 1884 he told the French Ambassador that 'Gladstone has made mistakes time and again and has no idea about the interests of his country'.[10] Gladstone, fully aware of this antagonism, wrote in 1874 that Bismarck's ideas and his methods were not like his own because they came from different traditions, but that his sympathies, though not in conformity with him, were more in favour than against him.[11] With regard to colonial affairs Gladstone had a co-operative attitude. 'I am prepared to satisfy Bismarck in the colonial question in any way';[12] 'they should take what they want, we can have no better neighbours than the Germans'.[13]

Bismarck motivated his reserve towards England by the reflection that public opinion in that country always remained the decisive factor of English policy, and in his view public opinion would never be won for political aims which were not made clear in public.[14] This was, in fact, a substantial difference between Bismarck and Gladstone: dependence on public opinion on the one side and no consideration for it on the other.

William II, though not a follower of Bismarck's policy, shared Bismarck's opinion about Gladstone. He knew that his mother, the German Empress Victoria, admired Gladstone. This was, for Bismarck, a decisive factor in his judgement on the Liberal statesman. It was, of course, not the only motive. In his view Gladstone was no longer popular in England. 'I saw the Grand

Old Man twice on the street. Nobody paid attention to him, nobody bowed or nodded to him.'[15] But the real reason for his personal antipathy to Gladstone could, probably, be found in certain critical utterances of the British statesman which had come to the Emperor's ears. The German Ambassador to Austria, Prince Reuss, reported on 1 August 1888 on a letter of 'a reliable and intelligent person' from Milan to Count Kalnoky, in which it was said that Gladstone had expressed his concern about a forthcoming war. 'In springtime next year the young firebrand who acceded to the throne in Berlin will surely go to war. Until this time we shall be in power again, and you will see how we shall force peace upon Germany. For this reason, don't chain yourself too much to Berlin and Vienna.'[16] There is no confirmation as to whether the text of this letter was in conformity with the speech quoted, but, the Emperor believed in the reliability of the source and he felt annoyed. When he learned of Gladstone's death and of Hatzfeldt's advice to express the condolences of the Imperial Government, he refused on the grounds that Gladstone had been the most dangerous adversary of monarchism both English and German and a 'sworn enemy of the Hohenzollern family and of Germany'. 'Majuba Hill, Alexandria, Khartoum—Gordon!' were his marginal notes. When the ambassador reported on the manifestations of sympathy of foreign sovereigns, including the German Empress Victoria, William II answered by the marginal: '*Neque tamen*.'[17]

The German press, however, did not ignore the decease of the Grand Old Man. The *Germania*, while hailing his achievements in internal policy, regretted 'the failure of his Home Rule project which was defeated by the House of Lords', and while emphasising his eloquence, his literary and political knowledge, as well as, his ingenuity in financial affairs, the paper remained, as frequently before, critical of his activity in foreign affairs.[18] The *Kölnische Zeitung* called him 'England's greatest Financier, one of the most powerful orators, probably one of her most significant theologians, too, and a statesman who would have been counted among the first of his century, if not of history, if his career had ended thirty years ago'. With regard to Home Rule the right-wing paper wrote that 'he intended to do the best but had not been able to achieve the worst' and concluding, it remarked that 'the individual German was not disliked by him but he hated the specific Prussian, the military demeanour and the bureaucratic behaviour'.[19]

A brief but impressive appreciation came from the paper which had frequently objected to his policy, the *Norddeutsche Allgemeine*: 'It was a life full of work and of love for his country, striving at the same time for noble humanity, which has come to an end. Nobody will minimise that a noble character has passed away and that Gladstone's objectives were of great significance.'[20] The Liberal *Vossische Zeitung* found in its comments that 'he was not an imperious figure like Bismarck, not a statesman with the characteristics of Richelieu, Cavour or Disraeli: his statesmanship was humanism applied to politics'.[21] The paper pointed out that the merit was due exclusively to Gladstone for having persuaded the United Kingdom of the indispensability to concede self-government to Ireland.[22] 'The Irish question was not a matter of political advantage for him; his engagement for the Irish people, who were far too long deprived of their rights, was rather an emanation of the same sense of justice, always incorruptible and never dominated by opportunist reflections, which had made him the attorney of all oppressed people, the more so because he had no relations with the Irish, neither of religion nor of racial character.'[23]

The *Deutsche Revue*, in an obituary, hailed Gladstone in a remarkable way. 'In spite of all differences of opinion, all members of Parliament feel that an elevated head, a noble face, a personality of picturesque charm, a sympathetic character, a rich source of thought and feeling, an inspiring politician and a man of initiatives has left us' the periodical wrote.[24] From the point of view of a German historian of the twentieth century and as an expert on England, Dibelius describes Gladstone as the most brilliant interior architect of the State based on commerce. 'Energetic and busy, clear and calm, but with an ethical buoyancy which swept along the English, he has exercised in his capacity as Finance Minister and Prime Minister a deeper influence on the destiny of the country than any other statesman.'[25] On the other hand he regards Gladstone's foreign policy as hesitant and incongruous, a view which became typical of the Liberals. Though following the principles of an ideal policy of humanity and shrinking back from the thought of a warlike development, they have never sacrificed really important British interests. 'The Conservatives never had a politician like Gladstone who seized the spirit of the nation, Disraeli remained an alien to the British hearts.'[26]

Gladstone died quietly in Hawarden on Ascension Day, 1898. 'Without a struggle he ceased to breathe. Nature outside—wood and wide lawn and cloudless far-off sky—shone at her fairest.'[27] The Iron Chancellor followed his great political opponent ten weeks later in Friedrichsruh. Gladstone was laid to rest in Westminster Abbey, and Salisbury hailed him in parliament as the great example of a Christian statesman who stands alone in history, while Bismarck had been refused congratulations on his eightieth birthday by the majority of the Reichstag. The most powerful figures of the nineteenth century left this world just before the century ended. The decline from greatness to insufficiency had begun in Europe.

When Gladstone was about to resign early in 1894 Lord Rosebery's chances of becoming his successor were made uncertain by the radical wing of the Liberal party. Already late in 1898, Hatzfeldt reported that Dilke and Labouchère intended to eliminate the Foreign Secretary from the cabinet, due to his friendly attitude towards the Triple-Alliance. This provoked the following marginal note of the Emperor: 'The only respectable man shall be pushed out by the disrespectable!'[28] Early in March 1894 the ambassador reiterated his concern,[29] which eventually proved unfounded. Rosebery's first steps were carefully observed by the embassy, obviously due to the fact that the new Prime Minister was persona grata in Germany. In the following reports Hatzfeldt informed of Rosebery's programmes with regard to Home Rule and organisation of the House of Lords which was meant to remain unaltered.[30] Rosebery's utterances that, in a forthcoming electoral contest, the question of this reorganisation should be the chief issue—'the House of Lords as a bulwark of Toryism is a challenge to all liberties'—were strongly rejected by Salisbury who threatened that the overthrow of the House of Lords could only be achieved by physical force and would never be approved by the people.[31]

Shortly after Rosebery had taken over, Hatzfeldt reported that 'Redmond has no trust in the new cabinet'.[32] This mistrust did not appear unfounded as far as the Irish question was concerned. In this context it is very interesting to read what Rosebery had intimated to his close friend, Herbert von Bismarck. According to Count Bismarck's record of 6 September 1887 Rosebery had declared it impracticable to restore order in Ireland by coercion after the Conservatives had repealed the Liberal coercion law in 1885 in order to gain the Irish support. 'Coercion is impracticable for the afore-mentioned reasons and because our democracy would not stand it and the Yankees would probably interfere. Since we launched Home Rule, we shall have to try it; should it prove a failure, as I suppose, we shall be backed by the English democracy if we decide to rout the Irish ruthlessly with fire and sword. In this case even the Americans would let us have our way. I see no way out of the problem through any of the means hitherto used. Ireland is like a weight at our feet, laming our force and taking our time'[33] Rosebery said. In a letter to him of 18 January 1888 Count Herbert wrote: 'I regret very much that you take such a gloomy view of Ireland; that question is indeed the stumbling block for every English government. . . . The whole of Europe is suffering from a sort of impotence which the state of Ireland brings upon England's position as a great power.'[34] In the area of foreign affairs Count Herbert expected a different policy—in vain. Under the Premiership of Rosebery, who was said to have remarked: ' If we come to war with Russia I know that it shall cost us more than 200 million pounds; but I shall not make peace until the Tsar sits in Claridge's Hotel.'[35]

Lyons states that 'the period between the death of Parnell 1891 and the re-emergence of the Irish Parliamentary party nineteen years later as a key factor in the balance of power at Westminster is often dismissed by historians as a kind of political vacuum, to be passed over as swiftly and silently as possible'.[36] This attitude of historians may appear understandable from the point of view that the 1880s presented so many problems and in such a concentrated form that the following time had to be felt as a phase of tranquillity, compared with the previous period. In some way a feeling of exhaustion also marked the diplomatic comments and those of the press and periodicals, combined, however, with an unspoken uneasiness, the lull before the storm, a storm which was expected by everybody who was wise enough to see that the English-Irish problems continued to smoulder under a thin surface. The worsening of Anglo-German relations had, moreover, made people more hesitant in commenting on matters which were not regarded as a controversial subject between the two empires whose time of honeymoon was over. Rosebery was out of power, and Salisbury, who had been supported for a rather long period by Bismarck and had been held in high esteem by the Emperor, was no longer persona grata in Berlin.[37] In June 1887 Herbert Bismarck had stated, in a long record on British politicians, that Salisbury, who had been regarded as an aggressive and dogmatic hotspur during Disraeli's lifetime, and in the opposition, had altered his character and moderated his temper, obviously under the influence of Hartington and Chamberlain.[38] The German press had hailed him during his previous Premiership because of his foreign policy. But after Bismarck's resignation, and following a brief euphoria of William II, private and official opinion in Germany became gradually adverse. The Boer War, in which clumsiness was shown on both sides, brought the climate, at least temporarily, almost to zero. Even during the Cecil decade, under the leadership of Salisbury and Balfour in Britain and under Hohenlohe and Bülow as Chancellors in Germany, it became manifest in both countries that an imperialism which was no longer dominated by moral principles and self-control was condemned to daring deeds.[39]

The situation of the Irish party in those years was not encouraging in so far as its activity was hampered by the split. The German embassy described the situation as chaotic, due—apart from the split of 1890—to another split into Healyites and McCarthyites. The embassy drew the conclusion that the Irish 'are not mature enough for Home Rule,'[40] but some months later the embassy reported, clearly satisfied, on Dillon's election as successor to McCarthy and leader of the anti-Parnellites, emphasising his outstanding social position and his qualities as an able parliamentarian and a highly cultivated man. 'He is the representative of pure Irish nationalism, of an Ireland for the Irish,' the report said.[41]

The history of the country in the years preceding the turn of the century was marked by the foundation of the People's Rights Association by Healy in 1897, and of the United Irish League by W. O'Brien in 1898. Beckett[42] states, in assessing the spirit of that period, with a certain resignation, that the excitement and enthusiasm of Parnell's time had been succeeded by apathy and cold cynicism, sentiments which seem typical of the period, not only of Ireland. Germany and England, in the decade following the resignation of Bismarck and Gladstone, could be described in a similar way.

One year before Queen Victoria's death the embassy reported on the celebration of St Patrick's day: ' Owing to a bright idea of the Queen the Shamrock is no longer a symbol of rebellion but of the visible amalgamation of the Irish with the British Empire.' These views provoked the following impulsive marginal note of the Emperor: 'England is getting more and more united! And we in Germany are lapsing more and more into the dirt of party life and into the muddiness of anti-national grumbling.'[43]

This euphoria, artificial though it was, rose again when the Queen paid her last visit to Ireland in April 1900; the embassy reported that she had applied the right tactics in paying attention to both communities. 'For the first time in Irish history representatives of the Catholic hierarchy were entertained at a Royal gala dinner, including Cardinal Logue and even Archbishop Walsh.' But the report on the visit concluded on a sober note by stating that, 'England's faults and sins towards Ireland in the past could not be wiped out at once'.[44]

In the same year, shortly before the Queen's visit, the reunification of both wings of the Irish party under John Redmond's leadership had put an end to the frantic agitation in which the Irish parliamentary situation had been since the secession from Committee Room 15 in December 1890. It was at the suggestion of Dillon that Redmond, still a true follower of the late Parnell and a member of the weaker section, became chairman.[45] But, as Lyons puts it, he was not regarded as 'pre-eminent', and the result of the election was open until the last minute.[46] The re-united party, though in a better position than before as to the Land question, faced a stagnation of the Home Rule issue during the Cecil decade. In those days the Home Rule idea was absolutely unpopular and was regarded as irrelevant. As Bonn[47] expressed it, the Conservatives were prepared to pay for the continuance of the Union with Land reforms, at the expense of the British taxpayer. In the same author's view the Land Commission, though not successful as an example of practical socialism— as they had been originally regarded—had contributed considerably to attaining a kind of social peace: 'The Land laws have abolished the ascendancy of the landlords and have made arbitrary evictions impossible.'[48] Bonn pays tribute in this context to the achievements of the Irish farmers who had bought their land and had managed their farms carefully. 'They had become part of the conservative elements of Irish life and had smashed English prejudices.'[49]

Looking back upon the period, it appears to be hardly conceivable that the men at the helm in Britain did not take the opportunity of the peace prevailing after the Boer War to pacify Ireland in the political field. As the course of history has proved, all agrarian and political measures, in particular the Irish Local Government Act of 1898,[50] and Wyndham's Land Act of 1903, though helpful and generous, did not lead to a satisfactory solution of the Irish question in the widest sense. The Conservative government, at that time still in full power and strength and not under pressure of an Irish party as a balancing force, could have got rid of 'the weight at the feet' through a spectacular action. But when Lord Dunraven started his Devolution Scheme in 1904, all Unionist associations came down upon him. Wyndham came into an awkward position, and the political profit of his Land Act went up in smoke. Inertia on the one hand was not balanced by political farsightedness on the other. The German embassy remarked that it had become evident in this new phase of development that the last Land Act had not satisfied the people in Ireland.[51]

This speculation may appear unrealistic if one takes into account the spirit of the age in England, in general, and the leading persons, Balfour and Chamberlain in particular. But after Gladstone's failure to dissipate the 'clouds from the west', the Conservative administration missed the next chance to make an ally out of a centuries-old adversary.[52]

It may be a poor parallel to point at Bismarck's policy towards the south-German states in 1866, in any case, he succeeded in getting rid of any presumable 'weight at the feet' which could have hampered him in subsequent foreign conflicts. In fact, the unrest in Ireland never ceased. The German ambassador—it was Count Metternich, the successor to the deceased Count Hatzfeldt, a diplomat of high standing and originally persona gratissima to the Emperor until he incurred William II's displeasure owing to his objection to the German naval policy—informed Berlin of the situation. 'There is further agitation in Ireland ...

H

in certain parts of the country a kind of martial law has been introduced . . . the governmental press demands the oppression of the United Irish League'[53]—something had to be done.

On 26 March 1903 the embassy reported on the introduction of the Land Bill in parliament and that it was welcomed by the Irish party and the press.[54] Six weeks later it reported the adoption of the bill, the Irish and the Liberals voting in favour,[55] and the Royal visit in July which was described as a success, resulting from the adoption of the Bill.[56] German newspapers expressed their interest both in the bill and the Royal visit which coincided with the death of Leo XIII. While the Catholic and the liberal papers informed their readers of the news through brief remarks, the national-liberal *Kölnische Zeitung*[57] dealt with the events at length. The paper took the opinion that Home Rule was postponed for years, but that the Conservatives and Liberal Unionists, had in mind to satisfy Ireland, if possible, in the economic field through the Land Bill. 'To everybody who has observed the Irish policy for any length of time it will appear doubtful, however, that this will be successful in the long run.' The paper was not optimistic about the further course of development. 'Although peaceful and reasonable feeling prevails within the ranks of the Irish party for the time being, the Home Rule movement will begin again with renewed strength as soon as the Land Bill has been enacted.' The paper accompanied the Royal visit to Ireland by friendly comments on the King but did not conceal the reserved attitude of the population.[58] Metternich quite clearly deemed it necessary to emphasise the intransigence of the Conservative and Unionist leaders with regard to Home Rule. He reported Chamberlain's utterances that the maintenance of the Union was the main programme of the Liberal Unionists and similar remarks of Balfour.[59] Even the Liberal party was said to have become lukewarm on the question, because of different opinions within their ranks. An indication of such an attitude was seen in a speech in which Lord Rosebery had suggested a postponement of Home Rule *ad calendas graecas*.[60]

Dunraven's above-mentioned Devolution Scheme, however, renewed interest in the Irish question, which had weakened after Wyndham's Land Act. While the German embassy[61] held that the Scheme, compared with Home Rule, was alike as one pea to

another, Lyons says that 'the devolution proposals were an interesting new departure, but they were a long way from Home Rule
and in any event never came remotely near being put to the test.
Yet in reality the episode was one of fundamental importance, for
it demonstrated conclusively the limits of constructive Unionism
at both the official and the unofficial levels.'[62] Despite its limited
and moderate aims, the Scheme aroused an unexpected amount
of attention within all ranks of the Unionists. On 21 February
1905 the German embassy reported on a letter to *The Times*
in which Wyndham had declared that the government had nothing to do with Dunraven's Scheme. 'Now it becomes clear that
the Lord Lieutenant of Ireland, Lord Dudley, and the Under
Secretary to Wyndham, Sir Anthony MacDonnell, had participated in drafting the plan', the embassy reported, adding that
Dudley, MacDonnell and even Wyndham might be compelled
to resign in order to calm the anger of the Ulster loyalists.
William II, who had been chary of personal utterances on
English-Irish affairs in the previous years, remarked: 'Wyndham
has told a lie. I know Dudley from his youth; a rather silly dandy
with an excellent wife!'[63] On 7 March 1905 the ambassador informed the Foreign Office in Berlin of Wyndham's resignation,
under pressure of the Ulster Unionists who had threatened to
withdraw their support from the government.[64] The *Vossische
Zeitung* commented on the Wyndham affair in colourful terms.
Under the headline 'Smear campaign against Sir Anthony Mac-
Donnell' the paper paralleled the actual situation with a comic
opera and told its readers that the Irish Unionists—'the Empire-
minded landlords'—were furious at Lord Dudley and Wyndham,
as well as, at MacDonnell and were thirsting for the blood of
MacDonnell because he had misused his official position by
giving support to Lord Dunraven with the approval of Wyndham, when 'this Lord, well-known in yachting circles, cooked up
his Home Rule project last August. Sir Anthony is an Irishman
and a Catholic and the whole hubbub is nothing but a mean
show. The Unionist party is threatened with decay due to
Chamberlain's tariff policy, and in order to restore unity the
Home Rule spectre is conjured up. There is the rub,' the paper
concluded.[65]

The *Kölnische Zeitung* described MacDonnell as 'a very able
Catholic Irishman, who had served for a long time in India and

who was designated to serve as a pleasant show in the shop-window, while he himself had taken up office in Ireland under quite a different impression, a man who was accustomed to a great autonomy in his actions, and a sharp plucky fellow when his own preferences are at stake'.[66]

The Cecil era expired in 1905. Already late in 1903, Metternich had expressed the view that the swing of the pendulum would go to the other side on the next occasion: 'The Liberal opposition is now united and a number of Unionists are prepared to secede. It would be most useful for us if such a hectic and unpredictable personality as Chamberlain were to lose his influence in the government.' William II commented bluntly: 'Yes!'[67]

The Liberal landslide did not turn out as progress for the Irish question, though Campbell-Bannerman was reported to have declared himself in favour of Home Rule. In the same report of the German Ambassador, Rosebery was said to have taken a different view. He had expressed himself against Home Rule under the auspices of liberalism, because recent history had demonstrated that concessions such as this had turned out to be wrong, the embassy said.[68] McCready, however, takes the view that 'the Liberals' commitment to Irish self-government was kept in the forefront of party-life by Lord Rosebery who, as an ex-Premier and Liberal Peer of immense prestige, lectured the party at intervals on the true lines of policy to be pursued' and that 'Irish Home Rule was his principal weapon' when he returned to politics in December 1901.[69] In the light of German observations and Count Bismarck's above-mentioned records regarding his friends' attitude, the quoted remarks do not appear quite clear and confirmed. However, the author is entirely right when he points out that 'the whole history of the matter would certainly have been radically different, the House of Lords would have been overwhelmed and the great advance in constitutional reform for Ireland would have been carried in a spirit of liberal reform rather than of political surrender'.[70]

This view seems to be another confirmation of the opinion expressed above, that the Conservative government would have been strong enough for a constitutional reform without any pressure from an Irish party. The Liberals, now provided with a large overall majority, followed their predecessor's example:

they did not take an initiative. The foundation of Sinn Féin may have been a result of this attitude.[71] On 9 September 1907 the German embassy reported for the first time on the new movement: 'An organisation of extremists who are striving for a separation of Ireland from England by the method of by-passing the English parliament and implementing an independent procedure of the Irish themselves.'[72]

But instead of taking notice of this writing on the wall, the Liberal government followed the old Conservative principles, which translated into modern slogans, would be; 'Economic concessions yes, Home Rule no.' In the course of further legislation a series of bills were enacted,[73] but a decisive break-through to the Irish did not take place. The Irish Council Bill, introduced in May 1907, was, as Lyons puts it, 'a Liberal version of the old devolution scheme'.[74] Metternich, reporting on the introduction of the bill, took the view that it was meant to please everybody and did in fact satisfy nobody. 'The government seems not to be very lucky in dealing with the Irish question.'[75] While the Irish party, including Redmond, voted in parliament in favour of the bill, the National Convention in Dublin rejected it unanimously on 21 May 1907.[76] Commenting on the bill, the German press was sceptical of its success. The *Germania* said that one could understand that a people who were struggling for their rights for twenty-five years would not be satisfied by half-measures. On the other hand the whole affair does not do credit to Redmond who would not be forced into forsaking either his own countrymen or the Liberal party.[77] The *Vossische Zeitung* took the view that the bill could not even be paralleled with the project elaborated by Chamberlain in the eighties, when 'he flirted with Parnell'.[78] The *Kölnische Zeitung* told its readers that the principal point of controversy had been the control of the police; while Birrel, the Chief Secretary, had been in favour of the Irish claim that the police should come under the control of the Council, Mac-Donnell had expressed himself against it. Therefore the Nationalists were now slandering him as a traitor.[79]

The failure of the government regarding the Council Bill gave rise to a comprehensive report by Metternich on Irish problems.[80] After some remarks on the situation in the cabinet as to Home Rule—the imperialist wing, Grey, Haldane and Asquith, were said to be against the introduction of a Home Rule Bill.[81] The report deals with the background of the rejection of the bill by the National Convention pointing out that the hierarchy, also had influenced the decision because of their fear of losing their say in educational matters. The Irish question becomes more and more critical in religious matters while, over the last twenty years, the Land question had been settled in favour of the small tenants. 'Injustice done in the past has to be dearly paid for in the present. By remedying it one does not delete it from the memory of people and the sting remains in their hearts. The effects of the benevolent legislation have not yet removed the inveterate mistrust. Time is not yet ripe in Ireland for a co-operation of both denominations. The spirit of the conqueror who despises the subdued race has by no means died out among the Protestant population of the North and the eminent landlords of that denomination living in other parts of Ireland.' Dealing with public opinion in England the ambassador took the view that it was yielding more and more to 'the Home Rule experiment'. Further reports informed of renewed unrest in Ireland, of dockers' strikes and arrests, as well as, the recommencement of cattle driving and maiming.[82] These outrages, as predicted by Redmond, took place subsequent to the Evicted Tenants' Bill which was amended by the House of Lords in a detrimental sense as regards the tenants. New reports emphasised an intensified activity of Sinn Féin and subsequently a more radical attitude by the Irish party[83] as well as Redmond's efforts in parliament regarding Home Rule.[84]

Campbell-Bannerman's career ended in 1908 by resignation due to illness. In Gwynn's opinion this was a severe blow to Nationalists, Asquith was regarded with much less cordial feelings.[85] The Anglo-German relations, tending more and more to freezing point, were characterised by Count Metternich in the following way: 'In the interests of peace, which we desire to maintain for as long as possible, it is by far better for us to have the Liberal party in power. The English Liberals have always liked the nation which is least popular here or which people fear most. Twenty years ago this was the Russians, while now it is us.' The Emperor, apparently pleased by this opinion, noted: 'Very good.'[86]

CHAPTER 5

The Unsettled Question

A Trap for the Lords—The Third Home Rule Bill—The Orangemen, Carson and Ulster—The Curragh Affair and Gunrunning—The King's Dilemma—Ireland and Europe in July 1914—Insufficiency prevails.

WHEN Asquith took over in 1908, he had to realise that the 'weight at England's feet' was still there, but being backed by an overall majority of his party and with regard to the comparatively inactive leaders in Ireland, he remained inactive himself. Nevertheless, he was quite aware that the Irish question could not be kept smouldering until the end of time, the more so, because he had to take into account a change of the majorities in the forthcoming elections. This took place when he had to go to the country in 1910 and 1911. In those years the Irish Party won eighty-two and eighty-four seats respectively and his own party lost much support, Home Rule was *en vogue* again.[1] But there was still the House of Lords which would have defeated any move in the direction of Home Rule as they had done in 1893 when Salisbury boasted afterwards in Cardiff about the rejection of Gladstone's second bill by the House of Lords 'which had expressed the views of the English nation'.[2]

The idea of a parliamentary reform aimed at the abolition of the peremptory veto of the House of Lords had been discussed already in the late 1800s. In a conversation with Herbert Bismarck on 10 July 1884 Chamberlain had declared: 'We shall stir up a tremendous agitation all over the country.'[3] If this agitation had been launched in conjunction with a Home Rule Bill, however, there is no doubt that it would have failed. But when the House of Lords, just as it had overrated its power and reputation in the twentieth century, rejected the Budget, its time was running out. The Budget, though rejected even in Ireland and with Irish representatives, due to its 'daring lines',[4] turned out to be a touch-stone for the Upper House and its constitutional functions. In consequence of the results of the two elections mentioned above, the House of Lords had to yield to the expressed will of the country and its elected representatives, as well as, to the threat of a batch of Peers.[5]

As Gwynn puts it, the abolition of the peremptory veto of the Lords through the Parliament Act of 18 August 1911 was to be the immediate prelude to the introduction of a Home Rule Bill.[6] In Colvin's view the 'capitulation' of the House of Lords 'left Ireland bare to the enemy' and he adds ominously that 'there was the stronghold where the fight could be continued, the Protestant North'.[7] The Parliament Act did not lift all barriers blocking the way to settling the Irish question, but it was no doubt a very important factor.

In the election campaigns, preceding the Parliament Act, Asquith had made remarkable statements on the Home Rule question. According to a report of Metternich he had declared Ireland to be the greatest fiasco of English politics.[8] In a further report on the elections and England's internal situation the ambassador expressed the opinion that England seemed to be sick of Home Rule. 'Two philosophies opposing each other in the struggle between Liberals and Unionists; the belief in the power of reconciling gentleness and balancing justice on the one side and the principle of powerful preservation of the status quo on the other. An adequate mixture of both seems to be hardly attainable in political life. Sometimes it emerges, after all, from the struggle of contradictory opinions: *du choc des opinions jaillit la lumière*. The Irishman hates the Englishman. The Irishman is imaginative and illogical while the Englishman is of a rigid and consistent character. The kindness bestowed upon Ireland is not done with elegance. Irishmen have told me that they would prefer to be German than English. Yet they would prefer to be French, if not independent' Metternich wrote.[9] A further report discloses the differences between Asquith and Redmond with regard to Home Rule. Redmond was said to be in agreement with the kind of legislation pursued by Gladstone while Asquith was only prepared to concede a more limited scheme of self-administration. 'An Irish-Conservative pact is not to be excluded, due to influential trends among the Conservatives' Metternich concluded.[10]

In his statements on the Irish question Asquith had been joined by Grey, who had confessed to be 'a determined advocate of Home Rule' and Churchill who referred to the creation of the South African Union despite the objection of the Lords. In the House of Commons, Asquith declared Home Rule for Ireland the next and most important task of the government after the enactment of the Parliament Bill.[11] But nothing was disclosed about the kind of Home Rule they had in mind. In any case, it was no longer the House of Lords which had the final say as to constitutional changes of the position of Ireland.[12]

Following his promise, Asquith introduced the third Home Rule Bill on 12 April 1912. He spoke of Ireland as a 'nation' which had been a subject of controversy in Great Britain for a long time. Colvin, Carson's biographer, calls this a 'fateful admission',[13] typical of the mentality of the ascendancy, which was prevalent even in the first half of the twentieth century among people whose philosophy was that of the nineteenth century.

The introduction was preceded by numerous utterances in favour of the bill among which the noble and audacious address of Winston Churchill in Belfast on 8 February was the most noteworthy.[14] This event in Belfast and everything connected with it, in particular its disgusting circumstances as regards the reception given to the speaker on his way to the meeting, provoked attention in the German press, despite the Tripolis and the Balkan Wars which filled the columns to a great extent. While the daily papers commented on the events rather briefly, stressing mainly the military measures taken, the *Kölnische Zeitung*, spoke of an 'audacious address despite a meagre argumentation and sentimental accompanying music'[15]—the *Preussische Jahrbücher* took the opportunity to make some comments of a particular character under the headline 'Religious Fanaticism', stating that whereas the Catholics of Ireland were demonstrating a tolerant feeling, partly by tactical reasons, partly because they were taught tolerance and indulgence during their long passion, the Ulster Protestants, particularly the Orangemen ill-famed for their hatred of Catholics, behaved more and more irreconcilably. With regard to what had occurred to Churchill in Belfast, the periodical stated that the Prussian State would be stirred up from top to bottom if one of its ministers was treated in such a way. 'One cannot express with certainty which state is more praiseworthy. The Prussian state exercises more pressure than England on freedom, but their achievements will be better in certain circumstances. This is not to say that the positive results of the British community are worse' the author concluded.[16]

The comments of the German embassy were subject to the crisis in which it had been plunged by the fact that Metternich was no longer persona grata with the Emperor, because his opinions on German naval policy were different from those of his naval attaché, Captain Widemann. After Metternich's resignation in June 1912 a brief interlude of a few months was occupied by Marschall von Bieberstein (a former State Secretary of the Foreign Office and successor to Herbert Bismarck in this capacity) who died in September. Prince von Lichnowsky, a Silesian magnate, was then appointed ambassador to the Court of St James—against the will of Bethmann-Hollweg, then Chancellor. He was a liberal in his way of thinking, but a wilful man and on bad terms with the Foreign Office, like Count Münster in his time.[17]

Despite this crisis, the embassy—as well as the press—carefully followed the parliamentary progress of the bill. Shortly before its introduction, the embassy reported on an anti-Home Rule rally in Belfast, with Carson and Bonar Law as speakers, in which Carson had expressed Ulster's intention to resist 'even if both parties in Great Britain were committed to Home Rule'—[18] a rally which was applauded by *The Times* with the comment that it was the assemblage of a nation to defend its existence, to plead against an attempt to suppress its identity, to plead and also to warn.[19]

On 12 April 1912 Berlin was informed of the formal introduction of the bill with a synopsis of the contents of the three Home Rule bills which had appeared in the *News Chronicle* of the same day. The embassy regarded the bill as a step in the direction of a further constitutional development of the Empire, alluding to South Africa and Australia. It also reported on Redmond's consent,[20] as well as, on that of the Labour leader, Ramsay Macdonald, who recommended the bill because 'there is now a prospect for the independence of Scotland and England, too,' a phrase which was underlined by William II with a big stroke. The report, however, did not conceal the brusque attacks of Carson.[21] In further reports the embassy dealt with some special problems of the bill and the reactions in England and Ireland. One took the view that the bill meant an attempt to reconcile Separatists and Federalists, a compromise which is always afflicted with weakness. Regarding the reactions of English politicians, the embassy reported on Morley's scepticism and Balfour's strong words against Federalism, obviously aimed at Ramsay Macdonald's opinions. Balfour was said to have used Bismarck's term 'blood and iron' as means to re-integrate Ireland and Scotland.[22]

Having reported on the meeting of the Irish National Convention in Dublin, which agreed to the bill, the embassy spoke of the reaction in England and their opinion that the Home Rule question did not arouse the same interest as in previous days. Conservatives, after King Edward's death, were said to have expressed their preparedness to support Home Rule measures during secret talks with the party-leaders, if they could make a bargain for the re-introduction of the Lords' peremptory veto. They were said, moreover, to prefer the settling of the Irish question before their return to power.[23]

After the second reading of the bill the Chargé d'Affaires, von Kühlmann, later State Secretary of the Foreign Office, gave a comprehensive description of the situation, dealing chiefly with the Ulster problem. 'In pursuing the policy of ruthless oppression of Ireland, England has abundantly relied on the Protestant Ulster people; since Cromwell's day a long history of cruelties has kept alive the religious hatred between Catholics and Protestants, more than in any other country of the world.' Carson is described as 'a grim and sinister looking man, who combines an inflexible character with eccentric and visionary qualities. Unionist leaders are instigating the Ulster people to armed resistance and are committing a grievous fault by identifying themselves with the treacherous Ulster movement.' Kühlmann mentioned 'the trend to partition' among Liberal party members and said, in concluding the long report: 'If the Conservatives succeed in overcoming the government and in torpedoing the Home Rule Bill, the Irish problem will come to the fore again. The disappointment of the Irish would probably provoke the worst cruelties, and the outrages in Parnell's time would appear ridiculous in comparison with them [William II: 'No disaster']. The resurgence of the Irish question as a living issue would weaken

England as a world power because of the influence the Irish exercise in America [William II: 'That would be a great boon'].[24] After a further report on Carson's instigations 'aimed at exciting the emotions' Lichnowsky informed Berlin of the adoption of the bill after the third reading, remarking that public opinion remained unconcerned.[25]

This first phase of the parliamentary procedure was commented on in the German papers partly by their own correspondents and observers. The *Vossische Zeitung* reminded its readers on this occasion of the history of the Act of Union—Gladstone was said to have called it a villainous trick, with its briberies and 'its rain of gold, orders and patents of nobility'—and reported on the several stages of the bill, not omitting, however, the Land legislation of the last decades on the one hand, and the difficulties of the Liberal party on the other. 'Without consent of the Lords, the bill cannot be enacted for two years. But will the Liberal cabinet still be in power at that time?' the paper asked. It confirmed, moreover, the opinion of the embassy about public opinion 'The country desires a solution leading to peace, no matter what.'[26] The *Germania* reported Redmond's declaration in favour of Home Rule, in which he claimed the same freedom of legislation that had been granted to Australia and New Zealand 'which were not yet discovered when Dublin was already one of the biggest cities in the world with a famous parliament'. Like the liberal paper, the *Germania*, having recalled the history of Ireland, in particular the expropriation of the land after the Battle of the Boyne, hailed the Irish people for their persistence in the struggle for freedom.[27] The *Kölnische Zeitung* commented in a somewhat discordant way. On the one hand it spoke of 'Asquith's portentous bill', reporting on the fear expressed by Englishmen and Protestants that the Irish would crush them economically, because freedom of conscience did not count for much there. 'They feel that it exists on paper only in other countries and must come to grief if the party in power depends on revolutionary secret societies or a fanatic clergy.' On the other hand the article spoke bluntly of the English conquest of the Emerald Island, which was achieved 'like a barbarous raid. . . . It looks as if the Moonlight Criminals, or the shrewd politicians who have replaced them, will take vengeance for sins of the past; it seems they intend to launch an attack which, by modern means, will prove more efficient than the blunt tactics used previously'. A few weeks later an editorial reported on Churchill's moderate and feeble intervention in parliament, adding that 'it makes people think that the Liberal leaders do not seem to be against a bargain with the rabid Northern Irish'. Confirming the general indifference to the bill, the paper reminded its readers of the political passion and emotion during the Home Rule debate in 1893, 'when Gladstone and other great leaders fought each other'.[28]

The unpredictable parliamentary outcome of the bill was observed in Germany with mounting interest, in particular the alternate play between the House of Commons, which always adopted the bill, and the House of Lords, which steadily rejected it, and at the end Lord Lansdowne's resolution to go to the country.[29] Curzon's remark that only England and Scotland should vote on the bill while Ireland should stand aside was answered by the *Germania* with the words: 'Does this man not feel ashamed of that demand?'[30]

Late in October 1913 the embassy reported on the firm intention, expressed by Asquith, to pass the Home Rule Bill in the next session under the auspices of the Parliament Act. Asquith was said to have underlined the priority of the Irish question among other problems of Federalism. In the embassy's view the government could not venture on an immediate exclusion of Ulster due to Asquith's declaration that 'the way to Ireland's unity must not be blocked by a peremptory and insurmountable obstacle'.[31] In further reports Berlin was informed of Grey's idea of 'Home Rule within Home Rule'—regarding Ulster—and of Bonar Law's and Carson's reply to Asquith and Grey who both agreed to Lansdowne's proposal to go to the country.[32] The deteriorating Anglo-German relations were reflected by a report in which the embassy took the view that it would be in the interest of German politics if the Unionists succeeded in again frustrating the great Liberal effort to restore peace in Ireland. 'So long as Ireland is in the foreground of internal policy, England's parties will be compelled to manage their foreign policy cautiously and with discretion.'[33] In an analysis of the situation in February 1914, in which the opinion that Home Rule would become law after all, though preparations were made for an armed resistance in Ulster, Lichnowsky compared the Irish

Nationalists with the Czechs in Bohemia who were objecting to the separation of the territorities with a German speaking population. 'The Unionists lack outstanding and popular leaders, as well as, a stirring slogan or a bold programme. Neither Lansdowne nor Balfour stir up the phantasy of the masses, they are taken as out-dated and pointless, Bonar Law is not like Disraeli.'

Recalling again English-Irish history, and drawing an analogy of the actual English situation with that of the Romans towards the end of the Republic, the Prince took the view that 'no other modern state demonstrates the contrast of poor and rich in such a harsh way as England, where the greatest luxury exists beside flagrant misery, and where the overwhelming part of the State, not only the rural and mining districts, are owned by a few hundred privileged people. . . . The English ascendancy in Ireland has been based on the interests of the Landlords; with the retrogression of the latter the rights of the oppressed Catholic-Celtic populace had to come into play.' William II with regard to the last phrase: 'Very good'.[34]

In the meantime, chiefly in the winter of 1913/14, there had been many contacts between the governmental parties and the Tory opposition with the aim of reconciling the contradicting views, particularly in regard to Ulster. Pointing at the danger which emerged—the disposition of the Liberal government to bend before the storm—Lyons recalls[35] that, as early as February 1912, the government had left open a line of retreat on the Ulster question by agreeing that while the bill as introduced should apply to the whole of Ireland, the Irish leaders should be granted such changes in the bill as fresh evidence of facts, or the pressure of British opinion, might render expedient (Asquith's report to the King). That meant in plain terms that the spirit of irresolution had already begun its work and replaced linearity.

Strong words had been spoken, but they remained words. The *Germania*,[36] reporting on Churchill's address in Dundee, in which he had spoken of the 'lawless boldness' (of the Ulster group) and of the danger of a 'bully's veto', commented that the government were obviously fully aware of the difficulties but that they should have been more forceful with the Ulstermen. The *Kölnische Zeitung* wrote about 'the fatal jam' in which the government found itself, perhaps due to their feeling that the opposition would prove so weak in a general election that the Liberals

would win again.[37] Only in September 1913 did the paper feel it
advisable to quote from the *Daily Chronicle* which had declared
that Asquith and his colleagues, though quite prepared to admit
each reasonable concession to Ulster, would never permit a pig-
headed minority to prevent Ireland from ruling herself according to her own ideas.[38] Early in March 1914, when Asquith had
formulated his concessions, the embassy reported on this compromise, according to which each county was to decide in favour
or against its exclusion from Home Rule for a six year period,
and which was called by Carson a 'stay of execution' (William II
remarked: 'Rubbish').[39] Churchill's strong words in Bradford,
where he had spoken of an 'outburst' of the English people, un-
imaginable to the Tories, in case of an attack on an English
soldier by an Orangeman,[40] were defied in the House of Commons by Carson who declared the compromise a failure and civil
war imminent.[41] The Emperor remarked: 'The army's views
will be clear very soon! I am not sure! The government must
give in and is lost', ominous words on the eve of the 'Curragh'.

The growing tension in Europe—before the Sarajevo murder
—influenced the further treatment of the bill which came, more
and more, into the realm of uncertainty. One of the most important and, incidentally, at this very moment, most ominous movements now became apparent. The Orange Order's role in Irish
history, its efforts to influence English politics in the nineteenth
century and its successes and rebuffs, make it necessary to note
its activities in the relevant time.

Churchill blamed them for the intemperance of their language
and for the religious bigotry 'which explains, though it does not
excuse it' and spoke of 'their worst excesses' of 'acts which are
in themselves cruel, wicked and contrary to law'.[42] Gwynn[43] recalls the Orange Order's role during the Home Rule debates in
1893, when the Lodges were characterised as the instigators and
promoters of the more violent and unreasoning features of the
Protestant agitation against Home Rule. Already in 1886 the
liberal *Vossische Zeitung*, a paper which had taken the side of
the State during the Kulturkampf, bluntly criticised the Order
in a long leader about 'the Orangemen of Ulster' pointing out
that religion and racial conflict had led to bloodshed throughout
Irish history, but that in modern times, since the Emancipation
Act and the Disestablishment Act, the Orangemen in Ireland

had proved intolerant and maniac persecutors to a much higher degree than the Catholics.[44]

It does not seem surprising that the Orange Order had attempted, during the Kulturkampf, to contact certain groups in Germany with the aim of fanning the flames of the Church-State struggle. In summer 1875 the Order submitted an address to Emperor William I, congratulating and hailing the government on its firm stand against the Pope. There is reason to believe that neither the Emperor nor Bismarck felt very happy at this unwelcome support, and before the Emperor made an answer to the address, Bismarck ordered an elaborate memorandum on the aims and history of the Order. In this memorandum, probably drafted by Bucher as an expert in British affairs, the history of the Order was depicted in a way which showed the lodges to be involved to some extent in subversive activity in political matters, directed mainly against the heiress to the Throne, then Princess Victoria. The memorandum did not conceal the precarious role of the Duke of Cumberland, later King Ernest August of Hanover, a member of a dynasty in rivalry with Prussia. This was most certainly the decisive motive for Bismarck to recommend a cool message of thanks, which was notified to the Grand Master Edward Harper by a letter of the Chargé d'Affaires on 26 August 1875. The Orange Order, in its turn, took this letter as an opportunity to give the matter more publicity by adopting a resolution which spoke of 'an exchange of Protestant ideas and feelings' and of 'the two powerful Protestant States England and Germany'.[45] Under these circumstances one can hardly agree with an opinion speaking of 'the apparently defensive character' of the Order.

It is true that it was 'by its very existence a threat to religious liberty', as Catholics claimed,[46] and so it remained for the years to come.

It is against this background that the development of the last months before August 1914 has to be assessed. It was, in any case, the ideological and sectarian sting that pushed the Unionist and Conservative zealots into rebellion against the government. A special correspondent of the liberal *Berliner Tageblatt* reported an interview with Carson in which he said that he would prefer open rebellion to Home Rule. The report added that the Anglo-Saxon Protestants since the Battle of the Boyne continued to feel the ascendant people. 'The Irish instigated by their Irish national feeling, want Home Rule, but the Orangemen with their Anglo-Saxon racial hubris do not want Home Rule, because they detest it; it looks as if religious intolerance and fanaticism are stronger in the North than in the South. While the Irish nationalists are gradually dropping their radical feelings, Ulster wants rifles. That is inconceivable for a civilised man of 1913', the correspondent declared.[47] This was the impression of the mentality of the 'grim and sinister looking man'[48] received by a German newspaperman just at the beginning of the renewed Ulster crisis, which had originally started in 1886 and continued in 1893. In the latter year the *Vossische Zeitung* had carefully registered the indications which led to the presumption mentioned above. In March 1893 the paper reported about 'preparations for civil war' and on the views expressed in Conservative newspapers that 'the Ulstermen would go into action like Cromwell's Ironsides: the Bible in one hand and the sword in the other,' and on the 'unscrupulous instigation of the Unionists'. It reported the opinion of the Duke of Devonshire as 'even at the cost of civil war Irish autonomy should be averted'.[49] Hatzfeldt reported in the same context that in Belfast Salisbury had declared an armed resistance of Ulster justified, in case the Home Rule Bill would become law.[50]

In 1913 nobody seemed to have added anything to his stock of knowledge since 1893. The lack of political insight and the absence of cleverness in handling precarious situations had quite clearly not diminished, chiefly due to the activities of Carson and Bonar Law.[51]

It is of particular interest to read the impressions a German writer received at a visit to Carson and Craig during the time of the crisis.[52] In his view Carson was a man who needed the excitement of travel and the thundering applause of enthusiastic audiences. 'He adds one argument to another, he is right or wrong, but he does not care a rap for political logic. The last analysis of the Ulstermen is their fixed idea, a religious prejudice and a strong political domineering.'

While the German embassy, apart from occasional remarks on the Carsonians and their activities in Ulster, withheld from comprehensive comments on the question of the North, before the Curragh events, periodicals and the press were very anxious to put their views on it. After the Covenant, the *Preussische Jahrbücher* in an article, having at first drawn parallels with the

I

Covenant of 1557, made some reflections of general character as to the threatening Ulster rebellion. 'The British nation seems to have trust in its abilities to tolerate and control an almost unlimited political freedom without danger to the existence of the community. For more than a year now the British government has quietly looked upon the treacherous activities in and around Belfast, quite an unthinkable phenomenon in Prussia,' the author said. In this context he took the view that a 'Protestant-Irish Covenant' could yet arouse much sympathy among the bulk of the British people, all the more so, because they violently opposed the government; the Liberals being no longer popular among the people.[53] In a comment on a work by Sidney Brooks[54] the *Jahrbücher*[55] emphasised the view of the author that 'the conflict between capital and labour in Ulster will thrust the religious hostilities into the background; and the recovery of the political situation in Ireland, aspired to by Britain, in admitting Home Rule, would be completed.' These remarks provoked the regrettable comment that religious hatred had destroyed the occasions for a reconciliation, although originally it appeared that even the Unionists could not neglect the weight of this argument.

The *Germania*, reporting on the economic impact of the unrest in Ulster—insurance premiums doubled in one year, industry was handicapped, emigration increased, great firms displaced—stressed the 'warfare plan' of the Ulster people and the constitution of an Ulster Government, calling Carson an 'agitator' and 'Irishmen-eater', who was addressing people in such a way that a man who acted likewise in another country would be jailed for high treason.[56] After a detailed description of the Ulster revolution, the paper reflected time and again, on the indulgence observed by the government. 'All around Europe the question has arisen why the government still tolerates the preparations for a genuine revolution which can no longer be taken lightly. The only grounds for this may be that the government does not wish to martyr Carson, in the hope that an agreement could be found before the outbreak of civil war, an optimism not being shared, however, by observers. Either Home Rule throughout Ireland or nothing.'[57]

The *Kölnische Zeitung* reported from Ulster in autumn 1913 that 'they do not parade with weapons, but like ex-servicemen elsewhere, with umbrellas and walking-sticks; but one should not forget that they have been training with weapons for a long time and that they are obsessed by the *furor Hibernicus* which presents itself in the Emerald Island through scuffles strongly suggestive of the people's pugnacity in Upper Bavaria.'[58] A remarkable portrait of Larkin was taken by the correspondent of the paper, who, reporting on a meeting in the Albert Hall, spoke of his 'golden honesty'. 'If Larkin speaks of matters in Dublin, with which he is fully acquainted one will hear a voice coming from the heart. He claims support for the great bulk of his worker-colleagues, who hold the belief, like himself, that they are enduring cruel injustice'[59]—a noteworthy opinion expressed by a paper which was said to be the big-business organ in the west of Germany before the First World War.

While the *Norddeutsche Allgemeine* refrained from detailed comments, the *Vossische Zeitung* regularly presented its views to its readers, emphasising in particular, that the fear of the Protestants in Ulster was unjustified due to the envisaged guarantees of religious freedom, and that the controversy over Ulster was 'more a matter of party tactics than of conscience'. 'The Irish question is too much for the politicians on the Thames, and they cannot get rid of the ghosts so deliberately conjured' the paper said.[60] In March 1914 things were in such a state of confusion that only statesmanlike ability and thoroughness could have unravelled it.

But in the last days of March the conjured ghosts did new mischief. The crisis began to undermine the allegedly unremovable basis of representative democracy in England and Ireland. The Curragh affair shook the country with far-reaching repercussions on the continent.

Lord Milner had written to Carson during the crisis: 'But it [the rebellion in Ulster] must fail unless we can *paralyse the arm* which might be raised to strike you.'[61]

The German public got its first briefing on the army's position through an article in the *Kölnische Zeitung* in autumn 1913, when a correspondent reported on letters he had received from serious older people in Ulster declaring that they were determined to risk everything, like the young hotspurs. 'Older and distinguished Englishmen have expressed their deep concern that one would have to face the probability of numerous officers, if not entire units, declining to fight against the Ulstermen.'[62] As early as February 1914 King George V expressed his concern to

Prince Lichnowsky about the situation in Ireland and the probability of a civil war: 'It is a dreadful thought that troops would be ordered to shoot at my most loyal subjects' the King said, blaming the government at the same time for having lifted the arms embargo a few years ago.[63] At any rate, the Curragh affair did not occur unexpectedly, neither to the English government nor to journalists or diplomats.

German newspapers reported on the affair on 21 March and the following days with sensational eye-catching headlines.[64] The *Vossische Zeitung* underlined that the cavalry officers of 'the most exclusive Curragh brigade' who refused to obey orders—to go to the North—were members of aristocratic and conservative families. 'It was a mutiny out of political motives. Why did the cabinet and parliament capitulate entirely before this military camarilla?' the paper asked, and it asserted that it was the King who had persuaded Asquith to yield to the rebellious officers.[65] In a further article under the headline 'Asquith's withdrawal before the Tory officers' the paper reported on the roles of French and Roberts and asserted that the Chief of Staff had been forced by Lord Roberts, who took the side of the mutineers, to confirm his weakness facing the 'Tory sons'. 'The Unionist party, which had arranged the revolt, has gone so far in its doggedness against the left wing parties that it helped a self-styled government into power despising all decisions of the parliamentary majority and reducing the sovereign parliament to a farce.'[66] The *Kölnische Zeitung* described the situation of the government in a biting comment. 'It has to be taken into account that the current leading English statesmen were never inclined to act resolutely during the time they were in office. They are neither heroes nor great men, but insignificant people who, having been made wise by long experience acquired in civil suits, prefer to reveal the weakness of an opponent, in order to exploit them, rather than meditate scrupulously upon an exchange of ideas.'[67] A further article in the paper dealt with the differing opinions in the cabinet, reckoning Seeley, Churchill and Lloyd George among the hardliners who pleaded for using a strong hand in Ulster. 'It seems to be quite certain that the Unionists' movement, which only amounts to humbug and bluff, will burst like a soap-bubble.' Churchill was regarded as the only man with practical experience and as the determinative personality, in contrast to Seeley, and to Haldane, who was a lawyer, philosopher and a thoroughly wise man, but without the ability to decide what could be expected of the officers.[68] Seeley's resignation drew forth the remark that he had become the victim of his own zeal and that, as a hardliner, he had been outvoted in the cabinet, the more so because his attitude had proved contradictory.[69]

The German embassy—as well as other embassies in London —had a boom period of reporting on the Curragh crisis. All reports, partly signed by the Military Attaché, Colonel Renner, partly by Lichnowsky, were of absolutely political character. For the first time the Attaché, a German officer, faced an approach (by officers) to military discipline which was quite different from his own. 'Ruthless agitation of the opposition begins to bear its fruits'; these first words of a series of reports appeared in all comments of the embassy. 'There is a deadlock here, the disaster provoked by the Irish crisis is big enough, even without civil war. Everybody is excited, many people have lost their heads. Even without exaggeration, the damage done to the army is great.' The Military Attaché laid stress upon the fact that only officers had made difficulties, not N.C.O.s or men. 'It goes without saying that this bad example has shaken the reliability of the troops considerably.' Then, dealing with the principles and guiding lines of the officers' vocation, the report described the role of the officer—'although it is denied'—as that of a politician. 'No wonder the officers adhere to the Unionist party considering the lack of interest the Liberal party has shown in the army. English discipline is not German discipline. We should never forget in assessing the events that English officers have an approach to their vocation different from ours.'[70]

In a cautious additional comment, Lichnowsky remarked that the government might have succeeded in averting the danger of a military *Pronunciamento*, but in fact the cabinet gave way in view of the mass resignation of the officers, which was presented to the public as an 'honest misunderstanding'. 'The discipline of the army has been seriously affected, creating a dangerous case of precedence' the ambassador concluded.[71] In further reports the Military Attaché pointed out that the Unionist party was responsible for the Curragh events. 'One must blame those who tried to use the army as an instrument of party politics. It is a "Pyrrhus victory" of the officers and of the opposition.' In the

Military Attaché's view the army's fighting power against an enemy from abroad would not be affected 'for the time being'. He reported that while younger officers were rejoicing the older ones were stupefied. 'A high-ranking officer of the War Office told me to-day that this is the gravest crisis in the army's history. The man really responsible is not the Secretary for War, but one high-ranking officer who did not like to see things as they were. It has been his duty to advise the Secretary correctly.' In the Attaché's opinion the officer did not hint at Paget (the C.-in-C. in Ireland) but at French. In a further report the Attaché wrote 'The officers have gone on strike and the highest military authority had to sound the retreat in a miserable way. So many foolish things have been done here in these days that it is difficult to say who did the worst. The blindness is great, the government has fallen between two stools, and they can satisfy nobody. The army's strike has made it impossible for them to unravel the knot by force.'[72]

Submitting the 'Correspondence relating to recent events in the Irish Command'—a document of parliament—to the Foreign Office, Lichnowsky reported on the two additional phrases of Seeley's letter to General Gough which was counter-signed by French and Ewart. These additions had not been covered by the cabinet[73] and when they decided that the phrases were not binding, Seeley resigned. Seeley, originally a hard-liner who had yielded to Gough, became the scapegoat.

French, originally a hard-liner too, was said to have been impressed by oral reports of officers stationed in Ireland. His attitude was perhaps revealed by the remark that his name under the letter may have been due to his distress.[74]

With the aim of pouring cold water on the gloating comments in the German press, the embassy sent a telegram to Berlin on 27 March 1914, requesting the Foreign Office to influence the papers in their coverage of the army crisis 'because all symptoms of gloating are noted here with touchiness. Derisive comments would be taken amiss in England on both sides and eventually turn out useful for the imperialist wing'. William II remarked: 'Quite right!' Bethmann-Hollweg, the Chancellor, also agreed to this proposal, remarking, however, that the ambassador should have tried to influence the British press in the Zabern affair also.[75]

In a concluding report of 15 April 1914, the Military Attaché described the reasons for the crisis once again and took the view that the officers had been too much engaged in politics during the last few years. 'The English army crisis should serve as a lesson to those in Germany who are enthusiastic about a parliamentary regime and would like to shake the position of the army and of the officers' the Attaché said.[76]

The different approach of officers to military discipline in England and Germany and all the questions closely linked with it became a popular subject of German public discussion. The *Germania* reported in an article entitled 'The Ulster Crisis' that Gough had boasted about his victory in public. The paper commented that 'an incredible event has happened in Dublin which stands beyond all German principles of military discipline'.[77]

The *Vossische Zeitung* tried to inform its readers of the position of the English soldiers by pointing out that there was no such thing as unconditional obedience in the English army. 'What is regarded as munity in our country, is for the Englishmen part of the law and one of their incontestable rights, even in the King's uniform. An army in peace-time is an unconstitutional institution in England. A standing army is only tolerated by the Mutiny Act to be passed by parliament every year.'[78] The *Kölnische Zeitung* drew the practical consequences of the Ulster Crisis, writing that officers and men would be justified to refuse obedience in case they were ordered to go into action against Orangemen, even if this would greatly affect the discipline.[79]

While the *Marine Rundschau* had dealt with the Curragh affair in a more descriptive way without substantial comments,[80] the *Deutsche Revue* published several essays by German officers. Under the headline 'Policy-making armies', one author[81] spoke of the 'disturbing event' which was a noteworthy symptom of the possibility that in the English army political views could jeopardise the execution of a military order. 'The German officer cannot understand that. There is no other rule for him than to serve truly, honestly and obediently, while the English oath of allegiance is not combined with obligations typical of a soldier's duty.' In the author's view the words 'according to law' in the English oath meant a substantial limitation of unconditional obedience. He expressed the opinion that the internal development of a country should go on 'without violence, in a peaceful arrangement of all determinant forces of the people'. 'Whenever the army must be mobilised to enforce certain aspects of internal policy, it is necessary to state beforehand, that the political substance of the country has been violated, either by rebellion of one part of the people, or of the people on the whole against the power of the state, or by a split through parties fighting each other,' the author said.[82]

The most noteworthy remarks on the subject from a general point of view are made by Ritter in one of his greatest works.[83] In a chapter on 'Army, society and state in England during the epoch of Liberalism' he emphasises the deep mistrust of the English nobility against standing armies. He reiterates—what has been said above—that for continental minds it was unheard-of that since 1688 the existence of the army depended on parliamentary decisions in force for just one year. 'The ruling classes in the nineteenth century regarded the hostility against armed forces as an attribute of genuine peace-mindedness, like the French bourgeoisie.'[84] In this context he praises Haldane as the man to whom England owes her new army 'the most gifted and the most active British Secretary for War since Cordwell' a man who called Germany his 'spiritual home-land' and who had, more than anybody else, made efforts aimed at an Anglo-German military-political arrangement.[85] But the most interesting remarks, regarding the Curragh affair, are to be found in his characterisation of General Wilson, the Director of military operations. 'He was the type of political general who did not confine himself to his technical duties but who pursued his own political target.' With regard to his activity in preparing a close collaboration with France in case of war against Germany, Ritter points out: 'In pursuing this target he did not shrink from political intrigue, and he conspired with the leaders of the opposition against the government.'[86] This characterisation hits the nail on the head in a striking and almost classical wording. It also applies to Wilson's activity during the Ulster crisis.[87]

It is a paradox of history that Wilson himself had to go to France in April 1914 to dispel the uneasiness which had been aroused in the camp of England's allies, and 'to reassure General de Castelneau, as best he could, on the singular situation'.[88] However, the damage had been done: to England, to her allies, to Ireland, to the Liberal party and as it was seen abroad, to the principle of the civil power of parliament in a democratic state.[89] The affair left, as Lyons puts it, 'an ugly legacy . . . a nagging anxiety about the loyalty of the forces,'[90] mainly due to the irresolution of Asquith and his advisers.[91] But the *Morning Post* felt satisfied and relieved when it wrote triumphantly: 'The army has killed the Home Rule Bill.'[92]

On 28 April Lichnowsky reported on the gun-running in Ulster with the comment that it was inconceivable that this smuggling had taken place without any knowledge of the government. 'I am inclined to believe in the information given to me confidentially that the customs' people in question have, at least, turned a blind eye to it.'[93] Asquith called this incident in the House of Commons 'a grave and unprecedented outrage'.[94] The *Germania* reported that the German government had briefed Westminster about orders concerning purchase of arms in Germany by the Ulster rebels, adding that 'Germany behaves as a better friend of England than the "Conservative patriots"'.[95]

In further reports the paper described the successful outcome of the gun-running as 'an aggravation of the Ulster crisis' stating that political circles had been upset by the fact that the government had not taken any energetic measures to prevent it. 'The Unionists landed weapons in Ulster with the arrogance to pose as persecuted little innocents.'[96] The paper reported on the demand for an investigation of the governmental measures in regard to the crisis and on the motion of censure tabled by the Conservatives, which was described by Churchill as a 'motion of censure by criminals against the police' and which induced him to comment that the balancing power in Europe could be temporarily shaken, and it remarked that 'a long and hard struggle has been fought out with poisoned weapons'.[97]

The landing of weapons in Ulster was another indication of Asquith's indulgence. As Lyons puts it, the decision to do nothing was influenced, it seems, not only by the King but also by Birrell, the Chief Secretary for Ireland, and Redmond who were convinced 'that a prosecution would magnify the offence into a martyrdom'.[98]

The state of affairs gave rise to a report of Lichnowsky in which he expressed the opinion that the responsible would shrink from using force, because it was to be presumed that, with or without general elections, the line of the leading statesman and his colleagues would triumph in the long run, provided that this kind of policy would, after all, spare the blood of British citizens,[99] a fair and understandable, though not very convincing explanation of the governmental attitude, given by a diplomat who was said to be a Liberal.

The *Preussische Jahrbücher* gave, as always, a remarkable résumé when they described the different spirit in which State affairs were dealt with in England and Prussia. 'Respect for law and order is also held in high esteem over there, but it is based more on voluntary co-operation than here, and therefore, is rather qualified and unreliable. Politically discontented people are wont to refuse obedience to the authority of the State—an obedience which they owe to this authority by the order of God and the law.' The author of this article also took the view that the Curragh affair and the 'strike of the officers' was grounded on that mentality—'a shady side of noble virtues we are not conversant with'.[100]

On 26 May 1914 Lichnowsky reported on the final adoption of the Home Rule Bill by the House of Commons, after the Lower Chamber had given its approval for the third time, with the addition that now the way was paved for a procedure in accordance with the Parliament Act, after the expected rejection by the Lords.[101] The German press informed its readers accordingly. But the tug-of-war behind the scenes went on, even after the proposal of a temporary exclusion of the Ulster counties. The *Kölnische Zeitung* commented that the government would commit suicide in case of further concessions. 'Home Rule without Ulster, the wealthiest, busiest, the financially most powerful part of the country and with the greatest taxable capacity, would appear as a dubious benefit to the rest of the island.'[102]

The Government, quite clearly, found themselves between two fires, with the unionists on one side and several members of the cabinet on the other. Lloyd George had said to O'Connor and Devlin that Churchill, for example, had stated openly he would have to resign if Ulster did not receive a reasonable offer before coercion were applied.[103] On another occasion he had hinted that the cabinet might lose Grey and Haldane and possibly even himself.[104]

It is against this background that the striving for the favour of the King intensified more and more. On 30 March 1914 Lichnowsky reported on the role of the King during the Curragh affair, expressing the opinion that owing to his mediating activity and interference a serious course of development had been avoided. 'The King has given proof that he regards himself as a constitutional monarch.'[105] The *Vossische Zeitung* published an article by its London correspondent, about speculations on the King's attitude, pointing out that 'according to the constitutional conception of to-day a King revolting against the will of parliament appears to be unthinkable'.[106] In a report of 2 October 1913 the embassy had taken the view, prematurely, that the hope of the Unionists that the King would refuse the Royal assent had failed.[107] In reality, the King bombarded Asquith during the summer of 1913 with inquiries about what was going to happen. He was extremely nervous about army loyalty and warned the Prime Minister 'that he must reserve his freedom to act'.[108] Asquith reminded the King 'that the Royal Veto was, literally, as dead as Queen Anne'.[109]

King George was convinced that the adoption of the bill would mean civil war in Ulster and that its failure would make the rest of Ireland ungovernable. He never doubted that Ulster would resist.[110] 'The King's peace of mind was disturbed by the flood of private, and often anonymous, letters which poured into Buckingham Palace.'[111] The whole dilemma of the King, was reflected by the exchange of letters between him and Asquith in summer 1913. Some remarkable phrases of his letters revealed the King's qualms of conscience. Time and again he pointed to the role of the army in case of disorders, partly anticipating the arguments of army leaders during the Curragh crisis ('our soldiers are citizens by birth, religion and environment, they may have strong feelings on the Irish question, . . .' 'Will it be wise, will it be fair to the sovereign as head of the army, to subject the discipline, and indeed the loyalty of his troops, to such a strain?'). Then he pressed again for an agreement 'such as leaving out Ulster from the scheme for a certain period' and hoped for a solution regarding 'so rich and flourishing a part of my dominions'.[112] It sounds like an outcry when he wrote in his memorandum of 11 August 1913: 'Whatever I do I shall offend half the population. No sovereign has ever been in such a position.'[113] Asquith, contrary to the King, did not see 'dimensions of civil war' but rather 'organised disorder' in Ulster, and opposed all Royal proposals for general elections as a way out. In his opinion elections would have settled nothing. Apart from his feeling that such an act, before the Home Rule Bill became law, would stultify the whole purpose of the Parliament Act, he feared armed risings in the south of Ireland.[114]

Nobody would dare to neglect the genuine embarrassment of the King as a sovereign who had to take into account the constitution on the one hand and his strong feeling as to the awkward position of the army with regard to his subjects on the other. As a 'constitutional monarch', as Lichnowsky had put it, he had to oppose every idea of a coup d'état. Only a resolute government could have relieved him from his dilemma. George V deserved the sympathy of everybody who understood the stresses of a genuine inner conflict.

The murder of the Austrian heir to the throne, Archduke Franz Ferdinand, on 28 June 1914, and the growing tension in Europe raised the question in all interested circles: What is going to happen first, war or Home Rule? The parliamentary procedure of the Amendment Bill suffered a heavy handicap by the tension. This tension, as it was felt in England and the parliamentary debates, influenced each other. That is the impression one has when studying the records of July 1914. The Home Rule question and the Ulster crisis were seen against a European situation, and the European tension was said to be influenced by the Ulster crisis. It is no exaggeration to assert that the whole situation was in a state of confusion. No doubt that the agitators, who were very anxious to draw advantages from this confusion, prevailed.

It was the Unionists' target to destroy even 'a very moderate measure of self-government'[115] which could in any case have proved unworkable after so many dilutions. The *Germania* had criticised the bill with the comment 'too little' quoting people from Dublin who compared the planned Irish parliament with a debating club.[116] It was Carson's intention, however, to wreck Home Rule by any means,[117] even a Home Rule Scheme which hardly deserved this name. He was full of mistrust towards the fiscal policy of a Dublin parliament which would be the master of Ulster's taxable capacity. 'You never wanted her [Ulster's] affections. You wanted her taxes.'[118]

The Unionists went so far in their objection that Bonar Law pleaded for foreign rule in the House of Commons in preference to Home Rule.[119] They expected help from 'the greatest Protestant nation on earth, Germany'.[120] Kuno Meyer, a German professor of Celtology, and his colleague Theodor Schiemann attacked this hope, pointing out that the Covenanters were living wholly in the ideas and sentiments of a by-gone age. 'We fear Ulster will wait in vain for another William to come to her defence.'[121]

It goes without saying that the German government came into an awkward position through these undesired approaches. The Emperor never wished to become a Gustavus Adolphus of the twentieth century. Under the headline 'Moral captures of the Chancellor' the *Germania* quoted Bonar Law's remarks and the various utterances of the Ulster press, in which the Unionists propagated the secession to Germany 'where Catholics are not in high esteem. Now we are making propaganda with intolerance and have real success in Ulster.'[122]

Conservative German voices also revealed an absolutely cool reaction to such approaches and to the whole Ulster movement. In a 'letter from London' the *Deutsche Tageszeitung*, a superconservative paper, opposed the movement as 'not being recognisable as conservative, from a German-conservative view and conscience'. In this context the paper pointed at the differences between Gladstone and Asquith in dealing with the Irish question. Gladstone regarded Home Rule as an emanation of the Liberal idea of self-government while Asquith was paying for the parliamentary assistance of the Irish. 'Redmond is the driver of the government's coach' the paper said.[123] A few days earlier the embassy had reported on a possible text of the referendum questions to be laid before the people of the Ulster counties concerned and mentioned Lord Lansdowne's efforts for a compromise in fighting against the 'diehards'.[124] In a report on the Lords' 'Amendments to the Amendment'—aimed at an anticipation of partition, in fact—Lichnowsky concluded his remarks by saying: 'It is noteworthy, in any case, that by the beginning of the twentieth century the danger of civil war has been created, primarily, by the denominational antagonism among a people regarded by many as the first civilised nation of the world.' (William II commented: 'War of Thirty Years!')[125]

After the total failure of the Buckingham Conference from 21 to 24 July,[126] Lichnowsky took the view that the government would restore the Amendment Bill in the original text with the aim of imposing on the House of Lords the odium of the failure of the compromise.[127]

The *Preussische Jahrbücher*, commenting on the Buckingham Conference and on the participation of Carson and Redmond, 'both of them backed up by their armies,' did not deem it impossible that the Unionists could be induced through the moral pressure of the foreign situation to sacrifice the Protestants. 'In any case, it is chiefly the Unionists and their Covenant adherents who render a solution of the Irish question by a peaceful agreement of the parties impossible.'[128] The *Vossische Zeitung*, dealing with the situation in the crucial days of July, strongly criticised the Unionist party because of its 'instigation of the masses'. 'The whole affair demonstrates a symptom of decay.' Carson was said to be 'bearing not a crucifix but a foolish fisted hand'. 'Nobody should publish his collected addresses in a book—that would be an anticlimax! "King" Carson hates, speaks and plays.'[129] Those were the last impressions received by German observers on the situation before war broke out.

There has been much discussion on the question as to whether Carson's preparations for what was called war had to be taken seriously or not. Redmond is said to have written to Australian friends that Carson never intended to go into action against regular troops, because he knew he would not have been able to withstand them for one week. He only intended to mislead the people in order to instigate the officers through social influence and to frustrate the will of the people.[130] James W. Gerard, the American ambassador to Germany, called the Ulster army 'one of the most gigantic political bluffs in all history which had no more revolutionary and military significance than a torchlight parade during our presidential campaigns'.[131]

Birrell, in an audience with King George on 24 July 1914, declared the situation to be artificial and discounted the seriousness of the state of things in Ulster; as to fighting, there would be no one to fight. A provisional government would not last a week as the whole county would be cut off from the outside world.[132] German voices, supporting these views, expressed the opinion that the Ulster leaders did not really believe that their troops could stand against a disciplined regiment of soldiers. 'An officer who would go into action against regular soldiers would be guilty of a massacre. As soon as the existence of the Ulster army is no longer needed, it would end in smoke.'[133] The *Germania* took the view that the Ulstermen would not win laurels in a civil war[134] and Meffert, relying on Casement, asserted that the bluff of the Ulster rising had not been taken seriously even by an English school-boy. 'European diplomats should learn their lesson before being posted to London. They should spend their years of training in Dublin.'[135] In the author's opinion it would have cost the government nothing to suppress the movement—if they had wanted to do so.[136]

The whole case is of a certain importance in the discussion of the further question as to whether the state of affairs in Great Britain in general and in Northern Ireland in particular has influenced, entirely or partly, the decisions taken by governments in Europe with regard to the growing tension after the Austrian Archduke's death. Bluntly, the question that mattered was: 'How strong is Britain after the Irish troubles?'

Mansergh asserts that as early as 1910 the Emperor, on his return from the funeral of King Edward VII, was 'apparently convinced that England was on the verge of civil war over the future of Ulster'.[137] This assertion does not seem to be more than an unproven presumption of the author. Another unproven presumption must be seen in the assertion that William II 'hopefully' anticipated civil war.[138] Other authors or politicians hold the view, even going beyond this assertion, that the war declarations of continental powers (meaning Germany and Austria in this case) could only be understood against the background of a possible civil war in the United Kingdom.[139] The American ambassador in Berlin also imputed to the Germans his belief that 'Ireland would rise in general rebellion the moment war was declared'.[140] Even a German voice, in a very tortuous way, however, expressed the opinion that the 'audacious decision' of the cabinet in Vienna (as regards Serbia) might have been influenced, at least partly, by the internal decay which had surprisingly hit the British state.[141] It is true that Fieldmarshal Conrad, the Austrian Chief of Staff, has mentioned in his memoirs that England was heavily threatened by the Irish question after the difficulties which had arisen from the parliamentary debate on the Home Rule Bill, the Curragh affair and the failure of the Buckingham Conference. He even uses the words: 'Civil war loomed up.'[142] A correspondent to Vienna is said to have telegraphed on 26 July 1914 that Austria expected a free hand in face of Serbia, partly due to the British government's absorption in preparing for the consequences of their internal policy.[143] In this context the German General von Bernhardi, is quoted as having uttered some speculative opinions about the possible event of an Anglo-German war.[144] General von Bernhardi, a retired officer and military author—obviously a kind of amateur politician—in two articles published in the conservative paper *Die Post* in September 1913 dealing with Germany and England, had indicated the weak points of England in the event of an emergency, in particular, the Irish situation. The first article, in which he had regarded the Irish as would-be allies, was strongly criticised by the *Kölnische Zeitung* and met with the Emperor's deep disapproval. The chief of the Royal Military Cabinet, von Lyncker, in communicating this displeasure to the Chancellor, asked for his opinion as to the political implications of the articles. In his reply of 8 October 1913, the Head of the Foreign Office, State Secretary Zimmerman, blamed the author for 'not being acquainted with the actual political situation' and pointed out that the opinions expressed were absolutely outdated. Everything should be avoided, Zimmermann wrote, that would allow the General's utterances to be taken as semi-official.[145] This is the story of General von Bernhardi which has been taken more seriously than it ever deserved.

Ryan takes the right view[146] when he calls it an exaggeration if people believe that Germany would not have risked her invasion of Belgium, unless a civil war was looming up in Ireland. However, there may have been people in Austria, Hungary and Germany who in their foolishness believed in an England unprepared for war due to the Ulster crisis, but it is beyond doubt that no responsible person, neither the Emperor, nor the government nor the General Staff of the German forces with its traditional and well-proved principle 'consider carefully and then take a chance' would have based a decision or an advice in a matter of life and death—such as a declaration of war or an invasion of another country—on a vague presumption, confirmed by agents or not, that civil war in a possible enemy country was imminent. The contrary assertion is a subjective assumption without proof.[147] Only half-wit chauvinist people, as a German author puts it, could have dreamt of military advantages to be drawn from civil war in Ireland.[148] Every responsible person in Germany, before the war, was fully aware of the difference in the British mentality on the question of internal difficulties or of a foreign war. One cannot even presume that Fieldmarshal Conrad, whose memoirs are mentioned above and who, according to these memoirs, had always been in close contact with the German Chief of Staff, the younger Moltke, could have nurtured unrealistic illusions. Historical research has made evident that grievous faults have been committeed on both sides in those fateful days, mortal errors had arisen, but the reproach of superficiality and recklessness against those responsible in Germany, is not justified in this particular case.

At this point it is worthwhile to reduce another story to its real substance: The alleged close relations between Carson and William II and the activity of Baron von Kühlmann, then Counsellor to the German embassy in London. There has been much talk about a meeting between the Emperor and Carson in Bad Homburg in the second half of August 1913. It is a fact that the Emperor attended a luncheon party of the District President, Dr von Meister, some day during the relevant time. The semi-official *Norddeutsche Allgemeine Zeitung* published on 23 August 1913 the following list of those entertained: The Emperor, Colonel-General von Plessen, Minister von Treutler (Diplomatic aide to William II), Prince Adalbert of Schleswig-Holstein, Sir Frank Lascelles, Lord Acton, General Sir Archibald Hunter, Major-General Charles Crutchley, Rear Admiral Sir Adolphus Fitzgeorge, Walter vom Rath.

Carson, who was said to have attended the party, was reported by a German paper to have been present, but did not appear in the published list. It cannot be denied, however, that he attended all the same. He used to come repeatedly to Germany because he liked the country and in particular the Homburg spa. He was, moreover, a member of the Anglo-German committee which worked for a mutual understanding of the two countries.[149] But it is an unproven assertion that he became the Emperor's particular friend. This consequence cannot be drawn from the talks the two men were said to have had.[150] William II sometimes used to seek the company of people like Carson, who played temporarily a more or less extraordinary role in their countries, and at

K

times became impressed by them. Such an appeal, however, may not have been a lasting one so far as Carson was concerned. Treutler, who during that time was the confidant of William, never mentioned Carson.[151] There were, moreover, no further indications of a closer contact between the Emperor and the Ulster leader. All other rumours which have come up in this context, in particular the news of 'an offer of help from a powerful European monarch', published by the *Irish Churchman* on 14 November 1913, are unfounded and a part of Carson's bluff-campaign.[152] The Ulster movement was not popular in Germany. The people had learnt its lesson during the Kulturkampf. Its reactions to the attempts of the Ulster leaders to make friends with the Germans as a Protestant power were cool, the more so, because the role of some British generals, who felt closely linked with the Ulster cause, was no secret in Germany. They were the same men who had been in permanent contact with the French army staff in preparing common military operations in case of war on the continent, or who were regarded with mistrust in Germany for other reasons.[153]

In this context it appears to be fantastic that Baron von Kühlmann should have served as the 'chief spy of the Kaiser' in Ireland. It was said that in July 1914 he had sent a dispatch from Ulster to Berlin, from where it was forwarded to Vienna.[154] Gwynn, who also alludes to the alleged stay of Kühlmann in Ulster during the crisis, deems it 'highly improbable' however, 'in view of Kühlmann's diplomatic position and his fine sense of diplomatic prudence'.[155] According to his memoirs, the Baron was on holidays in Germany in July and returned to London in the first days of August when Germany and Russia were already in a state of war.[156] Kühlmann was, moreover, optimistic on the Ulster question. He took the view that, taking into account the practical mercantile mentality of the Englishman who viewed the world in its entirety, there was every hope of a solution to the Irish question without civil war.[157] There is no serious indication at all that his records are untrue.

On 28 July 1914 Lichnowsky sent his last report on Ireland to Berlin, informing of the gun-running into Dublin and the dropping of the Amendment Bill from the agenda of the House of Commons.[158] All German newspapers of 31 July reported accordingly. Lichnowsky and Kühlmann left England after war had been declared. Further news reached Germany chiefly through her legation to the Netherlands in the Hague and other diplomatic missions in neutral states.

On 18 September 1914 the Home Rule Bill in the original text received the Royal Assent and the members of the House of Commons struck up the National Anthem. The bill reached the Statute Book together with the Suspensory Act—suspension for war time—following a declaration of Asquith in parliament on 15 September 1914 that the bill 'should not come into operation until parliament should have the fullest opportunity by an Amending Bill of altering, modifying or qualifying its provisions in such a way as to secure at any rate the general consent both of Ireland and the United Kingdom'.[159]

The Nationalists had reached their goal, but only on paper; what was given with one hand, was taken back with the other.

There had been much discussion before this date. A hard bargain had taken place behind the stage, beginning with Redmond's speech in parliament of 3 August, in which he had promised Ireland's support to Britain during the war and the defence of Irish coasts by the Volunteers in exchange for the withdrawal of British troops from the island. His greatest critic was Dillon who declared the speech a major blunder and a turning point in the party's history, expressing his negative views, moreover, in two letters of 5 and 6 August to T. P. O'Connor and to Scott.[160] Eventually, on 18 September, Redmond agreed to what had been done, without receiving, however, any conciliatory reactions from Carson who declared that the Home Rule conflict was only suspended by the war,[161] but he feared, however, that the government meant to betray Ulster by passing 'the Home Rule Bill over our heads' as he put it.[162]

All in all, 18 September, in fact, had brought nothing to the Irish cause. The whole arrangement appeared like the makeshift repair of broken windows after an air raid, which usually were glued up with pasteboard, a typical method dictated by emergency. But it would be a superficial judgement, a terrible simplification, even if one were to impose the responsibility for the outcome of the discussions on the third Home Rule Bill on one or more persons or groups of that time. It goes without saying that positions and problems together with inveterate prejudices could not be removed by the stroke of a pen.

The reasons for the failure of the attempt to solve the Irish question go back, of course, to 1886, when Chamberlain and Bright and their followers, that means the radical-imperialist wing of the Liberals, refused to follow Gladstone on his way to peace with Ireland, which he regarded, in his farsightedness, as the beginning of the reform of an Empire in its very prime, without any pressure from abroad. Gladstone's failure turned out to be the first sign of decay in the Liberal party; in fact, Chamberlain and his followers were the men who destroyed the substance and efficiency of the party to such an extent that it never really recovered from it. A united Liberal party might also have been able to overcome the opposing Lords in 1893.[163] The opportunity had been missed twice and it was missed a third time by the Conservatives during the Cecil decade when, as mentioned above, the government, in its shortsightedness, stayed rigid on the Irish Question, although it may not have been too difficult for them to assess the character of the world situation as a dangerous one. It was a time in which a cautious family man does not only let down the shutters of his house but extinguishes all fires inside it as well, or, at least, neutralises them.

The last attempt at coming to terms with the problem may have come too late. The longer the question stayed open, the more difficult the problem appeared to be. It was a real labour of Sysiphus, which the three key figures Asquith, Redmond and Carson, had to manage and for which extraordinary abilities, characters and personalities were needed. The question arises whether these men measured up to the demands of handling the case.

Eventually, in spite of an original good will and a good conscience, at least on two sides—which does not always coincide with bona fides—they did not. Asquith was a man almost completely lacking in imagination or enthusiasm, he was a moderate man in almost every respect.[164] His natural inclination was to concede 'not upon the merits of a well-established case at the outset, but under pressure'.[165] 'It was not his mission to find the raw materials of policy, but rather to shape and direct them . . . he lacked the Gladstonian sense of moral purpose and something of Gladstonian political artifice as well.'[166] As regards the Irish question, history knows that his politics were those of reason, not those of virtuous passion like Gladstone's.[167] What he lacked was the spirit of determination. A German paper wrote just at the time of the Ulster crisis: 'The Prime Minister is such a perfect *cunctator* that if he were asked officially what time it is, he would give an evasive reply either by postponing it to the forthcoming week or by requesting a question in writing for the next session.'[168]

After the Curragh affair, the *Vossische Zeitung* had remarked that the Conservative press had attempted to exonerate the government and had not succeeded, but 'probably only because, to use a simile, Asquith resemblanced the reed and not the oak'.[169] Churchill—despite his strong words in parliament after the Curragh crisis, when he accused the opposition members of leading the Army astray with the aim of using it as a political weapon,[170] and on other occasions—did not prove to be as assertive as expected from his behaviour. Lichnowsky informed Berlin of Churchill's cautious attitude towards Carson and of his opinion that Ulster's desire for exclusion from Home Rule could not be ignored without serious consideration.[171] Mansergh has confirmed, according to Churchill's own testimony, that he advocated the exclusion on the basis of county option.[172] Lloyd George always took the same view. Thus, it seems to be quite clear that if the Prime Minister had shown more determination in principle he would not have been forced out by his stronger ministers. But according to the judgement of his contemporaries, Asquith was not the man to make use of his prerogative to lay down the guiding-rules of the cabinet's policy in a forceful way.

Redmond, the second key figure, through his own fault, lost contact with the Irish people during his long presence at Westminster. In fact, he followed the policy of the Liberals, but he lacked the spirit of independence which Parnell had always regarded as indispensable for his struggle—close collaboration with the Liberals, but not entirely in their wake.[173] His main and actual fault, however, was his unreserved support of Britain in parliament and elsewhere. People in Ireland well understood his offer to defend Irish shores against an invader as a contribution to saving the Home Rule Bill, but they did not follow him when, after the Royal Assent, he offered his unreserved support in the war 'not only in Ireland but wherever the firing line extends, in defence of right, freedom and religion'.[174] Obviously, he felt strongly influenced by British war propaganda when he alluded in his speeches to the alleged German atrocities in Belgium, predicting the same fate for Ireland and her population.[175]

His sympathies for Britain and her cause seemed to have been stronger than those of the other leaders or of his people. He quite clearly found it difficult to 'stand up against the English' as Parnell had advised. He never appeared, despite the outstanding qualities of his character, as a personality comparable to Parnell with 'its ability and its fundamental national equipment'.[176] Lyons's view that it is difficult to arrive at a just assessment of Redmond, whose career ended in unrelieved tragedy,[177] is fair.

It was, in any event, a tragedy for his people, and in other respects also, that their destiny had been laid in the hands of a man who did not prove adequate to his function and task.

Carson, the third key figure, proved as insufficient as the two others in this triangle, but contrary to Asquith and Redmond, he was a resolute man—no matter if this resoluteness meant business or bluff.

The whole philosophy of his political attitude, though understandable from a purely human or even racial point of view, was determined by an outdated sectarianism, a spirit of intolerance which is always dominant in the age-old ascendancy of the conqueror, in other words, his attitude was the materialisation of a movement stemming from the dreadful events on the continent and on the islands during the sixteenth and seventeenth century.

The question why the parties concerned could not agree on a solution, as proposed by Grey and rejected by Carson and the Unionists, has not been answered in a convincing way.[178] The principle of federalism had succeeded well in other countries of the world. Britain would have gained more force and support in the imminent conflicts if she had settled the Irish question in that or a similar way. No British Dominion which had received that status in the years before the war refused to support England during the war, in spite of considerably divergent interests. In the case of Ireland, Britain barely succeeded in maintaining tranquillity and neutrality in the first years of the world conflict. The British achievement in Ireland on 18 September 1914 was far less perfect than the Central Powers' desperate attempt to restore an independent kingdom of Poland in 1916—a venture undertaken too late, however, and in an insufficient way.

Concluding this chapter, one must state again that almost

everybody engaged in this last phase of British-Irish relations before the war demonstrated a lack of political strategy and acted as mere tacticians. Everybody responsible played for time, typical of non-masterly minded and shortsighted men in crucial times, who resort to unsatisfactory compromise and are guided by a spirit of half-heartedness.

It is pure speculation to say what way Gladstone and Parnell would have acted in 1914 if they had returned from their graves. Probably they would have made use of their experiences of 1886, particularly regarding Ulster and the Ulster mind. In any case, the issue would have been entrusted to masterly minds which probably would have dealt with it accordingly.

But in the absence of real ingenious statesmanship, the last attempt failed and the Irish question stayed unsettled. Insufficiency had prevailed.

Epilogue

THE failure of Home Rule in 1914 was a victory of the spirit of the nineteenth century over the harbingers of a new epoch. Principles of integration, of religious and ethnical tolerance, of self-determination, of peaceful co-operation, as well as, of human rights and of necessary reparation of faults committed in the past had suffered a heavy setback.

The consequences were far-reaching. The Irish party received its death-blow. It never recovered from the fact that 'the issue was ultimately to be decided outside the house of commons'.[1] Sinn Féin took over and Parnell's party ceased to exist. The spirit of insurrection moved up and materialised shortly afterwards. It turned out also as a death-blow to the English Liberals, if not for English political liberalism on the whole. By gradually yielding to insubordination, political pressure, sectarianism, intolerance in the ethnical and religious field and to old prejudices about Ireland and the Irish,[2] English liberalism had destroyed itself. Their philosophy would have lost all political influence earlier than when it actually did, if war had not concealed the self-inflicted wounds. Lloyd George, Asquith's successor, was the last Liberal Prime Minister in the twentieth century.

Ireland had been faced with the problem of dismemberment— a word more to the point than the word partition. In dismembered parts of a living community the tendency to unite, either by rude diplomacy or by force, is always immanent, with all the dangers of an ethnical Irredenta. That is a lesson of history for which peoples and their leaders have paid and will pay considerably at any time.[3] The British in particular have paid and will pay, in every sense of the word. Britain's handicap in the nineteenth century, with regard to the Irish question,[4] persisted into the twentieth, for as Barker stated during the First War, 'a divided Ireland is an anomaly,' he added 'whatever the sectarian and political division by which Ireland is torn, she is really a unity'.[5] That means, in the last analysis, that everyone acting against this unity, no matter why, is dealing with the issue in an anomalous way.

MacDonagh, answering the question[6] what Great Britain had to fear from Home Rule or Dominion status or even a Republic of Ireland after 1900, states that even the more extreme Republicans were prepared to accommodate Britain on the issue of defence, because her concern for military security was accepted as reasonable. This has always been the view of impartial German observers, too. There was no longer a danger from France or the United States—and not even from Germany—because every possible aggressor would have to take into account an Ireland linked to Britain by genuine common interests. But, unfortunately, the solution to the Irish question fell victim to the outdated ascendancy-feeling.

The North-South antagonism has always been an enigma for continental and, in particular, German minds of the twentieth century. The German people had learnt its lesson in the seventeenth and nineteenth centuries, in so far as religious conflicts with political implications were concerned. The marginal note of William II: 'War of thirty years' on a diplomatic report during the Ulster crisis,[7] though perhaps meaningless at that time, has obviously won a tragic significance since the time when it was written. The War of Thirty Years, which devastated many parts of central Europe, had, no doubt, religious origins but implicated naked secular power politics. Gustavus Adolphus was not, as it was stated in many German school books before 1918, the 'saviour of German protestantism,' he had merely seized the opportunity to make Sweden a great European power. Religion was but the name, but imperialism as well as economic and social competition were behind it and rude power the objective on both sides. In history, religion has often been the mantle for sturdy political, military and economic interests.

Both the English-Irish and the North-South relations could also be assessed before this parallel background, at least *cum grano salis*. Britain's promotion of the North's industrialisation (which has now turned out, at least partly, as a miscalculation, provoking social unrest, tension and unemployment) and her support for the Protestant immigrants, as well as her sponsorship for their well-being in exchange for the settlers' guarantee to uphold the Union, seem to justify a comparison with the intrusion of foreign powers into German affairs in the seventeenth century. Fortunately, all these shadows over Germany disappeared in the course of history—until a later date.

Also the damage done to religious peace during the Kulturkampf had disappeared. This terrible period of German national and ecclesiastical history was, though not forgotten, not uppermost in the minds of Germans when war broke out in 1914. Shortly before his death in 1903, Pope Leo XIII declared with regard to German Catholics, in a conversation with the Emperor, 'Ils resteront absolument et infalliblement fidèles.'[8] The Pope was entirely right. German Catholics and Protestants fought and died together in the trenches during the Great War.

Even if one takes into account the peculiarities of character and the diversities of history in both islands, it is hardly understandable for German minds, especially with regard to their experiences described above, that no arrangements could have been made in order to come closer to an Ireland which 'is really a unity'. It appears to be extremely strange, that in the course of this fast-moving history all lessons learnt on the continent have not proved sufficient to produce better results in Ireland.

Burke once declared that the world is big enough for England and Ireland, adding: 'Let it be our care not to make ourselves too little for it.' Does this not seem to be applicable to North-South relations, too? Does it not express a general principle for the handling of each controversy existing or arising in the new Europe and threatening her growing solidarity and power so necessary for defending her menaced occidental heritage?

Notes

INTRODUCTION

1. Curtis jr, *Coercion and Conciliation in Ireland*, p. 1; Blake, *Disraeli*, p. 179; Lyons, *Ireland since the Famine*, p. 131.
2. Curtis jr, *op. cit.*, p. 2; Morley, *The Life of William Ewart Gladstone*, vol. 1, p. 383.
3. Bismarck to Count Münster: 'It is in contradiction to the regular practice and certainly against the rules.' Bismarck, Fürst Otto, *Die Gesammelte Werke*, vol. XIV/2; Nostitz, H., *Bismarcks unbotmässiger Botschafter*, p. 112.
4. Eyck, *Bismarck und das Deutsche Reich*, p. 267; Bismarck to Count Arnim, 21 Jan. 1874, in Eyck, *Bismarck*, vol. III, p. 136.
5. According to the German Constitution of 1871 the Emperor was not the Sovereign of the Empire. The sovereignty emanated from the Federation of the German States, represented by the Bundesrat. The Emperor was the President of the Federation in his capacity as King of Prussia.
6. Rep. 4 March and 30 March 1887 P.A. England 80 vol. 4.

CHAPTER I TWO EMPIRES

1. Ensor, *England 1870–1914*, Introduction xix.
2. Von Muralt, 'Die diplomatisch-politische Vorgeschichte', in Grote-Gersdorff (ed.) *Entscheidung 1870*, p. 9; *Grosse Politik der Europäischen Kabinette 1871–1914*, vol. II, No. 294.
3. Ensor *op. cit.*, pp. 3–4.
4. Gladstone had never shared the French view as to the Hohenzollern candidacy for the Spanish throne; 'We have in no way conceded that the acceptance of the throne by Prince Leopold would justify France's threatening with war.' Yet he recommended the renunciation of the Prince, see R. Buchner, 'Der Krieg und das Europäische Gleichgewicht', in Grote-Gersdorff (ed.) *Entscheidung 1870*, pp. 290–91 and *passim*.
5. Rep. 10 Feb. 1871 P.A. England 60 I A B b vol. 1; 'Public sympathy in England veered a good deal with the course of the war', Ensor *op. cit.*, p. 6.
6. Donoso Cortes (1809–53), Spanish statesman, diplomat and historian, Minister to Prussia (1849) and to France (1849–53), took

the view that Palmerston had recognised Napoleon's coup d'état against public opinion in Britain, see Veuillot, *Oeuvres de Donoso Cortes*, vol. 2, p. 398.

7. Eyck, 'Bismarck nach 50 Jahren', in Gall (ed.) *Das Bismarck Problem in der Geschichtsschreinbung nach 1945*, p. 3. In the same essay, however, he holds that Napoleon fell into a trap prepared by Bismarck, pp. 37–8.

8. *Op. cit.*, p. 6.

9. Rep. 10 Feb. 1871, P.A. England 60 I A B b vol. 1; Eyck, *Bismarck*, vol. III, pp. 30–31; Buchner, *op. cit.*, p. 291, on Disraeli's feeling about the results of the war, quoted from Buckle, *Life of Benjamin Disraeli*, vol. 5, p. 133.

10. Bismarck's address to the Reichstag on 16 May 1873: 'We laid the claim to the annexation of the land and its fortresses in order to have a bastion against the attacks which each generation of Germans has had to face for the past three hundred years', *Verhandlungen des Reichstags*, 1. Legislaturperiode, 4. Session 1873, vol. 27, p. 678.

11. Bismarck's opinion on this marriage had never been favourable. On 16 Nov. 1883 he called the Crown Princess 'a liberal English lady, a follower of Gladstone'. On 7 April 1888, after the death of William I, he remarked in a talk with Moritz Busch: 'The new Empress has always been an English lady, a channel for English influence', *Gesammelte Werke*, Gespräche, vol. II, pp. 448, 604.

12. *Ireland*, p. 136.

13. Curtis jr, *Coercion*, p. 27.

14. *Ibid.*

15. Letter of 2 Oct. 1887, *ibid.*, p. 13.

16. Curtis, jr, *Anglo-Saxons and Celts*, pp. 6–7.

17. See Annex: Curricula of the Ambassadors 1871–1914.

18. See above, Introduction, note 3; Sasse, *100 Jahre Botschaft in London*, p. 14.

19. Nostitz, *op. cit.*, p. 77; Rep. 8 Nov. 1875 P.A. England 64 I A B b vol. 6: in ten lines of text the word 'ultramontane' is used five times.

20. Rep. 8 Aug. 1871 P.A. England 60 I A B b vol. 2.

21. Rep. 2 Nov. 1871 P.A. England 60 I A B b vol. 3.

22. Rep. 18 Dec. 1872 P.A. England 61 I A B b vol. 2.

23. Rep. 10 Feb. 1871 P.A. England 60 I A B b vol. 1; 'By the beginning of 1871 the Queen had grown seriously unpopular', Ensor, *op. cit.*, p. 26.

24. Rep. 15 Dec. 1871 P.A. England 60 I A B b vol. 3.

25. Nostitz, *op. cit.*, pp. 70, 79, 95.

26. Rep. 8 May 1875 P.A. England 64 I A B b vol. 2 Bismarck's marginal note: 'Too rich'.
27. 21 March 1876 P.A. England 64 I A B b vol. 6.
28. 'It is inconceivable that a Jewish novelist without a penny can obtain such a position', Rep. 4 April 1876 P.A. England 64 I A B b vol. 8; 'The first Jew to become a Peer', Rep. 8 Feb. 1877 P.A. England 64 I A B b vol. 10; Bismarck's different opinion at the end of the Berlin Congress 1878: 'The old Jew, that is the man', Eyck, *Bismarck*, vol. III, p. 271.
29. Nostitz, *op. cit.*, p. 70.
30. Rep. 4 April 1876 P.A. England 64 I A B b vol. 8.
31. Nostitz, *op. cit.*, p. 123.
32. Rep. 4 April 1876 P.A. England 64 I A B b vol. 8; Bismarck's opinion on Salisbury in 1878 (Berlin Congress) was not very flattering. He compared him with a wooden lath painted the colour of iron. Eyck, *op. cit.*, p. 271.
33. Curtis jr, *op. cit.*, p. 31.
34. See note 10 above.
35. *Ibid.*
36. Rep. 14 May 1873 P.A. England 63 I A B b vol. 1.
37. Rep. 28 May 1873 P.A. England 63 I A B b vol. 1. with copies of the *Press* and *St James Chronicle* of 24 May 1873.

CHAPTER 2 RELIGION AND POLITICS

1. This term was first used by the Liberal member of the Prussian Abgeordnetenhaus, Professor Virchow, on 16 Jan. 1873.
2. (a) Law concerning the education and appointment of the Clergy (studies and examination in philosophy, history and literature besides theology prescribed).
   (b) Law concerning the ecclesiastical disciplinary power and the establishment of a Royal Court for ecclesiastical matters (interference of the state in every ecclesiastical affair, deposing of bishops and priests by judgement made possible).
   (c) Law concerning the limitation of the legal force of ecclesiastical sanctions and disciplinary measures (aimed at preventing the Church authorities from taking measures against priests who had violated Canon Law and major principles of the Church).
   (d) Law concerning the secession from the Church (aimed at favouring the establishment of the Old-Catholic communities in the relevant time).
   (e) Law concerning the administration of vacant sees (aimed at securing the temporal interests of the sees whose holders were deposed).
   All in May *1873*.

Other *Prussian* Laws of *1875* concerned the suspension of contributions of the State to dioceses and clergy ('bread-basket' Law, aimed at coercing 'unlawful' bishops and priests) and the treatment of religious orders and congregations (aimed at expelling their members from their houses).

An *Imperial* Law (of 1872) banned the Jesuits from the territory of the German Reich, another Law (of 1874) was aimed at preventing persons from 'unauthorised' practice in ecclesiastical activities.

3. Bachem, *Vorgeschichte, Geschichte und Politik der Zentrumspartei* vol. IV, p. 4; *Germ.*, 30 May 1892.
4. Schlözer, *Letzte Römische Briefe*, p. 3.
5. *Ibid.*, p. 47.
6. *Ibid.*, p. 68.
7. *Germ.*, 30 May 1901.
8. Kissling, *Geschichte des Kulturkampfs im Deutschen Reich* vol. I, p. 345.
9. *Ibid.*, p. 356
10. *Ibid.*, pp. 358–9, quoted from Poschinger, *Bismarcks neue Tischgespräche u. Interviews*, p. 68. In 1885 Bismarck asked Leo XIII to act as an arbiter in the conflict with Spain on the Caroline Islands. On New Year's eve the Pope awarded him the Order of Christ.
11. Buchheim, *Geschichte der Christlichen Parteien in Deutschland*, p. 202.
12. *Verhandlungen des Reichstags*, 1. Legislaturperiode, 3. Session 1872, vol. 24, p. 359. It was the same debate in which Bismarck declared, 'Do not worry, we shall not go to Canossa, neither physically nor mentally', p. 356.
13. *Verhandlungen des Reichstags*, 5. Legislaturperiode, 1. Session 1881/82, vol. 66, pp. 93–4; 'The Liberals believed in a permanent antagonism to the Church as an abstract antithesis', Eyck, *Bismarck*, vol. III, p. 91.
14. Windthorst's remarks as quoted above.
15. Rep. 7 Sept. 1874 P.A. England 64 I A B b vol. 1.
16. Bachem, *op. cit.*, vol. III, p. 93.
17. *Handbuch der Deutschen Geschichte* vol. III/2, Das Zeitalter Bismarks pp. 162–5; H. Holborn, 'Bismarks Realpolitik', in Gall (ed.), *Das Bismarckproblem in der Geschichtsschreibung nach 1945*, p. 248.
18. Bussmann, *Handbuch*, p. 170; Letter of Odo Russell to Lord Derby in 1874, Eyck, *op. cit.*, p. 107.
19. Rep. 7 Dec. and 7 Nov. 1874 P.A. England 64 I A B b vol. 3.

20. Rep. 4 Jan. 1874 P.A. England 64 I A B b vol. 1.
21. Eyck, *Gladstone*, p. 68.
22. Rep. 17 Nov. 1874 P.A. England 64 I A B b vol. 3.
23. *N.A.Z.*, 14, 17, 22 Nov. 1874.
24. Morley, *Life of Gladstone*, vol. II, pp. 507, 513.
25. Rep. 12 Jan. 1875 P.A. England 64 I A B b vol. 4.
26. Instr. 14 Nov. 1874 P.A. England 64 I A B b vol. 3.
27. Rep. 12 Jan. 1875 P.A. England 64 I A B b vol. 4.
28. Rep. 24 Feb. 1875 P.A. England 64 I A B b vol. 4.
29. Bucher was one of Bismarck's closest collaborators. He had lived in England for a long time as an emigrant after 1848. 'Whereas Bismarck was sick of the Kulturkampf since 1876, Bucher was the man who continued to instigate', Holstein, *Die Geheimen Papiere* vol. I, pp. 52, 59.
30. P.A. England 64 I A B b vol. 4; Gladstone's reply, *ibid.*
31. Eyck, *op. cit.*, p. 308; 'The pamphlets . . . had an immense sale . . . The second brought him a note of gratitude from the statesman with whom of all others he had least sympathy, Bismarck himself', Hammond, *Gladstone and the Irish Nation*, p. 136.
32. Bussmann, *op. cit.*, p. 251.
33. Bismarck, Fürst Otto, *Gedanken und Errinerungen*, p. 437; Holborn, *op. cit.*, p. 248; Schlözer, see note 4 above.
34. Bismarck, *ibid.*, p. 439; Schieder, '*Bismarck gestern und heute*' in Gall (ed.) *Das Bismarckproblem in der Geschichtsschreibung nach 1945*, speaks about the Kulturkampf as 'his most grievous political fault', p. 364.
35. Schlözer, *op. cit.*, p. 37.
36. *Germ.*, 30 May 1901.
37. Bachem, *Vorgeschichte*, Foreword and p. 133; *V.Z.*, 6 Sept. 1885: 'We are looking back upon the Kulturkampf laws with mixed feelings. They brought no success.' The liberal paper originally was one of the strongest advocates of the legal measures against the Church.
38. *Gladstone*, p. 163.
39. Rep. 13 Dec. 1873 P.A. England 63 I A B b vol. 2.
40. *The Times*, 11 Dec. 1873.
41. Recorded by Bülow 29 Jan. 1874 P.A. England 64 I A B b vol. 1.
42. Rep. 13 Dec. 1873, 4, 27, 28 and 29 Jan. 1874 P.A. England 63 I A B b vol. 2.
43. *The Times* 15 Dec. 1873; Rep. 15 Dec. 1873, P.A. England 63 I A B b vol. 2.
44. P.A. England 64 I A B b vol. 2.

45. The Queen on 6 Feb. 1873: 'A measure will be submitted to you at an early day for settling the question of university education in Ireland. It will be framed with a careful regard to the rights of conscience.'
46. Rep. 18 Feb. 1873 P.A. England 63 I A B b vol. 1; Moody, *The Course of Irish History*, p. 281: 'Gladstone's University Bill was a bold, ingenious and farsighted scheme.'
47. Morley, *Life of Gladstone*, vol. II, p. 443.
48. Rep. 9 and 16 March 1873 P.A. England 63 I A B b vol. 1.
49. Rep. 17 Nov. 1873 P.A. England 63 I A B b vol. 2.
50. *N.A.Z.*, 26 Nov. 1873.
51. See above, Introduction, note 6.
52. Rep. 28 and 29 Sept. 1873 P.A. England 63 I A B b vol. 2; Rep. 17 Feb. 1874 P.A. England 64 I A B b vol. 1.
53. Rep. 11 March 1874 P.A. England 64 I A B b vol. 1.
54. *Pr.Jb.*, 1873, vol. 31, p. 699.
55. See note 12 above.
56. Rep. 13 May 1875 P.A. England 64 secr., vol. 1, *The Times* 13 May 1875.
57. *Germ.*, 13 May 1875. Cookery was Münster's hobby.
58. *Germ.*, 19 May 1875.
59. Letter of Bülow to Münster of 20 May 1875 P.A. England 64 secr., vol. 1. Even the liberal *Fränkischer Courir* was very critical (Nürnberg), quoted by *Germ.*, 20 May 1875.
60. *The Times*, 14 May 1875.
61. See note 56 above.
62. The Maigesetze; as Prussian laws applied only to the Kingdom of Prussia, but neither to Bavaria nor to the other non-Prussian parts of the Empire.
63. See note 56 above, letter of 24 May 1875.
64. See note 56 above.
65. *Germ.*, 19 May 1875.
66. See note 56 above.
67. *Germ.*, 21 May 1875.
68. *N.A.Z.*, 22 May 1875.
69. Cf. Chapter 1 above, note 31.

CHAPTER 3 LAND WAR AND HOME RULE

1. The Irish question, see p. 21 above.
2. See above, Introduction, p. 13.
3. Rep. 28 March 1882 P.A. England 69 vol. 15.
4. Cf. Alter, *Die irische Nationalbewegung*, p. 45; Lyons, *John Dillon*, p. 29; Bonn, *Irland und die irische Frage*, p. 93.
5. Alter, *op. cit.*, p. 46.

6. Moody, *The New Departure in Irish Politics, Essays in British and Irish History*, vol. XVI, p. 303.
7. Moody, 'Irish-American Nationalism', *I.H.S.*, vol. XV, No. 60, p. 444.
8. Moody, *New Departure*, p. 325; cf. Lyons, *op. cit.*, p. 30.
9. *Ibid.*, p. 321; a definite compact was made along these lines by Parnell, Devoy and Davitt, approved of by Clan na Gael on 1 June 1879, *ibid.*, p. 329.
10. Moody, *Irish-American Nationalism*, p. 444.
11. Rep. 20 Jan. 1880 P.A. England 69 vol. 2.
12. Instr. 23 March 1880 P.A. England 69 vol. 3.
13. Rep. 2 April 1880 P.A. England 69 vol. 4; cf. Barker, *Ireland in the last fifty years*, p. 47: 'Elizabeth: 300,000 acres forfeited to the Crown; James I: 3 million acres confiscated; Cromwell: 11 million acres confiscated.'
14. *N.A.Z.*, 8, 14 and 17 Jan. 1880; cf. Rep. 3 Nov. 1880 P.A. England 69 vol. 8, in which the situation is described with almost the same words and by which the Foreign Office is informed on the investigation against Parnell, Dillon, Biggar, Sullivan and Sexton.
15. *Germ.*, 26 April 1880. In this context cf. Gladstone to Granville, 'To this great country the state of Ireland after 700 years of our tutelage is . . . an intolerable disgrace and a danger so absolutely transcending all others' Hammond, *Gladstone*, p. 85.
16. Rep. 2 Oct. 1880 P.A. England 69 vol. 7.
17. Rep. 5 Nov. 1880 P.A. England 69 vol. 8.
18. Rep. 10 Nov. 1880 P.A. England 69 vol. 8.
19. Rep. 12 and 19 Nov. 1880 P.A. England 69 vol. 8.
20. 29 Nov. 1880 P.A. England 69 vol. 8.
21. Cruise O'Brien, *Parnell and his Party*, p. 1.
22. MacDonagh, *Ireland*, p. 34; cf. Barker, *op. cit.*, p. 52, on Palmerston's thoughts: 'Tenant's right is landlord's wrong'.
23. *Lord Randolph Churchill*, p. 142.
24. Hansard 21 April 1893, quoted by Eversley, *Gladstone and Ireland*, p. 163.
25. *The Making of Modern Ireland*, p. 390.
26. Barker, *op. cit.*, p. 52; Lyons, *Ireland*, p. 164: 'It was a significant step forward.'
27. Eversley, *op. cit.*, p. 160, called the Bill 'a monument to Gladstone's skill, versatility, dialectics and tactics'.
28. Eyck, *Gladstone*, p. 385.
29. *Ibid.*, p. 387; cf. speech from the Throne on 27 Aug. 1881 with regard to Ireland, 'I earnestly desire that the condition of that country may so improve as to enable me to dispense with

L

or abate the use of temporary and exceptional provisions.' Rep. 28 Aug. 1881 P.A. England 69 vol. 12.

30. Rep. 8 April 1881 P.A. England 69 vol. 10.

31. Rep. 27 July 1881 P.A. England 69 vol. 11; Rep. 1 Aug. 1881 on the adoption of the Bill by the House of Commons, *ibid.*

32. Bismarck, *Gedanken und Erinnerungen*, p. 700.

33. Rep. 20 Sept. 1881 P.A. England 69 vol. 12.

34. *The Times* 26 Sept. 1881.

35. *Making of Modern Ireland*, p. 391; cf. Eyck, *op. cit.*, p. 388.

36. Emmet, *Ireland under English Rule* vol. I, p. 296, speaks of forty-five Coercion Acts from 1800 to 1886.

37. Rep. 18 and 28 Feb. 1881 P.A. England 69 vol. 9, 10.

38. Rep. 10 Oct. 1881 P.A. England 69 vol. 13.

39. See p. 45 above.

40. Rep. 14 Oct. 1881 P.A. England 69 vol. 13.

41. Rep. 17 Oct. 1881 P.A. England 69 vol. 13. 'The Land League insisting that peasant ownership and not the "three F's" was now the only satisfactory principle of settlement, refused to call off the agitation', Moody and Martin (eds.) *The Course of Irish History*, p. 286 ff.

42. Rep. 24 Oct. 1881 P.A. England 69 vol. 13. In Eversley's opinion—*Gladstone and Ireland*, p. 171—the arrest of Parnell was not in accordance with the Coercion Act: 'The Government will learn in a single winter how powerless is armed force against the will of a united, determined and self-reliant nation', p. 172.

43. Rep. 10 and 27 Nov. and 20 Dec. 1881 P.A. England 69 vol. 13.

44. *Ireland*, p. 166.

45. 21 March 1881 quoted by Winston Churchill, *Randolph Churchill*, p. 165.

46. *Ibid.*, pp. 163, 164.

47. Eversley, *op. cit.*, pp. 182, 211.

48. Rep. 5 May 1882 P.A. England 69 vol. 15.

49. Rep. 8 May 1882 P.A. England 69 vol. 16.

50. Rep. 12 May 1882 P.A. England 69 vol. 16. Eversley holds that one should have consulted Parnell before the Crimes Act 1882: 'He was never approached on that subject', *op. cit.*, p. 220. About the 'Kilmainham Treaty', the assassinations, the story of the 'Invincibles' and the special powers, see O'Broin's lecture on Radio Telefís Éireann, *Irish Times*, 18 Dec. 1970.

51. See pp. 25–28 above.

52. *Germ.*, 30 April 1880.

53. *Germ.*, 10 May 1880.

54. *Germ.*, 11 May 1880.

55. *Germ.*, 13 May 1882.

56. *Germ.*, 14 May 1882; cf. Cruise O'Brien, *Parnell*, p. 82: 'The futility of political assassination was seldom better illustrated than by this event, in which the assassins actually rescued their bitter opponents.'
57. *Germ.*, 18 May 1882.
58. *Germ.*, 21 May and 3 June 1882.
59. *Germ.*, 3 June 1882.
60. Bussmann (ed.) *Graf Herbert von Bismarck*, Aus seiner politischen Privat-korrespondez, pp. 22–37.
61. Letter of 8 Feb. 1882, Bussman, *Handbook*, p. 114.
62. *Ibid.*, p. 123.
63. *Ibid.*, p. 134; cf. see note 49 above.
64. *Ibid.*, Introduction p. 31.
65. Eyck, *Gladstone*, p. 249.
66. 'No more foolish vote is recorded in the annals of the Upper House, nor upon them rests a deeper stain', Chamberlain, quoted by Cruise O'Brien, *op. cit.*, p. 49. With regard to the consequences, O'Connor, *History of Ireland 1798–1924*, pp. 54–5, wrote: 'The landlords having sown the winds, were about to reap the whirlwinds.' The Queen was pleased and wrote to Disraeli on 5 Aug. 1880: 'I cannot be entirely silent now the event has taken place. I hope you are not the worse. Do you ever remember so many voting against the Government to whose party they belong? I do not', quoted by Cruise O'Brien, *op. cit.*, p. 49.
67. Five weeks before the murders, the embassy reported (in catchwords)—Rep. 1 April 1882 P.A. England 69 vol. 15, 'Eight Americans arrested as suspects. Irish agitation in New York, now strongly supported by German immigrants. Pressure on U.S. government who made a démarche in London in favour of the arrested people. About 700 held in custody without sentence. The state of affairs justifies the question; how would free Englishmen react if this would happen to another country?'
68. Eversley, *Gladstone*, p. 233: Salisbury did not succeed in wrecking the bill in the House of Lords.
69. Address of P. O'Hea on 26 July 1885, quoted by Alter, *Die Irische Nationalbewegung*, p. 150; cf. Lyons, *Ireland*, p. 170: The National League was more dependent on the Parliamentary Party than the Land League had been.
70. Rep. 8 Sept. 1882 England 69 vol. 17, in which the Chargé d'Affaires informed on the unrest within the R.I.C. because of their bad remuneration and on turmoil among military and police forces.
71. Rep. 16 Oct. 1882 P.A. England 69 vol. 17.

72. *Germ.*, 20 Feb. 1883.
73. Rep. 22 Jan. 1883 P.A. England 69 vol. 17.
74. Letter of 10 Jan. 1882, Bussmann, *op. cit.*, p. 144.
75. Letter of 11 Feb. 1883, *ibid.*, p. 146.
76. Letter of 6 July 1883 P.A. England 69 vol. 19; cf. above note 52 *Germ.*, 10 May 1880.
77. Rep. 27 Aug. and 25 Oct. 1883 P.A. England 69 vol. 20.
78. Rep. 3 May 1885 P.A. England 69 vol. 25. This report was made on the special request of Bismarck to the ambassador: 'It has struck His Majesty the Emperor and myself that Your Excellency has not reported on the trip of their Royal Highnesses the Prince and the Princess of Wales around Ireland. I hereby ask for your opinion as to whether the political purpose of the travel can be regarded as attained or as a failure.'
79. Letter of 22 June 1884 P.A. England 69 vol. 22.
80. Dibelius, *England*, vol. I, p. 254.
81. *Op. cit.*, p. 35 ff.
82. Eversley, *op. cit.*, p. 58: 'Home Rule, a phrase most happily devised by an eminent professor of Trinity College, Mr Galbraith, a conservative in politics who had recently been converted to the national cause.'
83. Butt, *Irish Federalism, its meaning, its objects and its hopes*, p. 39, quoted by Alter, *op. cit.*, p. 36.
84. Beckett, *Modern Ireland*, p. 377.
85. Thornley, *Isaac Butt*, p. 213, quoted by Alter, *op. cit.*, p. 40.
86. Hammond, *op. cit.*, p. 147.
87. Eversley, *op. cit.*, p. 86.
88. Beckett, *op. cit.*, p. 376.
89. *Ibid.*, p. 379.
90. *Ireland*, p. 51; see also Hammond, *Gladstone*, p. 151 on Shaw, the official leader: 'He was known in England as the leader of the Home Rule Party and in Ireland as the chairman of the Munster Bank.'
91. Lyons, *op cit.*, p. 163.
92. *Ibid.*, p. 148.
93. Rep. 21 March 1874 P.A. England 64 I A B b vol. 1.
94. Rep. 15 Aug. 1877 P.A. England 64 I A B b vol. 12.
95. Rep. 25 Feb. and 3 Mar. 1880 P.A. England 69 vol. 3.
96. Rep. 12 Feb. 1880 P.A. England 69 vol. 3.
97. Rep. 7 Jan. 1881 P.A. England 69 vol. 9.
98. Rep. 17 Jan. 1881 P.A. England 69 vol. 9.
99. Rep. 24 Feb. 1881 of the Embassy in Rome, copy in P.A. England 70 vol. 1—translation: 'Brave Patrick has too much intelligence.'

100. Rep. 25 May 1885 P.A. England 69 vol. 26.
101. *In actis* P.A. England 69 vol. 26.
102. Rep. 21 July 1885 P.A. England 69 vol. 27. This was Münster's second miscalculation as to the political development in England. In 1880 he had predicted Disraeli's victory in the General Election, cf. p. 41 above.
103. Rep. 26 Sept. 1885 P.A. England 69 vol. 29.
104. Rep. 7 Oct. 1885 P.A. England 80 vol. 1.
105. Rep. 10 Sept. 1885 P.A. Vereinigte Staaten von Amerika 1, vol. 5.
106. Including the *Germania*, curiously enough.
107. *V.Z.*, 2 Aug. 1885.
108. *V.Z.*, 24 Sept. 1885.
109. *V.Z.*, 30 Sept. 1885.
110. Eversley, *Gladstone*, p. 271, in whose view Carnarvon was a Home Ruler, see p. 274; cf. Beckett, *op. cit.*, p. 395, who recalls that Carnarvon had been largely responsible for the establishment of federal self-government in Canada and had later tried to work out a similar system for South Africa. 'He encouraged Parnell to believe that the Government might grant Ireland a status within the U.K. similar to that of a Canadian province within the Dominion.'
111. *Randolph Churchill*, p. 342.
112. *Ibid.*, p. 345.
113. Cruise O'Brien, *Parnell*, p. 100; in his view Chamberlain became a bitter foe of Irish aims from this time.
114. Alter, *op. cit.*, pp. 56–7; Hammond, *op. cit.*, pp. 67–82, 83–107; Beckett, *Modern Ireland*, p. 395, also speaks of conversion in 1885 and declares that Salisbury knew of it but ignored Gladstone's advances that he would support the government in case of a Home Rule motion.
115. *The Irish Question*, p. 129.
116. Cruise O'Brien, *op, cit.*, pp. 104–105. Mansergh speaks of a disastrous political blunder of his career, *op. cit.*, p. 143.
117. Cruise O'Brien, *ibid.*, (25 seats); Eversley, *op. cit.*, p. 284.
118. *Gladstone*, p. 462.
119. Cf. pp. 18, 19, 33–35.
120. *Pr.Jb.*, vol. 57, p. 83. Here one should remember that this right wing periodical, which usually followed national liberal principles and ideas, had obviously abandoned its attitude expressed during the Kulturkampf, cf. p. 33, Chap. 2, note 54.
121. *V.Z.*, 11 Dec. 1885.
122. Gladstone to Hartington, 'Besides the Parnell party there exists a party of separation or a Civil War party; and in due time the

question will arise which of them will carry the day.' In order to avoid civil war, one had to shake hands with Parnell; this was obviously Gladstone's idea, which was shared by Lord Spencer and Lord Granville: Eyck, *op. cit.*, p. 431.

123. *V.Z.*, 23 Dec. 1885.

124. Rep. 5 Jan. 1886 P.A. England 80 vol. 1.

125. Rep. 13 Jan. 1886 P.A. England 80 vol. 1.

126. *Ibid.*

127. 'We have done our best for you. Now we shall do our best against you.' Randolph Churchill to Justin McCarthy, quoted by Curtis jr, *Coercion*, p. 64.

128. Hammond, *Gladstone*, p. 436.

129. Curtis, jr, *op. cit.*, pp. 38, 46, 49.

130. *Ibid.*, p. 88; Salisbury: 'Carnarvon is getting so very green', *ibid.*, p. 94.

131. *Op. cit.*, p. 437.

132. Curtis jr, *op. cit.*, p. 87.

133. *N.A.Z.*, 25 Jan. 1886.

134. Stenographische Berichte des Preussischen Abgeordnetenhauses 1886, vol. 1. pp. 211–12.

135. The King of Saxony commented that Gladstone's return would mean *finis Britanniae* (like once *finis Poloniae*). 'There are parallels between the Parnellites and the Zentrum' [i.e. Catholic Party] and between Parnell and Windthorst', Rep. of the Royal Prussian Legation to Saxony of 28 Jan. 1886, copy in P.A. England 80 vol. 1.

136. See p. 21.

137. *The Times* 11 Feb. 1886; cf. Hammond, *op. cit.*, p. 465, who quotes from the same paper, speaking of Bismarck as 'Gladstone's Chief Enemy in Europe'.

138. The *N.A.Z.*, reported on these resignations and pointed out that 'the Whig Lords left the party on the grounds that they could not share Gladstone's Irish policy. Churchill's agitation in Ulster means pinprick tactics aimed at a curbing of the cabinet', 23 Feb. 1886. 'It seems doubtful whether the moral impression of such an exodus would leave the political prestige of the Premier untouched', 18 March 1886.

139. Rep. 25 Feb. 1886 P.A. England 80 vol. 1; cf. Winston Churchill, *Randolph Churchill*, p. 426: On 13 Feb. 1886, Lord Randolph spoke of two Governments in Ireland, the Government of the Queen and the Government of the National League, the Government of the Queen not being the stronger Government of the two in many parts of Ireland. The *V.Z.*, 25 Feb., spoke about Lord Randolph as a man who was on his way to

Damascus, preaching the religious strife in Ulster. Curtis, jr, *Coercion,* pp. 97–8, described Churchill's visit to Ulster and compares Gladstone to Macbeth, who hesitated before murdering Duncan: 'Gladstone, too, asked for time "before plunging the knife into the heart of the British Empire." '

140. *Op. cit.,* Preface.
141. Rep. 19 March 1886 P.A. England 80 vol. 1.
142. Instr. 24 March 1886 P.A. England 80 vol. 1.
143. Rep. 7 April 1886 P.A. England 80 vol. 2.
144. Rep. 9 April and 8 May 1886 P.A. England 80 vol. 2; cf. *V.Z.* of 10 May 1886 speaking of 'mounted gentlemen playing soldiers'.
145. P.A. England 80 vol. 2.
146. 22 April 1886, copy in P.A. England 80 vol. 2.
147. Rep. 22 April 1886, copy in P.A. England 80 vol. 2; cf. Rep. 16 April 1886 P.A. Vereinigte Staaten 1 vol. 6; Home Rule Bill was applauded in the House of Representatives.
148. Telegram, 21 May and 25 May 1886 P.A. England 80 vol. 2, Rosebery was a close friend of Count Herbert Bismarck.
149. Rep. 18 and 25 May, Telegram, 9 June 1886 P.A. England 80 vol. 3. In Rosebery's opinion one would now have to send 30,000 men over to Ireland (*ibid.*).
150. *N.A.Z.,* 9, 10, 13, 14 April, 11, 20, 21 May, 1, 2, and 5 June 1886.
151. *Germ.,* e.g. 10, 30 April 1886.
152. Winston Churchill, *op. cit.,* p. 485: 'Bright had parted from him [Gladstone] Forster was dead, Hartington and Goschen and James were gone, Chamberlain was a bitter and formidable foe. The Liberal party was shattered.'
153. *V.Z.,* 3 and 4 April 1886.
154. *V.Z.,* 8 April 1886.
155. *V.Z.,* 21 April 1886.
156. *V.Z.,* 29 May 1886.
157. *V.Z.,* 5, 8 and 9 June 1886.
158. *Pr.Jb.,* 1886, vol. 57 p. 300.
159. *Pr.Jb.,* 1886, vol. 57 p. 413.
160. *Ibid.* Bismarck himself took part in this 'twaddle', see his marginal p. 65.
161. Hammond, *op. cit.,* p. 493; cf. Winston Churchill, *op. cit.,* p. 481: 'A letter from Bright is said to have turned the scale.'
162. Mansergh, *Irish Question,* p. 141; O'Hegarty, *A History of Ireland under the Union 1801–1922,* p. 556: Letter of Chamberlain to Dilke of 30 April 1886: 'The Bill is doomed. I have a list of 111 Liberals pledged against the second reading.'

163. Churchill, *op. cit.*, pp. 440, 458.
164. *Ibid.*, p. 477.
165. Eyck, *Gladstone*, p. 483.
166. Curtis jr, *Coercion*, p. 106.
167. *Pr.Jb.*, 1886, vol. 58 p. 93.
168. Rep. 22 June 1886 P.A. England 80 vol. 3.
169. *N.A.Z.*, 10 June 1886.
170. *Germ.*, 11 June 1886.
171. *Ibid.*
172. *Ibid.*
173. *V.Z.*, 11 June 1886.
174. *V.Z.*, 19 June 1886.
175. *V.Z.*, 4 July 1886.
176. *Pr.Jb.*, 1886, vol. 58 p. 93.
177. Rep. 26 July 1886 P.A. England 80 vol. 3.
178. *V.Z.*, 17 July 1886.
179. *Pr.Jb.*, 1886, vol. 58 pp. 202–203.
180. *Ibid*; cf. Randolph Churchill's contrary view: 'Banish the Irish, and a house composed only of Englishmen and Scotsmen would sink to the conditions of a vestry', Winston Churchill, *op. cit.*, p. 90.
181. Gwendolin Cecil, *Life of Robert Marquis of Salisbury*, vol. III, pp. 302–303; Rep. 18 May 1886 P.A. England 80 vol. 3; the embassy speaks of 'ruthless policy'.
182. Gwendolin Cecil, *op. cit.*, vol. II, p. 39.
183. *Ibid.*, p. 49.
184. *Ibid.*, vol. III, p. 148.
185. *V.Z.*, 22 May 1886.
186. *Germ.*, 13 July 1886.
187. Rep. 18 Aug. 1886 P.A. England 80 vol. 3; *V.Z.*, 10 and 11 Aug. 1886.
188. *V.Z.*, 12 and 13 Aug. 1886.
189. *V.Z.*, 4 Aug. 1886.
190. *V.Z.*, 7 Aug. 1886.
191. *V.Z.*, 9 Aug. 1886.
192. Hammond, *op. cit.*, p. 291.
193. *Ibid.*, p. 455; cf. p. 602, Gladstone in a letter to Döllinger of 13 July 1889: 'It is in truth my completely accordant estimate of that [England's] vocation which makes me almost more anxious for Home Rule on England's behalf than on Ireland's. Ireland is at present a source of military weakness as well as of moral discredit.'
194. Curtis jr, *op. cit.*, p. 395.
195. *Ibid.*, p. 91.

196. *Ibid.*, p. 169.
197. MacDonagh, *Ireland*, p. 34.
198. Eversley, *op. cit.*, p. 330: 'Never . . . had a Coercion Bill been introduced with so little justification.'
199. Rep. 4 April 1887 P.A. England 80 vol. 4; see also *V.Z.*, 11 June 1887, in which details of evictions are reported.
200. Rep. 7 Nov. 1887 P.A. England 80 vol. 4.
201. Rep. 6 Oct. 1887 P.A. England 80 vol. 4. In July 1888 Hatzfeldt reported on a speech of Rosebery at Bolton where he had asserted that the Irish Question weakened England's influence abroad: 'While foreign Sovereigns are meeting amicably, England has to stand aloof and her power is miscalculated because her enemies are reckoning with her internal quarrels', Rep. 30 July 1888 P.A. England 81 No. 2 vol. 4; cf. Salisbury's admission, note 189 above.
202. Rep. 8 July 1887 P.A. England 80 vol. 4.
203. Curtis jr, *op. cit.*, p. 175; Eversley, *op. cit.*, p. 346: 'No passport to public credit and honour was so certain as that of having been imprisoned by Mr Balfour'; cf., report of the *Germania* of 21 Oct. 1891: 'Never before was a chief secretary hated so deeply in Ireland as Balfour'. The paper particularly mentioned the ruthlessness and cruelty of his coercive measures.
204. Curtis jr, *op. cit.*, p. 408.
205. *Ibid.*, p. 495; Eversley, *op. cit.*, p. 347.
206. Barker, *op. cit.*, p. 52 ff.; Alter, *op. cit.*, pp. 114–17.
207. Cruise O'Brien, *op. cit.*, pp. 201–205; also Hatzfeldt reported that Parnell had been against the campaign, Rep. 9 May 1888 P.A. England 81 vol. 4.
208. *Op. cit.*, p. 182.
209. Cruise O'Brien, *Parnell*, p. 209.
210. For more about the Plan, particularly the reactions of the Vatican and the clergy, see Chapter 3 below.
211. Rep. 7 May 1892 P.A. England 80 vol. 8.
212. Rep. 6 April 1893 P.A. England 80 vol. 9; cf. *N.A.Z.*, 5 April 1893, which reported on Balfour's address, adding that 'the phrases in party-rhetorics, however, have to be understood *cum grano salis*'.
213. *V.Z.*, 18 June 1892.
214. *V.Z.*, 22 June 1892.
215. *V.Z.*, 29 July 1892.
216. *V.Z.*, 13 Aug. 1892.
217. *V.Z.*, 19 Aug. 1892; cf. Rep. 16 Oct. 1892 from Copenhagen, *in actis* England 81 No. 2 vol. 9: 'Lord Rosebery is the safety valve in Gladstone's Cabinet.' (William II, 'Very good!')

218. *V.Z.*, 1 June 1892.
219. *V.Z.*, 1 July 1892.
220. *V.Z.*, 13 July 1892.
221. *V.Z.*, 12 June 1892; 16 June 1893.
222. *Pr.Jb.*, 1892, vol. 58 p. 307.
223. *Ibid.*, p. 308
224. Cf. Schieder, 'Idee und Gestalt des supranationalen Staates seit dem 19. Jahrhundert', *H.Z.*, vol. 184 p. 339, quoting from Lord Acton who had already in 1862 rejected the modern theory on nationality and had declared coexistence of several nationalities under the same state 'a test and the best security of its freedom': 'It indicates a state of greater advancement than the national unity which is the ideal of modern liberalism.' National unity was also mainly advocated by the liberals in Germany. Schieder maintained that in his time: 'The supra-national state in its various forms is, for Europeans, no longer a historical memorial but an appeal to our political will and political phantasy which cannot dispense with the historical model.' *Ibid.*, p. 365. Gerhard Ritter, 'Staattund Geselschaft in England', *H.Z.*, vol. 198 p. 24 quotes the same phrase of Acton.
225. Rep. 14 Feb. 1893 P.A. England 80 vol. 8.
226. Rep. 18 Feb. 1893 P.A. England 80 vol. 8.
227. Rep. 27 March 1893 P.A. England 80 vol. 9.
228. Rep. 26 Feb. and 2 March 1894 P.A. England 80 vol. 9.
229. Rep. 9 Sept. 1893 P.A. England 80 vol. 9.
230. *Germ.*, 15 Feb. 1893.
231. *N.A.Z.*, 18 Feb. 1893; cf. Curtis jr, *Anglo-Saxons and Celts*, p. 103, 'What really killed Home Rule in 1886 and 1893 was the Anglo-Saxon stereotype of the Irish Celt.' 'Among those Englishmen who were most influenced in their thinking about Ireland and the Irish by the Anglo-Saxonist attitudes of historians and ethnologists were the politically active members of the middle and upper classes who decided to oppose Home Rule in 1886 and thereafter', p. 98; cf. Hammond, *op. cit.*, p. 503.
232. *N.A.Z.*, 11 April 1893; in an earlier article the paper had expressed its doubts about the true intentions of the Home Rulers, pointing out that sincere members of the party were striving for a separate state, based on Celtic nationalism and Roman Catholicism, and drawing parallels with the United States. The paper put the question why the Americans had objected to a separate parliament of the Confederate South. 'A Parnellite parliament in Dublin would be the same as a Congress of the South.' *N.A.Z.*, 9 Nov. 1888.
233. *V.Z.*, 16 Feb. 1893.

234. *V.Z.*, 22 April 1893.
235. *Pr.Jb.*, vol. 72 p. 366.
236. *Ibid.*, p. 369.
237. Münster's and Bismarck's opinion on British aristocracy, see above p. 19; Herbert Bismarck's view see above p. 50.
238. *V.Z.*, 8 Sept. 1893.
239. *V.Z.*, 29 July 1893.
240. *Ibid.*, p. 532.
241. Justin McCarthy, *V.Z.*, 20 March 1893.
242. *V.Z.*, 20 March 1893.
243. See above p. 37.
244. Rep. 24 March 1882 P.A. England 69 vol. 15; cf. Larkin, 'Mounting the Counter Attack', in *Revue of Politics*, vol. 25, 1963, No. 2 p. 180: 'No one had more real influence in Rome with regard to Ireland than Manning'; cf. Rep. 26 March 1880 P.A. England 69 vol. 3, in which Münster had emphasised Manning's authority in the contest of 1880: 'Disraeli has won his confidence, Manning has instructed clergy and faithful to vote for the Conservatives'; cf. Manning's dispute with Gladstone, p. 26.
245. Alter, *Die Irische Nationalbewegung*, p. 30; Curtis jr, *op. cit.*, p. 232.
246. *Germ.*, 8 May 1882, after the Phoenix Park murders: 'Fenians are depraved hooligans who have been at variance with the Church for a long time.'
247. Alter, *op. cit.*, p. 95; Bonn, *Irland*, p. 179.
248. Letter of Gladstone to Newman, quoted by Eversley, *Gladstone*, p. 251. Gladstone's opinion was quite in accordance with his views expressed in his pamphlets on the Vatican Decrees and with the feeling of German liberals during the Kulturkampf.
249. Eversley, *Ibid.*
250. Rep. 24 Feb. 1881, copy in P.A. England 70 vol. 1.
251. Rep. 29 July 1881, copy in P.A. England 69 vol. 11; when Archbishop McCabe received the Red Hat in Rome, however, Leo XIII urged an Irish delegation attending the ceremony to follow its bishops in using legal means in love of peace and justice, *Germ.*, 8 May 1882.
252. *Germ.*, 2 May 1881.
253. The 'Castle Bishop' who had blamed Parnell after his visits to Victor Hugo and Rochefort in a Lenten Pastoral calling them 'impious infidels', Cruise O'Brien, *op. cit.*, p. 64.
254. Rep. 7 and 28 Nov. 1881 P.A. England 70 vol. 2; cf. O'Connor, *op. cit.*, p. 102: 'Errington seems to have been more silly than the usual run of the genus "busybody".' The *Germania*, in contrast, took him to be Gladstone's secret agent whose instructions

were to influence the Vatican in favour of the government against the majority of the clergy and the hierarchy, *Germ.*, 6 Nov. 1881.

255. Münster's report 17 Feb. 1882 P.A. England 70 vol. 2; cf. *St James Gazette* 12 May 1882 with a correspondent's letter, 'It is within my knowledge that Mr Errington submitted to the Vatican the secret reports on the state of Ireland which were presented by the police to the English Government.'

256. *Germ.*, 4 Feb. 1882.

257. Eversley, *Gladstone*, p. 251. There seems to be, moreover, no doubt that Errington also intervened in the issue of the appointment of the new Archbishop of Dublin in favour of the English candidate, Dr Donnelly, as Schlözer reported. Rep. 21 July 1885 P.A. England 70 vol. 2.

258. Rep. 16 May 1883 P.A. England 69 vol. 19.

259. *N.A.Z.*, 19 May 1883.

260. Eversley, *op. cit.*, pp. 250, 251, the Fund rose from £12,000 to £39,000.

261. *Germ.*, 26 May and 9 June 1883. The *Kleine Journal* of 4 June 1883 described Errington's activity in Rome and the man himself: 'A lean and long-faced man with white sidewhiskers'.

262. *Germ.*, 23 May 1883. Archbishop Croke of Cashel was the leading Irish churchman supporting the Irish nationalism at that time. The paper denounced the motives of the Parnell Testimonial Fund: 'It would be regrettable if the Irish people were to falter in its loyalty to the Holy See.'

263. Count Ledochowski was deposed during the Kulturkampf; after having been jailed for some time he was called to Rome and received the Red Hat; cf. p. 22.

264. Eyck, *Bismarck III*, pp. 80–7; cf. pp. 23–24.

265. Cf. above p. 22.

266. Buchheim, *op. cit.*, p. 235. Schlözer was in high esteem of the Vatican. Very often he received letters from Galimberti with the following text: 'Il Santo Padre desidera di vedere S.E. il Signor Ministro di Prussia in tutta confidenza.' Schlözer, *op. cit.*, p. 65.

267. Eyck, *Gladstone*, pp. 463–4; Buchheim, *op. cit.*, p. 236. A German paper wrote on the party's feeling: 'Never defeated by foes, never forsaken by friends, but disavowed by the Pope, for whose rights and claims it had fought and suffered for seventeen years.' (Schlözer, *op. cit.*, p. 109.)

268. The expulsion of the Jesuits was repealed in 1917.

269. In his letters to the Pope, Bismarck always addressed Leo XIII as 'Sire' instead of 'Votre Sainteté'. When Schlözer presented to him the first letter of this kind, the Pope remarked 'He recog-

nised me as a sovereign', Schlözer, *op. cit.*, p. 71; Bismarck, *Die Gesammelten Werke*, Briefe, No. 1766 vol. XIV/2.

270. There was also another important difference as regards the treatment of the Catholics in Germany and in Ireland. In Barker's view (*op. cit.*, p. 101) 'there has never raged in Ireland a struggle such as raged in Germany in the days of Bismarck between the Government and the Roman Church'. In the interest of historical truth the phrase should be corrected into the following version: There has never raged a struggle in Germany in the days of Bismarck between the government and the Roman Church such as raged in Ireland until the Emancipation Act.

271. *Germ.*, 14 Feb. 1886, quoting the *Moniteur de Rome* and commenting: 'One must hope that he will not send Errington again, who has a bad record in Rome.'

272. Rep. 20 Feb. 1886 P.A. England 90 vol. 1.

273. Rep. 27 Feb. 1886 Legation to the Vatican, P.A. England 90 vol. 1.

274. Rep. 9 Dec. 1887 P.A. England 90 vol. 1.

275. Instr. 14 Dec. 1887, copy in P.A. England 90 vol. 1, on the Duke of Norfolk's special mission to the Pope on the occasion of Leo XIII's jubilee of his priesthood. See Correspondence, submitted to Parliament Nov. 1887–Jan. 1888. *Ibid.*

276. *Germ.*, 27 Jan. 1888.

277. 4 Feb. 1888 P.A. England 80 vol. 5.

278. The Political Archives of the German Foreign Office filed the reports and instructions in a special series of the records, 'England 90, England und der Vatikan'.

279. Rep. 4 May 1888 P.A. England 90 vol. 1; cf. Salisbury's conversation with Hatzfeldt, footnote 274 above.

280. Rep. 3 May 1888, Legation to the Vatican, P.A. England 90 vol. 1.

281. Rep. 30 Oct. and 12 Nov. 1888 P.A. England 90 vol. 1; cf. Curtis jr, *op. cit.*, p. 275: Simmons gave briefings to the Curia about good or bad priests in Ireland and gave advice as to candidates for bishoprics.

282. Rep. 11 Feb. 1889, Legation to the Vatican, P.A. England 90 vol. 1.

283. Rep. 9 Jan. 1890, Legation to the Vatican, P.A. England 90 vol. 1.

284. Instr. 18 Jan. 1890 P.A. England 90 vol. 1.

285. Rep. 4 Feb. 1890 P.A. England 90 vol. 1; the *V.Z.*, on 18 April 1888, took the opinion that the mission of the Duke of Norfolk had proved a failure in the principal matters, the Curia not being inclined to take into account the desires of the Conservative

cabinet aimed at an adverse position of the Vatican towards the Nationalists in Ireland. The *Daily News* (28 April 1888) shared this opinion, while *The Times* (25 April 1888) took the opposite view.

286. Rep. 11 April 1890, Legation to the Vatican, P.A. England 90 vol. 1.

287. Rep. 14 Feb. 1893 P.A. England 90 vol. 2; The *N.A.Z.*, 9 April 1893, reported that several politicians had expected the Pope to speak against Home Rule in Ireland. On the occasion of pilgrimages to Rome, however, he did not mention it. Already on 26 Aug. 1892 the *Germania* had emphasised that, because of the Irish problem, the Vatican had welcomed the Gladstone administration. 'Home Rule would neutralise the elements of revolutionist propaganda.'

288. Rep. 13 June 1893, Legation to the Vatican, P.A. England 90 vol. 2.

289. Eyck, *op. cit.*, p. 533. Salisbury to Herbert Bismarck: 'Let us leave the proposal on the table, without yes or no.'

290. See pp. 75–76 and the respective notes.

291. *Germ.*, 5 May 1888.

292. Rep. 1 May 1888 P.A. England 80 vol. 5; cf. Morley, *Gladstone III*, p. 383: 'The government had lively hopes of the emissary, and while they beat the Orange drum in Ulster with one hand, with the other they stealthily twitched the sleeve of Mgr Persico.'

293. Cruise O'Brien, *Parnell*, pp. 221, 222; the same author points out that the Rescript had to be taken more seriously than the other interferences: 'It was a pronouncement approved by the Pope himself in the sphere of morals' (p. 215). He speaks of consternation and confusion among the hierarchy, but 'Dr Croke seems to have been made of sterner stuff' (p. 216).

294. Rep. 9 May 1888 P.A. England 81 vol. 4.

295. Rep. 25 May 1888 P.A. England 80 vol. 6; Curtis jr, *op. cit.*, p. 274; 'Archbishop William Walsh', in *Shaping of Modern Ireland* (ed.) Cruise O'Brien, pp. 101–102: 'Croke and Walsh became the Pollux and Castor of the National Movement led by Parnell. Croke continued (after the Rescript) to support what was condemned, but Archbishop Walsh saved the situation—Manning . . . saved Walsh in Rome. It was a case of appealing from an ill-informed Pope (by Persico) to one better informed (by Manning)', like Luther's letter to Pope Leo X. 'Walsh lost the Red Hat, and of him as of other great but Hatless archbishops, there may be said to be cases when the man is too big for the Hat and not vice versa,' p. 107.

296. *V.Z.*, 2 May 1888.
297. See pp. 86–87 above.
298. *V.Z.*, 4 May 1888; in this context it should be recalled what Fieldmarshal Count Waldersee wrote, when the Pope interfered with the Septennat affair in 1887: 'Everybody rejoices at the Pope's interference, I don't do that. Now he can raise the claim to have a say everywhere', Denkwürdigkeiten I, p. 314, quoted by Bachem, *op. cit.*, IV, p. 173.
299. *V.Z.*, 23 May 1888.
300. *V.Z.*, 25 May 1888.
301. *Germ.*, 5 and 6 May 1888.
302. *Ibid.*
303. *Germ.*, 7 July 1888.
304. *V.Z.*, 4 June 1888.
305. '*Die Insel der Heiligen und der Rebellen*', pp. 153–4.
306. *Recollections*, vol. I, pp. 236, 239, 240.
307. *Op. cit.*, p. 7.
308. *Op. cit.*, p. 366.
309. *V.Z.*, 4 Dec. 1890; cf. Cruise O'Brien, *op. cit.*, p. 354: 'Not a particular affection for democracy.'
310. *Irland und die Irische Frage*, p. 97; Oxford and Asquith, *Fifty Years of Parliament*, p. 184: 'Parnell's character and career are, and are likely to remain, one of the unsolved enigmas of history. He was not only not a demagogue; he was not, and never pretended to be, a democrat.'
311. See p. 40 above.
312. It is very interesting to take note in this context of the essay by Henry A. Kissinger on 'The white revolutionist; reflections about Bismarck' *Daedalus, Journal of the American Academy of Arts and Sciences, 1968*, pp. 888–924; translated into German, it appeared in 'Das Bismarck-Problem in der Geschichtsschreibung nach 1945', pp. 392ff. The author emphasises the opinion that even an arch-conservative point of view can undermine the political and social structure, if it neglects its limits, for institutions are adapted to a mediocre standard of performance. It goes without saying that institutions are inevitably shaken by the work of a great man. The situation Bismarck had created could only have been handled by leaders of extraordinary abilities. 'It was Bismarck's tragedy that he left a heritage of a greatness not to be mastered by any successor.'
One may add that this was Parnell's tragedy, too. Nobody after him has been able to operate in the same way as he had done. Neither Bismarck's successor Caprivi, who was characterised by Schlözer (*op. cit.*, p. 158) as a mere executive organ of the

Emperor ('One could appoint a battalion commander Chancellor, that would be just as good') nor Parnell's successors ever reached the standard of their respective predecessors. Nobody had the character of that which is cherished both in Germany and in Ireland and which is now called Vaterfigur.

313. W. O'Brien, *The Parnell of Real Life*, pp. 40, 45, 143: 'The Catholic Church is the only one that can make a man die with any real hope.'

314. *Op. cit.*, p. 28. This suspicion was obviously enhanced by the fear of heresy and atheism, imported from England, the continental countries and the U.S.A.; Winston Churchill (*op. cit.*, p. 460) quoting from a letter of Randolph Churchill to Salisbury of 29 March 1886: 'John Morley spells God with a small g; but he spells Gladstone with a big G, and that satisfies the Archbishop [Walsh].'

315. Cf. the *Germania*'s comments with regard to the Papal Rescript in 1888, see pp. 93–94 and notes 301, 302, 303 above.

316. W. O'Brien, *op. cit.*, p. 79: 'Parnell towered amongst his marshals. The least noisy member of the orchestra himself, he was the Maestro without whose eye the fiddles and reeds soon end in discord.'

317. Cruise O'Brien, *op. cit.*, pp. 250, 252, 254; Cruise O'Brien (ed.), *Shaping of Modern Ireland*, p. 168; Lyons, *Fall of Parnell*, pp. 24–6; Eyck, *Gladstone*, p. 377.

318. O'Hegarty, *op. cit.*, p. 575; cf. Hammond, *op. cit.*, pp. 580–81, 584, with the text of the forged letters.

319. Rep. 5 Oct. 1888 P.A. England 80 vol. 6; Oxford and Asquith, *op. cit.*, I, pp. 176–8, Asquith, who was Parnell's counsel, knew from the beginning that the letters were forgeries.

320. Rep. 27 Feb. and 2 March 1889 P.A. England 80 vol. 6.

321. Rep. 6 Feb. 1890 P.A. England 80 vol. 6.

322. *Germ.*, 6 Feb. 1890.

323. *Germ.*, 28 Feb. and 2 March 1890.

324. *Op. cit.*, p. 702; Randolph Churchill harshly denounced the government: 'What, with all your skill, with all your cleverness, has been the result? A ghastly, bloody rotten, foetus, Pigott! Pigott!! Pigott!!!' Curtis jr, *Coercion*, p. 295.

325. *Pr.Jb.*, vol. 63 p. 308.

326. *Life of John Redmond*, p. 6, the Attorney General had to admit the charge was unfounded, but he did so without regretting the affair: Eversley, *op. cit.*, p. 356. Eversley takes the view that, had there been a general election in the summer of 1890, there was no doubt of a majority in England being in favour of Home Rule (p. 359).

327. O'Brien, *Parnell of Real Life*, Preface.
328. *Pr.Jb.*, vol. 65 p. 225; cf. Cruise O'Brien, *op. cit.*, p. 117: 'The disastrous O'Shea'; O'Hegarty, *op. cit.*, p. 579: O'Shea was a political adventurer of a dashing but meretricious character; Lyons, *op. cit.*, p. 55: 'The conclusion that O'Shea was in the fullest sense a conniving husband is irresistible'; was he conniving because he waited for the inheritance of 'Aunt Ben' who died on 19 May 1889?
329. Cruise O'Brien, *op. cit.*, p. 283: 'He [O'Shea] was always short of money.'
330. *Pr.Jb.*, vol. 66, pp. 648–9.
331. Lyons, *op. cit.*, p. 38.
332. Lyons, *John Dillon*, pp. 114–15.
333. See Cruise O'Brien, *op. cit.*, p. 171.
334. *Ibid.*, p. 167; as to the exchange of letters between Mrs O'Shea and Gladstone, Hammond, *op. cit.*, p. 679; O'Hegarty, *op. cit.*, p. 582.
335. *Op. cit.*, p. 282; cf. O'Hegarty, *op. cit.*, p. 582, 'Chamberlain encouraged O'Shea and Chamberlain was the one person who could have stopped O'Shea with a word.' The author compares Chamberlain with Iago in Shakespeare's *Othello*.
336. It seems to be fantastic that Liberal leaders were surprised by the trial. As Hammond (*op. cit.*, p. 669) reports, Harcourt had told his colleagues that Mrs O'Shea was Parnell's mistress, a fact he had discovered when his detectives were following Parnell's movements. Gladstone had spoken of 'rumours'; Ensor, *op. cit.*, p. 183.
337. Rep. 1 and 5 Dec. 1890 P.A. England 80 vol. 7; the manifesto was published in the *Freeman's Journal* on 29 Nov. 1890. It dealt first with Gladstone's letter to Morley, written with the aim to influence the election of the party leader, then described the details of the Hawarden talks. Gladstone was said to have revealed his intentions as to the next Home Rule Bill (32 Irish members in Westminster, no Irish competence on the land question, the police under the authority of Westminster for a further 12 years) concluding: 'Because of its independence it has forced upon the English people the necessity of granting home rule to Ireland. I believe that party will obtain home rule only provided it remains independent of any English party', Lyons, *Fall of Parnell*, p. 320; as Cruise O'Brien reports, Gladstone had told McCarthy that Parnell was absolutely mistaken on the Hawarden conversation. He quotes from a letter of Harcourt in which he gave an account of Parnell's proposal that Gladstone, Morley and himself should sign a letter 'containing

M

terms to be binding on us in the final settlement of home rule which he, Parnell, undertook to keep an unviolable secret'. Harcourt felt this proposal was inconceivable, *op. cit.*, pp. 313, 319.

338. *Pr.Jb.*, vol. 67 p. 119, in the view of the Liberal leaders, Parnell was now regarded as untrustworthy; Morley remarked: '[It] reveals an infamy of character which I had never suspected' Lyons, *Fall*, pp. 111, 144. It should be recalled in this context that it was Morley who had induced Gladstone to add the P.S.: 'Parnell's re-election would render my retention of the leadership of the Liberal party almost a nullity' to the letter of 24 Nov. 1890. Gladstone had omitted this passage from the final draft. To Harcourt he had remarked: 'What, because a man is what is called leader of a party, does that constitute him a judge and accuser of faith and morals? I will not accept it', O'Brien, *Parnell of Real Life*, pp. 150, 165.

339. *Germ.*, 2 Dec. 1890.

340. *N.A.Z.*, 26 and 28 Nov. 1890; cf. Lyons, *Fall of Parnell*, p. 81, Gladstone had to take into account the impact of an alliance with a man 'who had flouted one of the society's most rigid rules'; Cruise O'Brien, *op. cit.*, p. 294, holds that the attitude of the Liberals was based solely on the movement of English public opinion, 'moral indignation of the lower middle class, a force which hardly anyone in Victorian England, and certainly not the Liberal party, could withstand for long'.

341. *N.A.Z.*, 3 Dec. 1890.

342. *Köln.Ztg.*, 18 Nov. 1890.

343. *Köln.Ztg.*, 4 Dec. 1890.

344. *Köln.Ztg.*, 4 and 5 Dec. 1890.

345. *V.Z.*, 18 Nov. 1890.

346. *V.Z.*, 7 Jan. 1890.

347. *V.Z.*, 28 and 29 Nov. 1890.

348. *V.Z.*, 1 Jan. 1890; cf. Lyons, *Fall*, p. 80, Manning wrote to Gladstone that Parnell as a leader was intolerable; *ibid.*, p. 116. In Archbishop Walsh's view the manifesto was political suicide; *ibid.*, p. 76, Manning wrote to Walsh that 'bishops, priests and people in Ireland would be seriously affected in the judgment of all English friends or of the chief of them' (Gladstone); Archbishop Croke of Cashel wired to J. McCarthy: 'All sorry for Parnell, but still, in God's name, let him retire quietly . . .' (Morley, *op. cit.*, p. 449; Cruise O'Brien, *op. cit.*, p. 310); from a non-clerical side, from Cecil Rhodes came a telegram, 'Resign, marry, return!' (Beckett, *op. cit.*, p. 403). A German paper, however, reported that it was Carnegie who wired this text (*Köln.Ztg.*, 1 Dec. 1890).

349. Cruise O'Brien, *op. cit.*, p. 348.
350. *Op. cit.*, p. 55.
351. Rep. 9 Dec. 1890 P.A. England 90 vol. 7.
352. Lyons, *op. cit.*, p. 159; *V.Z.*, 11 Dec. 1890.
353. *Köln.Ztg.*, 8 Dec. 1890.
354. *Köln.Ztg.*, 22 Dec. 1890; *V.Z.*, 17 and 24 Dec. 1890. In this final report on J. McCarthy's victory the paper commented that this would be promising for the future 'if one had to deal with a less changeable nation than Ireland'! Emmet Larkin, *op. cit.*, p. 182, dealing with the hierarchy's role in the destruction of Parnellism, points out: 'Why clerical power was more apparent than real during the destruction of Parnellism cannot be explained simply in terms of the happy inaptitude of the Irish bishops, or in the archaic or inflexible apparatus of the Irish Church or even in the long-term undermining and rebuilding of a new episcopal complex from Rome.' While the author described the harsh way in which the campaign of certain bishops was made upon Parnell's followers, he stressed Archbishop Walsh's good will in attempting to achieve a reasonable settlement in a letter to Gladstone of 28 Jan. 1891 (pp. 171, 177). Archbishop Croke, however, did not appreciate O'Brien's conciliatory communiqués from America (p. 182). His letter to O'Brien: 'Be staunch and steady and no surrender' Lyons, *Fall*, p. 194. After the breakdown in Boulogne Redmond blamed priests and bishops: 'They cannot by reason of their sacred office lose their civil rights or evade their duties as patriotic Irishmen', Lyons, *Fall*, p. 26.
355. *Germ.*, 13 Dec. 1890.
356. Rep. 26 Jan. 1891 P.A. England 80 vol. 7.
357. *Ibid.*, this is contrary to the opinion of Randolph Churchill who wrote in a letter to his wife of 3 Dec. 1890: 'The Government will be fools if they do not dissolve. This crash of the Home Rule party, this repudiation by Parnell of Mr Gladstone's scheme, is the most complete and glaring justification of the Unionist cause', Winston Churchill, *op. cit.*, p. 724.
358. Lyons, *Fall*, p. 305.
359. *Köln.Ztg.*, 9 Oct. 1891.
360. *Germ.*, 8 Oct. 1891.
361. *V.Z.*, 8 Oct. 1891.
362. *Pr.Jb.*, vol. 68 p. 752.
363. See *Fall*, pp. 309–10, *Ireland*, p. 195.
364. MacDonagh, *op. cit.*, p. 54.
365. *Recollections* I, p. 251.

CHAPTER 4 GREATNESS AND INSUFFICIENCY

1. *Fifty Years of Parliament,* I, p. 217.
2. Eyck, *Gladstone,* p. 544.
3. Rep. to the Emperor of 22 Oct. 1883; *Die Gesammelten Werke,* vol. 4X.
4. Letter of 14 Feb. 1882 to his father (Bussmann, *Handbuch,* p. 119) in which he says that Gladstone's foreign policy might be summed up in the gravedigger's reply in *Hamlet,* V, 1, when asked why Hamlet was sent to England: 'Why, because he was mad: he shall recover his wits there; or if he do not, it's no great matter there. . . . 'Twill not be seen in him there; there the men are as mad as he.'
5. Instr. 17 Jan. 1874 P.A. England 64 I A B b vol. 1.
6. Rep. 12 Jan. 1875 P.A. England 64 I A B b vol. 4.
7. Rep. 31 March 1880 P.A. England 69 vol. 4.
8. 'Das Problem Bismarck' in Gall (ed.) *Das Bismarck-Problem in der Geschichtsschreibung nach 1945,* p. 100.
9. Eyck, *Bismarck III,* p. 408.
10. *Ibid.*
11. Rothfels, 'Probleme einer Bismarck-Biographie' in Gall (ed.) *Das Bismarck-Problem,* p. 73.
12. Eyck, *op. cit.,* p. 407.
13. Letter of Professor Müller, Oxford, of 1 Dec. 1885, quoted by Schlözer, *Letzte Römische Briefe,* p. 73, who wrote, moreover, that Gladstone's reserves as to Germany were based on personal grounds.
14. See Eyck, *op. cit.,* p. 346.
15. Letter of Prince William to Bismarck of 8 July 1877, copy in P.A. England 81 No. 2a vol. 2.
16. P.A. England 81 No. 2a vol. 2.
17. Rep. 19 and 21 May 1898, P.A. England 81 No. 2a vol. 3.
18. *Germ.,* 21 May 1898.
19. *Köln.Ztg.,* 20 May 1898.
20. *N.A.Z.,* 21 May 1898.
21. Cf. W. O'Brien on Gladstone in *United Ireland* 12 June 1886: 'A white old man, with a face like a benediction and a voice like an archangel's', quoted by Cruise O'Brien, *Shaping of Modern Ireland,* p. 193.
22. Cf. Hammond, *Gladstone,* p. 485: 'He [Gladstone] knew that he was the only man who could persuade England . . . if he could appeal to her imagination. He could draw the bow of Odysseus, but no other.'
23. *V.Z.,* 20 May 1898; twelve years earlier (30 June 1886) the

paper had quoted from Carlyle: 'Heavens, what a conscience he has!'

24. *Dt. Rev.*, 1898 vol. 23 p. 279.
25. *England*, p. 239.
26. *Ibid.*, pp. 243–4.
27. Morley, *Gladstone*, vol. III, p. 528.
28. Rep. 21 Dec. 1892 P.A. England 81 No. 2 vol. 9.
29. Rep. 2 March 1894 P.A. England 81 No. 2a vol. 2.
30. Rep. 13 March 1894 P.A. England 81 No. 2 vol. 10.
31. Rep. 29 and 30 Oct. 1894 P.A. England 81 No. 2 vol. 11.
32. Rep. 10 March 1894 P.A. England 80 vol. 9.
33. Bussmann, *Handbuch*, p. 470; cf. *op. cit.*, p. 454, where Count Herbert is quoted as having the same sentiments.
34. *Ibid.*, p. 499; this remark was strictly along the lines of Count Herbert's father.
35. Letter of 4 Oct. 1887 to Bülow, Bussmann, *op. cit.*, p. 475. Both Rosebery and Count Herbert had apparently no secrets between each other. In October 1890 the latter brought over to England the notes he had set on paper 'about the history of the crisis which led to my father's [i.e. the Chancellor's] resignation' (Letter of 29 Oct. 1890 to Rosebery, Bussman, *op. cit.*, p. 573) and left them with Rosebery in a safe place. Already on 18 March he had written to Rosebery that 'the Emperor wishes to get rid of my father: His Majesty wants more elbow-room, and my father is in his way' (Bussmann, *op. cit.*, p. 563) and on 30 March—after the resignation—he had spoken of 'a camarilla which would sooner or later have put my father and myself in a more than awkward position' and of 'the new Chancellor, who is our best General but who never knew a word about foreign politics' (Bussmann, *op. cit.*, p. 566). On 28 February 1901 he expressed his concern about the ill-feeling in Germany towards English policy and that 'the paramount cause is the distrust of my countrymen in the wisdom of the German foreign policy' (Bussmann, *op. cit.*, p. 583). In previous years, however—in 1880 and 1882—Rosebery had been described as 'a clever and ambitious but rather light-minded man, who had dissipated his means on racecourses' before he married Hanna Rothschild who kept her Jewish religion and who was said to have spent £60,000 for the Liberals in the contest of 1880 (Letter of Münster to William I of 20 March 1880, P.A. England 69 vol. 3, and Münster's report of 6 April 1880, P.A. England 69 vol. 5). Count Herbert, in letters to his father of 19 Feb. 1882 and 12 Feb. 1883, had confirmed these reported facts, adding that the dowry of Lady Rosebery had amounted to four million pounds

and that Mentmore Castle, the Rosebery's residence 'is over-loaded with gold and valuable rarities. The content of one room is estimated to a value of £30,000' (Bussmann, *op. cit.*, pp. 122, 150).

36. *Ireland*, p. 196.
37. In a letter of 22 May 1899 to his grandmother Queen Victoria, one year after Gladstone's death. William II complained bitterly about the attitude of Salisbury and his government towards the misbehaviour of navy men in Samoa—ten years after the Emperor had been appointed Admiral of the Fleet cf. P.A. Preussen No. 1 [Pers.] vol. 4.
38. Bussmann, *op. cit.*, p. 446; cf. Hammond, *op. cit.*, p. 291: 'No man was so ready to use his taunting tongue for brilliant mischief.'
39. Dibelius, *England*, pp. 243–6, points chiefly at Chamberlain, Landsdowne and Curzon. In his view the Liberals followed the same line when they came to power again in 1905; in this context cf. Hatzfeldt's report of 16 Nov. 1900, 'Lansdowne is not a shining light. One should treat him well for the time being and not deter him by brusque demands', P.A. England 81 No. 2 vol. 13.
40. Rep. 8 Oct. 1895 P.A. England 80 vol. 9.
41. Rep. 19 Feb. 1896 P.A. England 80 vol. 9; cf. Lyons, *John Dillon*, p. 133: 'Parnell had always found Dillon an able but not very amenable lieutenant, while Dillon, though respecting Parnell's political mastery, had never succumbed to his dominant personality.'
42. *Modern Ireland*, p. 414.
43. Rep. 19 March 1900 P.A. England 80 vol. 9.
44. Rep. 1 May 1900 P.A. England 80 vol. 9; only in 1899 Cardinal Logue was said to have denounced the English government because of their objections to the establishment of a Catholic university in Dublin. 'I have no longer any trust in English statesmen' the Roman paper *Civilta Cattolica* quoted. (Rep. 3 Aug. 1899, Legation to the Holy See, P.A. England 90 vol. 2.)
45. See Mansergh, 'John Redmond', in *Shaping of Modern Ireland* (ed.) Cruise O'Brien, p. 40.
46. *Fall of Parnell*, p. 313; although it seems to be premature to deal at length with Redmond in this chapter, it should be pointed out here that since the time of the split German opinion was hesitant in recognising his abilities: 'Redmond uses strong words, but he is not a strong character', *V.Z.*, 27 Oct. 1891.
47. *Irland*, p. 107.
48. *Ibid.*, p. 119.

49. *Ibid.*, p. 131.
50. Lyons, *Ireland*, p. 207, says that this Act deservedly ranks as one of the most important measures of conciliation passed during the whole period of the Union.
51. Rep. 30 Sept. 1904 P.A. England 80 vol. 10.
52. Cf. Lyons, *Ireland*, p. 218, 'The tragedy of Irish Unionism is that so few of this class could see the writing on the wall, or could react to it in any way but by clinging stubbornly to a status quo which many of them must have known in their hearts was doomed.'
53. Rep. 17 and 19 April 1902 P.A. England 80 vol. 9.
54. P.A. England 80 vol. 10; as to the details of the Bill see Barker, Ireland, p. 58 ff., Lyons, *Ireland*, p. 214.
55. Rep. 8 May 1903 P.A. England 80 vol. 10.
56. Rep. 27 July 1903 P.A. England 80 vol. 10.
57. *Köln.Ztg.*, 9 May 1903.
58. *Köln.Ztg.*, 22 July 1903.
59. Rep. 15 July and 4 Oct. 1904 P.A. England 80 vol. 10; cf. Rep. 30 Sept. 1904, note 51.
60. Rep. 17 Aug. 1904 and 20 March 1905 P.A. England 80 vol. 10.
61. See Rep. note 51 above.
62. *Ireland*, p. 217; cf. note 52 above.
63. P.A. England 80 vol. 10; cf. Lyons, *Ireland*, p. 216, who writes about the Scheme as of a 'document which MacDonnell helped Dunraven to produce (it would be more accurate to say, produced for him)'.
64. P.A. England 81 No. 2 vol. 23.
65. *V.Z.*, 21 Feb. 1905; Lyons, *Ireland*, p. 216, speaks of Mac-Donnell as 'a forceful and choleric character (even his friends called him "the Bengal tiger")' because of his previous office in India; cf. Asquith, *op. cit.*, p. 23, who characterises Wyndham as being totally without the toughness and phlegm of the Anglo-Saxon race.
66. *Köln.Ztg.*, 23 Feb. 1905.
67. Rep. 26 Nov. 1903 P.A. England 69 vol. 36. In Dangerfield's view (*The strange death of Liberal England*, p. 10) the Liberal party was already doomed when it came back to power at Westminster. 'It was like an army protected at all points except for one vital position on its flank.'
68. Rep. 27 Nov. 1905 P.A. England 80 vol. 10.
69. The Liberal party 1899–1906, *I.H.S.*, 13, pp. 323, 327.
70. *Ibid.*, p. 316.
71. *Ibid.*

72. P.A. England 80 vol. 10.
73. 1906 Town Tenants' Act, 1907 Evicted Tenants' Act, 1909 Land Act.
74. *Ireland*, p. 261; the author quotes Grey: 'Things must advance towards Home Rule, but I think it must be step by step', *ibid.*, p. 260.
75. Rep. 8 May 1907 P.A. England 80 vol. 10; cf. *V.Z.*, 15 May 1907.
76. See Gwynn, *Redmond*, p. 147: 'The atmosphere was electrical, in view of the strong rumours that the Irish party desired to carry a resolution supporting the Bill'; as to the principal point of the resolution rejecting the Bill see *ibid.*, p. 148.
77. *Germ.*, 28 May 1907.
78. *V.Z.*, 22 May 1907.
79. *Köln.Ztg.*, 24 May 1907.
80. Rep. 29 May 1907 P.A. England 80 vol. 10.
81. Cf. *V.Z.*, 15 May 1907, the paper told its readers that Campbell-Bannerman and Morley were in favour of Home Rule, while Asquith, Grey and Haldane were not.
82. Rep. 8, 13 and 29 Aug. 1907 P.A. England 80 vol. 10.
83. Rep. 19 Sept. P.A. England 80 vol. 10; cf. Gwynn, *op. cit.*, p. 150: 'Sinn Fein gained considerably in importance by the rejection of the Irish Council Bill.'
84. Rep. 31 March 1908 P.A. England 80 vol. 10.
85. *Op. cit.*, p. 154; cf. Dangerfield, *op. cit.*, p. 16: 'When Sir Henry Campbell-Bannerman died in 1908 it was like the passing of true liberalism.'
86. Rep. 3 April 1908 P.A. England 80 vol. 10; Baron Schwabach recorded on 28 May 1908, *ibid.*: The English have taken into their head that Germany is their real adversary.

CHAPTER 5 THE UNSETTLED QUESTION

1. Beckett, *Modern Ireland*, p. 427, 'It is hardly an exaggeration to say that both British parties were prisoners of their Irish allies. The legislative Union forced upon an unwilling Ireland a century earlier had brought its Nemesis.' At this point it is noteworthy to mark the opinion expressed by Grey, in a conversation with Metternich, that he did not think that the Irish would succeed with Home Rule, because the country would vote against—as in 1886, Rep. 18 Nov. 1909 P.A. England 80 vol. 10.
2. Rep. 29 Nov. 1893 P.A. England 81 No. 2 vol. 10.
3. Recorded in P.A. England 69 vol. 23.
4. Gwynn, *Redmond*, p. 161, speaks of serious revolt in Ireland over the liquor tax. Redmond: 'There is absolutely no excuse

for maintaining this tax which will ruin the whiskey industry in Ireland.' *Ibid.*, p. 180; cf. Asquith, *op. cit.*, II p. 78: 'The House of Lords rejected the Finance Bill, not because they love the people but because they hate the budget.'

5. The government had the consent of King George V to the creation of 400 Peers. 'The Lords submitted and passed the Bill, but from that moment the Tories were determined to destroy the Liberal party', Gallagher, *Indivisible Island.*

6. Gwynn, *op. cit.*, p. 191.

7. Marjoribanks-Colvin, *Carson*, II, p. 66; cf. Lyons, *Dillon*, p. 327; 'The resistance of the Ulster Unionists had begun to take shape as soon as it became clear that the Parliament Act deprived them of the protection of the House of Lords.'

8. Rep. 11 Dec. 1909 P.A. England 80 vol. 10.

9. Rep. 30 Dec. 1909 P.A. England 80 vol. 10.

10. Rep. 24 Feb. 1910 P.A. England 80 vol. 11.

11. Rep. 3 Dec. 1910 and 16 Feb. 1911 P.A. England 80 vol. 11.

12. Also Peers with Irish interests could no longer influence constitutional measures. In 1914 there were still 104 Peers who had Irish interests, 28 being Irish representative Peers, and of the total, 86 had interests in the south of Ireland, P. J. Buckland, 'The Southern Irish Unionists and British politics 1906–1914', *I.H.S.* 15 p. 246.

13. *Op. cit.*, p. 114; cf. *The Times* of 6 Nov. 1911 with Balfour's views on the Irish question—'the rotten hybrid system' represented by the Home Rule schemes.

14. Text of the speech, *The Times* 9 Feb. 1912.

15. See *Germ.*, 9 Feb. 1912; *Köln.Ztg.*, 11 Feb. 1912; *V.Z.*, 6 Feb. 1912.

16. *Pr.Jb.*, vol. 147 p. 553; cf. Ryan, *Mutiny*, p. 35, on Churchill's return through back streets: 'The Orangemen triumphantly added the reflection that Lord Randolph Churchill had been welcomed like a King (in 1886) while his son had slunk away like a thief in the night.'

17. See Sasse, *100 Jahre Botschaft in London*, pp. 26–36.

18. Rep. 10 April 1912 P.A. England 80 vol. 12.

19. *The Times* 10 April 1912.

20. Lyons, *Ireland*, p. 301, 'On the face of it, it is more difficult to see why Redmond should have been prepared to accept such a modest form of self-government than why the Unionists should have been prepared to take arms against it'; Cf. Leslie Shane in *Shaping of Modern Ireland*, O'Brien (ed.), p. 103, Archbishop Walsh, one of the ecclesiastical protagonists of the Home Rule movement, 'could not accept Redmond's satisfaction

with the last Home Rule Bill as a full and complete settlement.'

21. Rep. 12 April 1912 P.A. England 80 vol. 12; see Ryan, *op. cit.*, p. 45, Lord Hugh Cecil declared that the Bill reduced Ireland from the status of wife to that of mistress.
22. Rep. 13 and 16 April 1912 P.A. England 80 vol. 12; cf. Gardiner, editor of the *Daily News*, in *Frankfurter Zeitung* of 25 Dec. 1913, who supports the view that the Ulster question presents the only occasion to restore the full power of the House of Lords.
23. Rep. 24 April and 2 May 1912 P.A. England 80 vol. 12.
24. Rep. 14 Sept. 1912 P.A. England 69 vol. 43; It is noteworthy to state that the Emperor's remarks with regard to Ireland became more biting after the English-German antagonism in the navy question appeared to be insurmountable and after Haldane's visit to Berlin had proved a failure.
25. Rep. 16 Sept. 1912 and 17 Jan. 1913 P.A. England 80 vol. 12.
26. *V.Z.*, 9 Feb., 17 April and 8 May 1912.
27. *Germ.*, 17 and 23 April 1912.
28. *Köln.Ztg.*, 11 April, 2 and 8 May 1912.
29. *V.Z.*, 15 and 16 July 1913.
30. *Germ.*, 13 Sept. 1913.
31. Rep. 27 Oct. 1913 P.A. England 80 vol. 12; Dillon's characterisation of Asquith in this context as 'a statesman . . . and brave friend of Ireland' (*The Times* 27 Oct. 1913) proved premature.
32. Rep. 28 and 30 Oct. 1913 P.A. England 80 vol. 12; cf. Dugdale, *Balfour*, vol. II, p. 98; 'Balfour did not believe the government could proceed to the coercion of Northern Ireland without a new mandate from the country.'
33. Rep. 10 Nov. 1913 P.A. England 80 vol. 12.
34. Rep. 9 Feb. 1914 P.A. England 80 vol. 12; cf. Gardiner in the *Frankfurter Zeitung* 25 Dec. 1913: 'A certain rebellious spirit is the consequence of neglecting social problems in the last years.'
35. *Dillon*, pp. 328–9.
36. *Germ.*, 9 Oct. 1913.
37. *Köln.Ztg.*, 4 Jan. 1913.
38. *Ibid.*, 10 Sept. 1913.
39. Rep., 10 March 1914 P.A. England 80 vol. 13.
40. *Germ.*, 16 March 1914.
41. Rep. 20 March 1914 P.A. England 80 vol. 13; all German papers reported on the pandemonium in the House and Carson's departure to Belfast.
42. See Ryan, *Mutiny*, p. 54, Letter of Churchill to Sir George Ritchie in Dundee.
43. *Redmond*, p. 81.

44. *V.Z.*, 19 May 1866.
45. P.A. England I A B b 66 vol. 1; cf. Rep. 11 Aug. 1875 *ibid.*, in which Lord Oranmore, who had made an interpellation in the Lords concerning the rank of Manning, was characterised by the Chargè d'Affaires, von Brincken, as an 'Orangist who tries to express his Protestant feelings with more zeal and harshness than delicacy', a reproach made to the Orangemen very often; The story presented to the Emperor in the memorandum is confirmed by Lynch, *Ireland's Vital Hour*, p. 163; The report of the Select Committee, set up by parliament in 1835, said: 'The obvious tendency and effect of the Orange Institution is to keep up an exclusive association in civil and military society, exciting one portion of the people against the other, to increase the rancour and animosity too often, unfortunately, existing between persons of different religious persuasions', quoted *ibid.*; On the history of the Order in the nineteenth century see *Irish Times* of 9 Nov. 1970, Thomas Davis lecture of Professor H. Senior, Montreal, and of 4 Jan. 1971, lecture of Mr Aiken McClelland; On the role of the Duke of Cumberland see also *Pr.Jb.*, vol. 156 p. 181ff.
46. Stewart, *Ulster Crisis*, p. 45.
47. *Berliner Tageblatt* of 31 July 1913, copy in P.A. England 80 vol. 13.
48. See Kühlmann's portrait p. 163; cf. McDowell, in *Shaping* (ed.) Cruise O'Brien, p. 87: 'Carson . . . provided for his opponents a cartoonist's conception of the upholder of autocratic and alien law'; Lyons, *Ireland*, p. 298: 'He looked as a dyspeptic pessimist, he was in addition a hypochondriac who enjoyed his ill-health to the full.'
49. *V.Z.*, 10 March, 25 April and 25 Aug. 1893; cf. Beckett, *op. cit.*, p. 428, in whose view Protestants of all ranks were preparing to fight for the threatened Protestant ascendancy in Ireland.
50. Rep. 25 May 1893 P.A. England 81 No. 2 vol. 9.
51. Stewart, *op. cit.*, p. 39, takes the view, however, that in private Carson frequently expressed doubts and second thoughts about issues on which he was adamant in public. But there is no indication whatever that this applied also to issues in connection with the Ulster crisis. Healy is said to have remarked: 'I would trust my soul to Carson', Marjoribanks-Colvin, *op. cit.*, I, p. 1; Pointing at Bonar Law and F. E. Smith, MacDonagh, *op. cit.*, p. 59, expresses the opinion that the Conservative party 'ridden by these demonic spirits, moved close to a position which a later generation might call fascist'; Dangerfield, *op. cit.*, p. 80, on Bonar Law: 'He had the unfortunate habit of saying the wrong

thing in debate, excessively Tory in the matter of having no political imagination whatsoever.'

52. Bermann, *Irland*, pp. 168–82; a noteworthy contribution as regards Carson's historical image has been brought in by the remarks of Dangerfield (*op. cit.*, pp. 130–131) that, in fact, Carson was by no means hated by the southern nationalists. 'Here was an Irishman who not only defied the English parliament but defied it successfully and forcibly and with threats of bloodshed. That he defied it in the name of loyalty to England scarcely mattered; the point was that what he could do other Irishmen could do.'

53. *Pr.Jb.*, vol. 154 p. 382

54. *Aspects of the Irish Question*, Dublin and London 1912.

55. *Pr.Jb.*, vol. 155 p. 396.

56. *Germ.*, 30 Aug. 23 and 26 Sept. 1913.

57. *Germ.*, 29 Sept. and 4 Oct. 1913; cf. Gwynn, *op. cit.*, pp. 224–5; The Irish nationalists were against prosecution of the Ulstermen 'no Irish jury would convict'. In Redmond's view an arrest of Carson would have enforced him and would have created an atmosphere in which all hope for conciliation would have to be dropped. Asquith, too, expressed the opinion that no Irish jury would give a verdict, of either the guilt or innocence of the accused (Asquith, *op. cit.*, II, p. 141); although Churchill in Bradford on 14 March 1914, called Carson's convention in Ulster 'a self-elected body, composed of persons who, to put it plainly, are engaged in a treasonable conspiracy', *ibid.*, p. 147; 'Let us go forward together and put these grave matters to the proof', Churchill on the same occasion, Marjoribanks-Colvin, *op. cit.*, II, p. 294. The *Köln.Ztg.*, of 16 March 1914 takes the view that his strong feeling in the Ulster question was his return service to the Liberal party for having agreed to his navy budget.

58. *Köln.Ztg.*, 20 Sept. 1913.

59. *Köln.Ztg.*, 22 Nov. 1913.

60. *V.Z.*, 17 March 1914.

61. Marjoribanks-Colvin, *op. cit.*, II, p. 241; cf. the same authors, *ibid.*, p. 243, 'The Army was at that time largely officered by the Irish gentry. They went to Sandhurst and Woolwich. Almost to a man they were Loyalists; Home Rule was not for them a political question.'

62. *Köln.Ztg.*, 23 Sept. 1913; Bonar Law appealed, on 28 Nov. 1913 in Dublin, to the army to refuse orders from the government and asked the Prime Minister to turn his mind to the history of the Great Revolution. 'The army refused to fight for James II in 1688.' Gwynn, *op. cit.*, p. 239.

63. Rep. 11 Feb. 1914 P.A. England 69 vol. 43.
64. *Germ.*, 21 March; *N.A.Z.*, 22 March; *V.Z.*, 23 March; *Köln. Ztg.*, 22 March 1914.
65. *V.Z.*, 24 March 1914; as to the extent of the resignations see Ryan, *Mutiny*, p. 139.
66. *V.Z.*, 25 March 1914; the *Germ.*, 26 March 1914, took the same view about Roberts's position.
67. *Köln.Ztg.*, 22 March 1914.
68. *Köln.Ztg.*, 24 March 1914; cf. the contrary opinion of Ryan, *op. cit.*, p. 16, and of Stewart, *op. cit.*, p. 108, 'Haldane soon won the respect of the generals . . . Had he remained at the War Office instead of becoming Lord Chancellor it is probable that the Army crisis of March 1914 would have been averted.'
69. *Köln.Ztg.*, 26 March 1914.
70. Rep. 23 March 1914 P.A. England 71 vol. 60; it is a regrettable fact that the records of the Prussian War Ministry, of the General Staff of the Army and of the Royal Prussian Military Cabinet have been destroyed following an air raid on Potsdam on 14 April 1945. Thus, a most valuable source is no longer available for historical research; all the marginal notes, remarks and instructions following the reports from London, both of civil and military authorities, have been lost. A part of the archives is said to be shelved in East Germany, that means, for the time being, unattainable.
71. Rep. 23 March 1914 P.A. England 71 vol. 60.
72. Rep. 24 and 25 March and 25 April 1914 *ibid.*; also the *Germ.*, of 24 March 1914 spoke of a Pyrrhus victory and of the 'two stools'.
73. 'H.M.G. must retain their right to use all the forces of the Crown in Ireland or elsewhere to maintain law and order and to support the Civil Power in the ordinary execution of its duty. But they have no intention whatever of taking advantage of this right to crush political opposition to the policy or principles of the Home Rule Bill', Rep. 26 April 1914 P.A. England 71 vol. 60; The *Köln.Ztg.* of 26 March 1914 regarded the 'Correspondence' as an unpleasant paper, criticising the heads of the military authorities.
74. Rep. 27 March 1914 *ibid.*; cf. in this context the Order of the Army Council of 28 March 1914 (*The Times* 28 March 1914) which was aimed at restoring the authority of the civil and military authorities. 'In particular it is the duty of every officer and soldier to obey all lawful commands given to them through the proper channel, either for the safeguarding of public property or the support of the civil power in the ordinary execu-

tion of its duty or for the protection of the lives and property of the inhabitants in the case of disturbances of the peace.'

75. P.A. England 71 vol. 60 and 78 vol. 95; Bethmann-Hollweg's remark hinted at the troubles in Zabern (Alsace), where a serious conflict had broken out between the 99th regiment of Infantry and the Alsatian inhabitants of the town.

76. P.A. England 71 vol. 60.

77. *Germ.*, 26 March 1914.

78. *V.Z.*, 26 March 1914; cf. Gwynn, *op. cit.*, p. 251, Asquith was expecting that the opposition in parliament would not approve the Army Bill unless they knew how the army would be employed in Ulster.

79. *Köln.Ztg.*, 26 March 1914.

80. *Mar.Rdsch.*, 1914 I, pp. 681, 810.

81. General v. Beseler, *Dt. Rev.*, 1914, April–June, pp. 129, 131.

82. Another author, General v. Falkenhausen, *ibid.*, p. 151, expressed the same views, alluding to 'recent events'.

83. *Staatskunst und Kriegshandwerk*, vol. II.

84. *Ibid.*, pp. 44–7.

85. *Ibid.*, p. 62.

86. *Ibid.*, p. 91.

87. See Ryan, *op. cit.*, p. 100: 'It was said of him that he was the greatest intriguer who had ever worn the King's uniform.' Wilson himself told Bonar Law that 'there was much talk in the Army and that if we were ordered to coerce Ulster there would be wholesale defections. Forty per cent of officers and men would leave the Army', p. 103; cf. Gwynn, *op. cit.*, p. 291, Wilson had been informed by telegram of the Curragh events earlier than the War Office. 'He was in permanent contact with the politicians of the opposition', p. 281; cf. Stewart, *op. cit.*, p. 149, who says that in the Belfast headquarters (of Carson) everything that happened in the War Office was known. 'French informed Wilson on all decisions taken in the morning. In the evening he dined with Milner, Jameson and Carson and presumably told them all he knew of the Government's plans'; cf. Asquith, *Memories and Reflections*, II, p. 185; 'Wilson was voluble, impetuous and an indefatigable intriguer' quoted by Dangerfield, *op. cit.*, p. 347.

88. Gwynn, *op. cit.*, p. 331.

89. *V.Z.*, 22 March 1914 on Lloyd George's address in Huddersfield: 'The system of a representative constitution is in jeopardy; if the Liberals recede now they will no longer be able to govern the Empire.'

90. *Dillon*, p. 348.

91. Lyons, *Ireland*, p. 307, speaks about Asquith's inclination 'to prudence, rather than valour'.
92. Gwynn, *op. cit.*, p. 297.
93. P.A. England 80 vol. 13.
94. *Ibid.*
95. *Germ.*, 28 March 1914; this briefing refutes all rumours saying that the German government had approved of the purchase of arms and supported the whole action. It is interesting to note that Lord Roberts congratulated Carson on the successful outcome of the gun-running, Gwynn, *op. cit.*, p. 305.
96. *Germ.*, 28 and 29 April 1914.
97. *Ibid.*, 29 April 1914.
98. *Dillon*, p. 349; cf. Gwynn, *op. cit.*, p. 305 : 'Everybody in Ireland, whether Orangeman or Nationalist, believed, very naturally, that the Government had been outwitted or afraid to interfere.'
99. Rep. 13 May 1914 P.A. England 80 vol. 13.
100. *Pr.Jb.*, vol. 156 p. 181.
101. P.A. England 80 vol. 13.
102. *Köln.Ztg.*, 4 April 1914; cf. edition of 27 May in which the paper expressed its doubts after the bill had been passed by the House of Commons.
103. Lyons, *Dillon*, p. 343.
104. *Ibid.*, p. 341; cf. Gwynn, *op. cit.*, p. 256, who maintains that Churchill and Lloyd George had proposed to exclude Ulster before the bill was ever introduced.
105. P.A. England 80 vol. 13; cf. p. 176, note 63 above.
106. *V.Z.*, 20 June 1914.
107. P.A. England 80 vol. 12.
108. Lyons, *Dillon*, pp. 330, 347.
109. *Ibid.*, p. 347.
110. Mansergh, *op. cit.*, pp. 203–204; cf. Nicolson, *King George the Fifth* p. 199.
111. Nicolson, *op. cit.*, p. 221.
112. *Ibid.*, pp. 225–7.
113. *Ibid.*, p. 223.
114. *Ibid.*, p. 225.
115. Mansergh, *op. cit.*, p. 196.
116. *Germ.*, 8 April 1914.
117. Mansergh, *op. cit.*, p. 199.
118. Carson to Redmond on 11 Feb. 1914, Marjoribanks-Colvin, *op. cit.*, I, p. 282.
119. Ryan, *op cit.*, p. 65; Churchill hit back: 'Latest Tory threat—Ulster will secede to Germany'; cf. Gywnn, *op cit.*, p. 205,

Crawford, Andrews and Craig would prefer the German rule to Home Rule, *Morning Post*, 10 Dec. 1910, 9 Jan. 1911.

120. From a leaflet, quoted by Ryan, *op. cit.*, p. 165.
121. *Ibid.*
122. *Germ.*, 9 Jan. 1913.
123. 10 July 1914, quoted in P.A. England 80 vol. 13.
124. Rep. 26 June and 2 July 1914 P.A. England 80 vol. 13.
125. Rep. 15 July 1914 P.A. England 80 vol. 13.
126. See Asquith, *op. cit.*, II p. 155; Lyons, *Dillon*, p. 353, who quotes Churchill's famous phrase about the 'muddy by-ways of Fermanagh and Tyrone'.
127. Rep. 25 July 1914 P.A. England 80 vol. 13.
128. *Pr.Jb.*, vol. 157 p. 363.
129. *V.Z.*, 14 and 18 July 1914.
130. Gwynn, *op. cit.*, p. 298.
131. Gerard, *My four years in Germany*, p. 100.
132. Nicolson, *op. cit.*, p. 220.
133. *V.Z.*, 28 March 1914.
134. *Germ.*, 11 July 1914.
135. Casement, *Gesammelte Schriften*, p. 138, quoted by Meffert, *Englische Verbrechen am Katholischen Irland*, p. 104.
136. *Ibid.*
137. *Op. cit.*, p. 271.
138. *Ibid.*, p. 272.
139. See, e.g. Lloyd George on 9 Sept. 1924, quoted by Gallagher, *op. cit.*, p. 104: 'It is very problematical if war would have been declared if Britain had not been believed on the Continent of Europe to be so completely absorbed in serious civil dissension over the Irish Question, that she could not intervene in a European struggle.' Churchill takes the same view in pointing out that, following reports of their agents, German politicians were convinced that England was on the brink of civil war and therefore could not be regarded as a factor to be reckoned with in European matters. Die Weltkrise, I, p. 135; see also Gwynn, *op. cit.*, p. 349.
140. Gerard, *op. cit.*, p. 100.
141. *Pr.Jb.*, vol. 157 p. 363.
142. Conrad v. Hoetzendorf, *Aus meiner Dienstzeit 1906–18*, vol. III, p. 675.
143. Stewart, *op. cit.*, p. 227; Gwynn, *op. cit.*, p. 350.
144. Stewart, *ibid.*, p. 22.
145. P.A. Deutschland 121 No. 6 vol. 3.
146. *Op. cit.*, Prelude XVI; the same author speaks without any basis of 'the Kaiser's war' (Prelude XIV).

147. Cf., Bauer, *op. cit.*, p. 201.
148. Bermann, *op. cit.*, p. 171; it must be noted here—although this is not verified—that the German staff, as Gwynn *op. cit.*, p. 350, puts it, took a different view than the American ambassador (who held that Carson's threat was a bluff).
149. See Bermann, *op. cit.*, p. 171.
150. See Marjoribanks-Colvin, *op. cit.*, II, p. 193, the author mentions the rumours of a desperate intrigue between the Ulster rebels and the arch-enemy (*sic*) of England; Stewart, *op. cit.*, p. 226.
151. See Janssen, *Graue Exzellenz*, who published the records and letters of Treutler including the conversations he had had with the Emperor in August 1913.
152. See Wolf, *Sir Roger Casement und die deutsch-irischen Beziehungen*, p. 14.
153. See, e.g., Sir Henry Wilson, Ritter, *op. cit.*, pp. 95, 96, in whose view Wilson was a Francophile; Lord Roberts (*Frankfurter Zeitung* 23 Oct. 1912 and Rep. 24 Oct. 1912 P.A. England 78 vol. 92) who was reported to have spoken in favour of conscription, which was needed owing to the 'German danger'; and Lord Beresford who was said to be a great Ulster friend and who always greeted 'Good morning, one day nearer the German war', Stewart, *op. cit.*, p. 256, note 12.
154. Stewart, *op. cit.*, p. 228.
155. *Op. cit.*, p. 350.
156. See Kühlmann, *Erinnerungen*, pp. 389–90. There is no reason to mistrust his records. Moreover, his absence from Great Britain during the month of July 1914 has been confirmed to the author by Baron von Kühlmann-Stumm, Member of the German Bundestag and son of the late Baron von Kühlmann.
157. Rep. 22 Sept. 1913 P.A. England 80 vol. 12.
158. P.A. England 80 vol. 13.
159. Asquith, *op. cit.*, p. 158; Lyons, *Dillon*, p. 358, says that after the mass withdrawal of Unionists the assent was promulgated amid cheers of Liberal, Labour and Nationalist members. 'It is difficult not to feel, in retrospect, that if the Unionists had stayed to cheer and the Home Rulers had left the House in protest this would have been a more appropriate comment.'
160. To T. P. O'Connor: 'The world is now reaping the bitter harvest of the Triple Entente and Grey's foreign policy which for years I have denounced to deaf ears.' To Scott 'It is the greatest crime against humanity perpetrated in modern times and I cannot help feeling that England must bear a considerable share of the responsibility', Dillon Papers, quoted by Lyons, *Dillon*, p. 355.

N

161. Cf. Letter of Redmond to Asquith of 4 Aug. 1914, Asquith Papers, quoted by Lyons, *Dillon*, p. 351; Bauer, *op. cit.*, p. 206.
162. Marjoribanks-Colvin, *op. cit.*, III, p. 25.
163. Dangerfield, *op. cit.*, p. 348, speaks of the Curragh affair as a perpetual reminder 'not merely of the party treacheries and follies of men but of the strange ways in which a great political philosophy can come to grief and the government of a great country can be put to shame'. The Curragh affair and its handling by the Liberal government was, in fact, the virtual end of the Liberal party's importance. Cf. Chamberlain to Carson during the crisis: 'I would fight it out to the finish', Marjoribanks-Colvin, *op. cit.*, II, p. 233.
164. Dangerfield, *op. cit.*, p. 17.
165. Mansergh, *op. cit.*, p. 176.
166. *Ibid.*, pp. 170, 174.
167. *Ibid.*, p. 174.
168. *Köln.Ztg.*, 14 July 1914.
169. 31 March 1914; it should be recalled here that the Prime Minister was regarded by Germans as a waverer because of his attitude on the question of assistance to France in the event of a continental war. His declaration in the House of Commons that England had not undertaken to send troops to the continent (Lichnowsky's report of 11 March 1913 P.A. England 78 vol. 93) had given rise to uneasiness in France. (Rep. von Schoen, ambassador in Paris, 12 March 1913 P.A. England 78 vol. 93.) On 21 Dec. 1912 the Military Attaché in London reported that, as long as the Liberal government was in power, only a part of the expeditionary force would be shipped over, but that reasons might be found for not sending any troops at all. According to this report the English government had made provision for reserves for Ireland and India, P.A. England 78 vol. 93; cf. Ritter, *op. cit.*, II, pp. 94–5.
170. *V.Z.*, 31 March 1914.
171. Rep. 9 Oct. 1913 P.A. England 80 vol. 12; cf. *Köln.Ztg.*, 2 May 1914, which reported on his inclination to flexibility.
172. *Op. cit.*, p. 198; cf. Gwynn, *op. cit.*, p. 213, quoting from a letter of Churchill to Redmond of 12 Aug. 1912 with the comment: 'This letter was an ominous symptom of the uneasiness which was spreading through the Liberal ranks. He and Lloyd George had been the most vigorous advocates throughout the country. Lloyd George was at all times an uncertain factor.'
173. Cf. Beckett, *op. cit.*, p. 420. No wonder that under these circumstances the Sinn Féin movement grew rapidly. Griffith on the third bill: 'If this is liberty, the lexicographers have deceived

us', *ibid.*; cf. Dangerfield, *op. cit.*, p. 74, who compared him with Parnell: 'He was never hurt by scandal . . . never touched by that cold flame which burned in his former leader'; cf. Mansergh on Redmond in *Shaping of Modern Ireland*, p. 45, in whose view Redmond encouraged Asquith's policy of 'wait and see'.

174. MacDonagh, *op. cit.*, p. 73.
175. See *The Times* 26 Sept. 1914; Bauer, *op. cit.*, p. 206, calls his speech in Dublin of 25 Sept. 1914 'undignified' and 'servile'. He asserts that Redmond, when visiting the trenches of Flanders, 'preached' against Germany and fired a cannon-shot against the German trenches.
176. O'Hegarty, *op. cit.*, p. 605; cf. Lyons, *Ireland*, pp. 257, 309; cf. MacDonagh, *op. cit.*, p. 62, who presents more contrasts between both leaders.
177. *Ireland*, p. 257.
178. See Asquith, *op. cit.*, II, p. 145; cf. Mansergh, *op. cit.*, p. 193, who deals with this subject with regard to the first attempts to settle the question while taking into account particular Ulster interests.

EPILOGUE

1. Lyons, *Fall of Parnell*, p. 319.
2. In Goschen's view Irishmen had ineradicable and incurable vices and a sort of double doses of original sin. Colonel Saunderson (Ulster) believed that Ireland did not deserve to be free until such time as she became strong enough to free herself, Curtis, jr, *Anglo-Saxons and Celts*, pp. 100, 102.
3. The late Federal Chancellor, Adenauer, in a personal conversation about Ireland with the author, expressed the view that partitions of countries were mostly grounded on indecisiveness, insufficiency and lack of imagination on the part of the politicians concerned.
4. 'There has not been a Foreign Minister in this country during the last fifty years who has not felt, and indeed often stated, that the strength of England was diminished, and her moral influence jeopardised by the unsolved position of the Irish question', Lord Curzon in the House of Lords on 14 Dec. 1921, quoted by Mansergh, *op. cit.*, p. 268.
5. *Ireland in the last fifty years*, p. 92.
6. *Ireland*, p. 19.
7. See p. 143 above.
8. Wilhelm II, *Ereignisse und Gestalten 1878–1918*, p. 178.

Chronological Table

1870–71 Franco-German War
1871   Proclamation of the German Empire (18 Jan.)
         Peace Treaty of Frankfurt (10 May)
1872   Beginning of the Kulturkampf in Germany
1874   Disraeli, Prime Minister (Feb.)
1877   Parnell, President of Home Rule Federation (Aug.)
1878   Death of Pope Pius IX (7 Feb.)
         Leo XIII Pope (20 Feb.)
         Berlin Congress (June–July)
1879   Austro-German Alliance
1879–82 Land War in Ireland
1879   New Departure in Irish politics (June)
         Land League founded; Parnell, Head of the League (Oct.)
1880   Gladstone, Prime Minister (April)
         Parnell, Head of the Irish Parliamentary Party (May)
1881   Forster's Coercion Act (March)
         Land Act
         Land League declared unlawful
1882   Arrears Act
         New Coercion Act
         Kilmainham Treaty (April)
         Phoenix Park Murders (May)
         Triple Alliance, Germany, Austria, Italy (May)
         National League founded (Oct.)
1885   Salisbury, Prime Minister—Caretaker Cabinet (June)
1886   Gladstone's third Cabinet (Feb.)
         First Home Rule Bill introduced (8 April)
         Bill defeated (7 June)
         Salisbury's second Cabinet (Aug.)
         Balfour, Chief Secretary for Ireland
         Parnell's Tenants' Relief Bill defeated (Oct.)
         Plan of Campaign announced (Oct.)
1887   Balfour's Crimes Bill
         Mgr Persico in Ireland
         'Parnellism and Crime' in *The Times* (April)

End of the Kulturkampf in Germany
1888   Death of William I (9 March)
          Frederick III, Emperor
          Death of Frederick III (15 June)
          William II, Emperor
          Roman Circular condemning Plan of Campaign
1888–90 Parnell Commission
1889   Pigott forgeries exposed (Feb.)
          Bismarck's offer of an Anglo-German Alliance
1890   Report of Parnell Commission
          Bismarck's resignation (March)
          General Caprivi, Chancellor
          Mrs O'Shea divorced (17 Nov.)
          Parnell's Manifesto (29 Nov.)
          Committee Room 15 (1–6 Dec.)
          Split of the Irish Party
1891   Death of Parnell (6 Oct.)
          Redmond, leader of the Parnellites (Dec.)
1892   Gladstone's fourth Cabinet (Aug.)
1893   Second Home Rule Bill introduced (13 Feb.)
          Passed in third reading (1 Sept.)
          Bill defeated by the House of Lords (8 Sept.)
1894   Gladstone's resignation (3 March)
          Lord Rosebery, Prime Minister
1895   Salisbury's third Cabinet: Beginning of Cecil Decade
1898   Death of Gladstone (19 May)
          Death of Bismarck (30 July)
1900   Reunification of the Irish Party under Redmond (Feb.)
1901   Death of Queen Victoria (22 Jan.)
          Edward VII, King
1902   Balfour, Prime Minister (July)
1903   Wyndham's Land Act
          Death of Leo XIII (20 July)
          Death of Salisbury (22 Aug.)
1904   Dunraven's Devolution Scheme
1905   Resignation of Balfour (Dec.)
          Campbell-Bannerman, Prime Minister
1906   Town Tenants Act
          Sinn Féin founded (5 May)
1907   Evicted Tenants' Act
          Irish Council Bill
1908   Resignation and Death of Campbell-Bannerman (22 April)
1909   Land Act

1910   Death of Edward VII (6 May)
       George V, King
1911   Parliament Act (Aug.)
1912   Haldane's visit to Berlin
       Third Home Rule Bill introduced (11 April)
       Carson's Ulster Covenant (28 Sept.)
1913   Ulster Volunteer Force established (Jan.)
       Third Home Rule Bill defeated in the House of Lords (Jan.)
       Third Home Rule Bill passes House of Commons again and
          is defeated in the House of Lords (July)
       Irish Citizens' Army and Irish Volunteers established (Nov.)
1914   Curragh Affair (20 March)
       Larne Gun-Running (24 April)
       Home Rule Bill passed again by the House of Commons
          (26 May)
       Archduke Franz Ferdinand of Austria murdered (28 June)
       Buckingham Conference (21–24 July)
       Austrian Ultimatum to Serbia (23 July)
       Howth Gun-Running (26 July)
       British Declaration of War on Germany (4 Aug.)
       Royal Assent to the Home Rule Bill
       Execution of Bill suspended for war time (18 Sept.)

Curricula of the Imperial German Ambassadors to the Court of St James

ALBRECHT GRAF VON BERNSTORFF
Born 1809 at Dreilützow in Mecklenburg, entered the Prussian diplomatic service in 1832; Minister Plenipotentiary in Munich, Vienna, Naples, and in 1854 London, 1861 Prussian Minister of Foreign Affairs in Berlin; 1862 Ambassador of Prussia in London; 1868 Ambassador of Prussia and of the North German Federation in London; 1871 Ambassador of the German Empire in London; died 1873 in London.

GEORG HERBERT GRAF ZU MUNSTER – LEDENBURG
Born 1820 in London, entered the diplomatic service of Hanover in 1856; Minister Plenipotentiary of the King of Hanover in St Petersburg 1857–65 (then a colleague of Bismarck, who was Prussian Minister Plenipotentiary during a part of the same period); 1867 Member of the North German Bundestag; 1871 Member of the German Reichstag; 1873 Ambassador in London; 1885 Ambassador in Paris; 1899 Fürst Münster von Derneburg; retired 5 January 1900; died 28 March 1902 in Hanover.

PAUL GRAF VON HATZFELDT – WILDENBURG
Born 1831 in Düsseldorf, entered the Prussian diplomatic service in 1859; held diplomatic posts in Paris and The Hague; 1868 Counsellor and close collaborator to Bismarck in Berlin; 1874 Minister Plenipotentiary in Madrid; 1878 Ambassador in Constantinople; 1882 State Secretary and Head of the Foreign Office in Berlin; 1885 Ambassador in London; died 1901 in London.

PAUL GRAF VON WOLFF – METTERNICH ZUR GRACHT
Born 1853 in Bonn, of oldest Rhenish nobility, entered the diplomatic service in 1882; 1885–87 Second Secretary; 1890–95 First Secretary in London; 1895–97 Consul General in Cairo; 1897–1901 Minister Plenipotentiary of Prussia in Hamburg; 1901 Ambassador in London, called back 1912; died 1934 in Heppingen.

ADOLF FREIHERR MARSCHALL VON BIEBERSTEIN
Born 1842 in Karlsruhe, Public Prosecutor in Mannheim; 1878–81
Member of the Reichstag; 1883 Minister Plenipotentiary of the Grand
Duke of Baden in Berlin; 1890–97 State Secretary and Head of the
Foreign Office in Berlin; 1897 Ambassador in Constantinople; 18
May 1912 Ambassador in London; died 24 September 1912 in
Badenweiler.

KARL MAX FURST VON LICHNOWSKY
Born 1860 at Kreuzenort, of Silesian nobility, entered the diplomatic
service in 1884, served in the Foreign Office, 1892–99 in Stockholm,
Constantinople, Bucharest and Vienna; 1895 First Secretary; resigned
1904; Member of the Prussian Herrenhaus; 1912 Ambassador in
London; 3 June 1914 Hon. Degree Oxford; left London 6 August
1914; died 1928 at Schloss Kuchelna.

Bibliography

Alter, P., *Die Irische Nationalbewegung zwischen Parlament und Revolution*. Munich – Vienna 1971.

Bachem, K., *Vorgeschichte, Geschichte und Politik der Zentrumspartei*, vol. III u. IV, Cologne 1927.

Barker, E., *Ireland in the last fifty years, 1866–1916*, Oxford 1917.

Bauer, R., *Irland, die Insel der Heiligen und der Rebellen*, Leipzig 1938.

Beckett, J. C., *The Making of Modern Ireland 1663–1923*, London 1966.

Bermann, R. A., *Irland*, Berlin 1914.

Bismarck, Fürst Otto, *Gedanken und Erinnerungen*, Stuttgart – Berlin 1928.

Bismarck, Fürst Otto, *Die Gesammelte Werke*, vols. II, XIV/2, LX, Berlin 1926/29.

Bismarck, Graf Herbert, *Aus seiner politischen Privatkorrespondenz*, edited by W. Bussmann, Göttingen 1964.

Blake, R., *Disraeli*, London 1966.

Bonn, M. J., *Irland und die Irische Frage*, Munich – Leipzig 1918.

Buchheim, K., *Geshichte der christlichen Parteien in Deutschland*, Munich 1953.

Bussmann, W., Das Zeitalter Bismarcks, in: *Handbuch der Deutschen Geschichte*, vol. III/2, Konstanz 1956/57.

Cecil, G., *Life of Robert Marquis of Salisbury*, vols. II and III, London 1921.

Churchill, W. S., *Lord Randolph Churchill*, London 1906.

Churchill, W. S., *Weltkrisis*, vol. I, Deutsche Ausgabe Leipzig 1924–30.

Cruise O'Brien, C., *Parnell and his Party*, Oxford 1957.

Cruise O'Brien, C. (ed.), *The Shaping of Modern Ireland*, London 1960.

Curtis, E., *A History of Ireland*, London 1950.

Curtis jr, L. P., *Coercion and Conciliation in Ireland*, Princeton 1963.

Curtis jr, L. P., *Anglo-Saxons and Celts*, Bridgeport 1968.

Dangerfield, G., *The Strange Death of Liberal England*, New York 1961.

Dibelius, W., *England*, vol. I, Berlin – Stuttgart 1951.

Dugdale, B. E. C., *Balfour*, vol. II, London 1936.

Emmet, Th. A., *Ireland under English Rule*, vol. I, New York 1909.

Ensor, R. C. K., *England 1870–1914*, Oxford 1936.

Eversley, G. J., *Gladstone and Ireland*, London 1912.

Eyck, E., *Bismarck*, vol. III, Erlenbach – Zürich 1944.

Eyck, E., *Bismarck und das Deutsche Reich*, Erlenbach – Zürich 1955.

Eyck, E., *Gladstone*, Erlenbach – Zürich – Leipzig 1938.

Gall, L., (ed.) *Das Bismarck-Problem in der Geschichtsschreibung nach 1945*, Cologne – Berlin 1971.

Gallacher, F., *The Indivisible Island*, London 1957.

Gladstone, W. E., *The Irish Question*, London 1886.

Grote – Gersdorff, Fed. *Entscheidung 1870*, Stuttgart 1970.

Gwynn, D., *The Life of John Redmond*, London 1932.

Hall – Albion – Pope, *A History of England and Empire-Commonwealth*, Boston – New York 1962.

Hammond, J. L., *Gladstone and the Irish Nation*, London 1964.

Holstein, F., *Die Geheimen Papiere*, herausgegeben von N. Rich und H. M. Fischer, Deutsche Ausgabe von W. Frauendienst, vol. I, Göttingen 1956.

Janssen, K. H., *Die Graue Exzellenz. Zwischen Staatsräson und Vasallentreue*. Aus den Papieren des Kaiserlichen Gesandten Karl Georg von Treutler, Frankfurt – Berlin 1971.

Kissling, J. B., *Geschichte des Kulturkampfs im Deutschen Reich*, vol. I Frieburg 1911.

Kühlmann, R., *Erinnerungen*, Heidelberg 1948.

Larkin, E., Mounting the Counter Attack: The Roman Catholic Hierarchy and the Destruction of Parnellism, *Revue of Politics*, vol. XXV, University of Indiana (Notre Dame) 1963.

Lynch, A., *Ireland's Vital Hour*, London 1915.

Lyons, F. S. L., *The Fall of Parnell*, London 1960.

Lyons, F. S. L., *John Dillon*, London 1968.

Lyons, F. S. L., *Ireland since the Famine*, London 1971.

MacDonagh, O., *Ireland*, Englewood Cliffs (N.Y.) 1968.

Mansergh, N., *The Irish Question 1840–1921*, London 1968.

Marjoribanks-Colvin, *The Life of Lord Carson*, vols I, II, III, London 1932/34.

Meffert, F., *Englische Verbrechen am Katholischen Irland*, Mönchengladbach 1917.

Moody, T. W., *Irish-American Nationalism*, I.H.S. vol. XV no. 60.

Moody, T. W., *The New Departure in Irish Politics*, Essays in British and Irish History, vol. XVI, London 1949.

Moody–Martin, *The Course of Irish History*, New York 1967.

Morley, J., *The Life of William Ewart Gladstone*, 3 vols, London 1904.
Morley, J., *Recollections*, vol. I, London 1917.
Nicolson, H. *King George the Fifth, His Life and Reign*, London 1952.
Nostitz, H. *Bismarcks unbotmässiger Botschafter, Fürst Münster von Derneburg*, Göttingen 1968.
O'Brien, W., *The Parnell of Real Life*, London 1926.
O'Connor, J., *History of Ireland 1798–1924*, London 1924.
O'Hegarty, P. S., *Ireland under the Union*, London 1952.
Oxford and Asquith, H., *Fifty Years of Parliament*, vol. II, London 1926.
Ritter, G., *Staatskunst und Kriegshandwerk*, vol. II, Munich 1960.
Ryan, A. P., *Mutiny at the Curragh*, London 1956.
Saase, H. G., *100 Jahre Botschaft in London*, Bonn 1963.
Schlözer, K., *Letzte Römische Briefe*, Berlin – Leipzig 1924.
Stewart, A. T. Q., *The Ulster Crisis*, London 1967.
Veuillot, D., *Oeuvres de Donoso Cortes*, vol. II, Lyon 1877.
Wilhelm II, *Ereignisse und Gestalten 1878–1918*, Leipzig 1922.
Wolf, K., *Sir Roger Casement und die deutsch-irischen Beziehungen*, Historische Forschungen, vol. V, Berlin 1972.

COMPILATIONS
Encyclopaedia Britannica.
Grosse Politik der Europäischen Kabinette, 1871–1914, vol. II, Berlin 1924–27.

RECORDS
Akten des Politischen Archivs des Auswärtigen Amtes 1871–1914.
Stenographische Berichte des Deutschen Reichstags.
Stenographische Berichte des Preussischen Abgeordnetenhauses.

NEWSPAPERS AND PERIODICALS
Daily News
Daily Telegraph
Deutsche Revue, edited by Richard Fleischer.
Die Post
Germania
Irish Times
Historische Zeitschrift, edited by Heinrich von Sybel, later by Friedrich Meinecke, Theodor Schieder and Walter Kienast.
Kölnische Zeitung
Marine Rundschau
Morning Post

Norddeutsche Allgemeine Zeitung
Preussische Jahrbücher, edited by Heinrich von Treitschke, later by
   Hans Delbrück.
The Times
Vossische Zeitung

Index